Challenge the Moment

By Michael Kiel

© 2019 Michael Kiel

DEDICATION

For Pop and Madre

Amy and Pete

Jack and Ben

because of you, I am

Table of Contents

PROLOGUE - The Preciousness of Life

I don't remember exactly when this dawned on me, but I do remember how and in vivid detail. One of my favorite things to do is find a comfortable spot outside when the weather is nice, recline my chair facing the sun, close my eyes and focus on everything I don't see. With all the thoughts bouncing around inside my head it's sometimes rather difficult, but over time I've become pretty good at it. The things that then take charge bring a type of peace that rejuvenates the soul. Surprisingly enough, they are nothing unordinary yet absolutely profound. They are the sounds of leaves fluttering in a breeze, water flowing along rocks and - even more elemental - the warmth of the sun upon my face. Some would call it meditation, others might call it a nap, but the bottom line is, it brings a sense of calm I find nowhere else.

I had become so relaxed late one afternoon that I hadn't noticed the sun was beginning to set. When it dipped below the tree line and the warmth began to fade, I opened my eyes to one of the deepest sunsets I have ever seen. Between the tree line and overall geography of where I live, the remnants of the day are often noteworthy, but this one seemed to capture my mind like none before. I remember staring at the golden sky with its deep red tint and thinking if I ever had the power to stop time that this would be the moment I would choose. It was beyond beautiful, bordering on spiritual, and almost demanding the acknowledgment of God. But like all sunsets it quickly diminished until the sky became a colorless gray.

I remember closing my eyes with an unrealistic sorrow in the pit of my stomach. Logic and reason told me that of course it couldn't last, that brevity is the nature of a sunset and one of the defining characteristics that make it so beautiful. But logic and reason, while valuable at times, have no authority in the realm of hope and heart. So I sat and mourned the fleeting nature of the good we experience in life. It seemed only fair that as the bad we experience in life eventually passes, so must that which brings us joy. As my mind worked in overdrive to find a balance between reason and emotion, the cool night air was bringing me back to reality and I opened my eyes again. I didn't realize the lateness of the hour and therefore never expected the site I saw next. The stars were already out and brighter than I had seen them in years.

I've always loved astronomy and especially its ties to Greek mythology. As a child my family would go camping near Kittanning, PA at a secluded region on the Allegheny River. We referred to it as Captain Charlie's, after the man from whom we rented the campsite. The lack of light from any civilization, coupled with its terrain, provided a view of the night sky that to this day we refer to as a "Captain Charlie's sky." I remember once again thinking I had been graced with the perfect moment. I saw a beauty residing far above, stretching forth throughout the universe to infinity. It reinforced a presence far greater than anything here on Earth. But the brevity of the sunset, still fresh in my thoughts, reminded me again that this too shall quickly pass, and I was once more disheartened. It wasn't until the following morning that I finally understood what I had been missing. The greater picture came to light in the form of a majestic sunrise flooding through my window.

I've always been good at staying in the moment, especially since my spinal cord injury. Not only has it allowed me to avoid the pitfalls of becoming overwhelmed with the demands of paralysis, but it's blessed me with the ability to appreciate the preciousness of life. The old adage tells us to stop and smell the roses, to recognize the value of each and every second. What it neglects to emphasize though, is that as each of those seconds fade, as each heartfelt experience passes, another opportunity for the next profound moment ensues. Everything we find in this world, from the simplest of sunsets to the awe-inspiring feeling of falling in love, defines the value of life. And while they may pass and leave a scar when they go, it's merely because they must so that the next inevitable moment can realize its greatness. Besides, I've always liked the premise that our scars should remind us of where we've been, not dictate where we go.

PART ONE – Growing Up

We search the skies, beyond the fireflies
seeking out life's elusive reason
why does the deer leap, across the mountain so steep
while season changes season

I sit and think, while the sun sinks
into an ocean of bluest calm
what is our purpose, when even the birds chirp less
and destiny eliminates our freedom

Does God's plan, for woman and man
belittle our freedom of choice
if going through life, wherein full of strife
what then have we to rejoice

Is our task on earth, beginning at birth
simply to reach heaven's palace
if so why wait until eighty or ninety-eight
and drink now from the reaper's chalice

No, this meaning we seek, is more humble and meek
and the essence of life no doubt
with destiny fulfilled, and reaching heaven's guild
we'll find the journey is paramount

-   M Kiel

Chapter 1 - Run

BANG! The crack of the pistol shattered the air and I was gone - the rest of the world, a blur. I could feel, even hear, the blood and adrenaline pumping through me as my vision began to narrow. I was propelling myself toward the first obstacle as the blocks faded quickly behind me. I was already at full speed well before I got to the first one. I kicked my right foot up, my momentum carrying me over the hurdle as it grazed the back of my thigh before snapping my left leg down. Up, over, down. Bam, Bam. Up, over, down. Only three steps were allowed between the hurdles, otherwise my lead leg would alternate. Three steps, but it always felt like two. Up, over, down. Bam, Bam. Up, over, down. It was rhythmic, and it needed to be. If I slowed or hesitated my timing would be completely off when I reached the next hurdle. That would mean even if I was lucky enough to clear it the following one would be a nightmare and each hurdle after that exponentially worse. There were ten in a row and I needed to stay at full speed through every single one. There was no time to think, no time to process, just flow forward with everything I had, otherwise each hurdle would become more and more difficult.

I loved running track. I just never wanted to run all that far. As a kid I ran all the time, of course everyone did in the 70s and 80s. The only time you didn't was when you were riding your bike. One of my most vivid memories of childhood is of running. If I close my eyes, I can still envision it.

Faster and faster I ran, wind gushing against my face, my arms pumping as fast as they could. It felt like wind beneath the soles of my shoes rather than the hard asphalt road. I was airborne. I was free. A sharp pain began to stab into my side. It didn't matter. They would be there soon if they weren't already! I needed to move. I had just talked to Grandma about 30 seconds ago, but at 9 years old that was plenty of time for my cousins to have pulled into the driveway. I ran faster. The 200-yard stretch of road between my parents' house and my grandparents' house was my Olympic track, and there I was king. Faster. Tiny pebbles and dirt kicked up behind me, telltale souvenirs from the coal trucks traveling their regular route, once the lifeblood of the small town in Pennsylvania. Who would get there first? O'Dowds? Soulsbys? Aunt Gigi? No, definitely not Gigi - she is always late. Faster. Tranters? Kensingers? Faster. Faster. My heart racing and my lungs on fire, but I never felt more alive. Uncle Joe? Uncle Pat? There's no way; he is probably hitchhiking from Virginia again. Lord only knows when he'll get here. I hit the grassy front lawn and collapse, completely drained but content. I see there are no new cars. All is quiet as the shale driveway lay undisturbed. I knew it - there is no way they could have gotten there faster than me! I own that road, always have.

Growing up in a massive Irish Catholic family I always loved the times everyone in my father's family would come home. My dad's parents raised him and nine brothers and sisters in a small three-bedroom house that during my youth still served as the focal point for everyone's homecoming. Two grandparents, 16 aunts and uncles and roughly 24 cousins would gather during the holidays in this tiny little home. It was wonderful. The adults sat around the table in the kitchen while the oldest cousins sat in the living room and the younger ones sat along the stairs. The higher up the staircase the younger the kid. I, being one of the youngest, spent most of my time in the upstairs hallway with my sister Amy and cousins Danny Boy, Robbie, Stevie, Kathleen and Colleen. It wasn't until after my grandparents' deaths that we began congregating at my parents' house where there was much more room.

It may seem odd to some people why we would continue to spend holidays in such cramped quarters when a much larger house lay not more than two football fields away. Looking back now it would seem odd even to me had I not experienced the love and warmth that seemed to permeate that little home. My grandmother was 100 percent Irish and loved everything about her heritage. Maybe she put slightly too much stock into the old Irish blessing, "May your home forever be too small to hold those who love you."

Likewise, my mother's parents raised six kids in a small, three-bedroom house. The ethnic background there was a little more evenly distributed though: Irish from my grandfather and German from my grandmother. It was also a more traditional household, with my grandfather working at the railroad and my grandmother a stay-at-home mom. It was a very typical post-World War II household. My grandfather, "Moose," had a very colorful history, which included running booze during prohibition before he was a teenager. It also included multiple medals of valor from World War II, including The Silver Star and The Purple Heart. With both of my parents working since before I was born, I needed somewhere to go during the day. I began my life spending my days at my mother's parents' house driving Moose crazy with my invisible friends - one of which was named Maria. She was 24 and lived in my treehouse. Several of my uncles spent an awful lot of time searching that treehouse for her. When I reached school age, I began going to my father's parents' house after Catholic school since it was closer to home.

Chapter 2 - St. Joe's

When first grade rolled around my parents enrolled me in St. Joseph's elementary school. My father's entire family had gone to St. Joe's dating back many generations. Thus began my parochial school experience. I still remember Mike Harrison climbing out the window on or about that initial day of first grade. He put on his spacesuit/backpack outfit and literally climbed out the window and made a run for it. I don't quite remember how or when they caught him, all I remember is seeing that space suit climbing out the window and falling three feet to the ground outside. I smile every time I think of that image. I guess Mike eventually became more comfortable with the idea of school. Well, at least he never tried to go out the window again. The rest of us guys were not very concerned with leaving our parents for the first time; we had bigger things to worry about. First grade was nothing. We had to get ready to make our First Communion the following year in 2nd grade.

We all knew that most of our parents had traveled this exact path through Catholic school while growing up. And we all knew the agenda that was laid out before us. It began with First Holy Communion, then for the guys it was becoming an altar boy. Next was either football or cheerleading, then came confirmation, and finally graduation. All the while listening to the priests and nuns so we could become "such nice young men and women." I still remember complaining to my father that I didn't understand why I had to give up some of my Saturday afternoons to clean up and help maintain the grounds around the school and church. His response of, "Because when I was your age, I was a nice young man, and now it's your turn to be a nice young man!" just drove me crazy. It was almost as bad as his garden rationalization. He loved planting a garden every year and, of course, he had two kids that could provide free labor. So, every year, Amy and I had to help plant the garden. Then, when it came time to maintain it, we had to help weed the garden. Every time I complained, I received the same response: "You have to weed the garden, you helped plant it." Then, come harvest time, we had to help gather everything from the garden. Again, when I complained, my dad's response was, "You have to harvest it, you planted it and weeded it." Finally, when everything was gathered and canned and taken care of, it would be included in some of the family dinners. Of course each time a vegetable landed on my plate that I didn't care for, there was no way out because, you guessed it, I planted it, weeded it, gathered it and helped prepare it. I had no choice but to eat it. The fact that I wanted no part of any of that process in the first place I think was just icing on the cake for my parents' amusement. Thinking back now, some of the problems I had during my middle years at St. Joe's could probably be directly attributed to rebelling against being a nice young man. Then again, many of the convictions and morals I hold so very dear can as well.

I was an altar boy, very respectful to my grandparents and all of their friends, helped out in any way they needed, but I had a temper. I seemed to get angry fairly easily with other kids and when I got angry, I simply started swinging. It was not an easy childhood during report card time, keep in mind they always put the child's last name first and first name last. "Kiel, Mike" was an anthem sung at the end of each nine weeks. By third grade, the school began to intervene. I'm not sure if it was because of a specific incident or just an overall observation, but someone decided a counselor needed to get involved. I remember having five little squares on the top of my desk in which the stickers our teacher occasionally handed out as a reward for good behavior would fit perfectly (collecting stickers was extremely popular at that time, no idea why). We had a guidance counselor who came by once a week. There was no free space inside, so he used a motor home as an office, which he parked outside along the street. It's kind of creepy to think about nowadays, but it was the norm back then. He made me a deal that if I could go an entire day without getting into a fight the teacher would give me a sticker for my desk. If I could collect five stickers, five days in a row, I would be allowed to skip a class of my choice and bring a friend to his "office" and play a game of my choice.

It took me several weeks to collect five stickers in five consecutive days. Every Monday I had to start from scratch, which was rather frustrating. Eventually I got my five stickers within the five-day school week. I don't really remember receiving my reward and going out to play the game. But I do remember that I had chosen Monopoly, and I remember choosing Chris Sossong as the friend who went with me. Overall, I'm not sure if the attempts at behavior modification actually worked as I seemed to have a chip on my shoulder throughout most of my youth and into high school. When we got our report cards, the thing to do was get everyone to sign the envelope, sort of like a yearbook. I still remember my fourth-grade teacher Mrs. Woomer signing the envelope and writing below it "Put up your dukes." She was one of my favorites, and one of the best teachers I ever had.

You would think that an attitude like that would serve me well when my father started pushing me towards football. Wrong. I don't think I broke 100 pounds until I was in eighth grade. So basically, I had the mouth and attitude but nothing behind it, which ironically enough made my attitude all that much worse. Probably because it was based on insecurities. I was never very comfortable with my body image. I was probably close to 5 ft. 9 in. by the time I went out for football in seventh grade, but that didn't mean very much since all my friends were six feet tall and outweighed me by an easy 20 pounds. As far as my father pushing me towards football, he tried for two years until I finally decided to try it. Of course I loved it, but my dad is a sharp character. He knew I would really enjoy football, so once I was firmly entrenched and completely enjoying playing, he and my mom decided that would be useful leverage. Those two definitely knew what they were doing. They went from "You should really go out for football. You'll really like it" to "Well, we're glad you're enjoying football, but if you don't make the honor roll you won't be allowed to play." Shady characters those two, but like I said they knew what they were doing as parents. I wasn't about to let something stupid like grades interfere with my newfound sports career.

It wasn't very difficult for me to comply; I was a pretty good student and things came easily. I typically got As and Bs with minimal effort. However, one of the criteria we were graded on in parochial school was conduct. In the rare event I did not make the honor roll, conduct was typically the culprit. There was more than one occasion in which I found myself staring at a perfect report card, all As with the exception of that great big letter C next to conduct. Those were the times I hated coming home after school. I knew I was in for it. The consequences levied at home were much more of a concern than anything my teachers ever implemented. I rarely got grounded, I didn't have a room full of toys or video games they could take away, and we only got two channels on TV. I had little to worry about in that regard, but my father was in construction, so there was always plenty of hard labor waiting to be done. Trust me when I say that at 11 or 12 years old a day full of carrying shingles up a ladder, hanging drywall or digging ditches for free is a much greater deterrent than most anything else. Looking back, I realize that while I had much more work to do on average than any of my friends the consequences and punishments my parents handed down were just. More importantly, even though they were firm and occasionally strict, they were understanding when real problems arose. A good example is a meltdown I had in eighth grade.

I don't remember how it started, but I was arguing with the other boys in the class. There were only 13 students in my eighth grade, six boys and seven girls, and I was fighting with every one of my friends, all five other boys. I have no idea what we were fighting about, but it escalated to the point where I lost it. I shoved one, grabbed another and threw him over a desk, and started a fist fight with a third. I was so angry I felt like I was going to explode. It's weird how the intensity of that emotion at that time has stuck with me over the years, yet I have no idea why I was so upset. Somehow everything got broken up and I went stomping over to my desk. I remember sitting down, my hands shaking, wanting to throw something through the window beside me. I just wanted to smash something. Just then, the girl behind me, Julie, said in a laughing tone, "I'm afraid to sit next to him!" That was it. My entire body was trembling, and I felt like I was going to burst into tears. I got up and walked straight out of the classroom. When the teacher tried to step in front of me, I pushed right through him.

I walked out the door, down the steps and straight out the front door. By the time I reached the street I was in a dead sprint. I had no idea where I was going. I couldn't go home -- I just walked out of school after a fight in the middle of the day. My parents were going to kill me. I ran down a side street toward the train tracks where there were several abandoned cars. I quickly climbed up the side, throwing my legs over the top and sliding down inside. The second my feet touched the bottom and I came to a stop the flood gates opened and I began to sob uncontrollably. I have no idea how long I sat there, knees curled up to my chest, trembling and weeping at the bottom of that rusted train car. I also have no idea how I ended up at home. I'm assuming I just gathered myself together somehow and climbed back out, walking the rest of the way home. I never expected what was waiting for me.

My parents didn't flip out or unload on me as I was expecting. I actually didn't get into trouble at all. They talked to me. They talked about growing pains and adult behavior. They talked about why everything happened and what was behind it. They talked about how most of the other guys were a lot older than me, almost a full year in some cases. They also talked about how easily I allowed myself to get upset and that in any circumstance, if I looked hard enough, I could find something to upset me. They made it clear that leaving school like that, just walking out, was unacceptable. However, their main focus was the underlying issue, the cause of the problem in the first place.

Those last few years of Catholic school were filled with some definite growing pains and, looking back, some amazing life lessons. My parents didn't have much money, hell I don't think we had much of anything. We always laugh about the little front living room that had the only heat source when I was a kid. There was a little potbelly stove that would get red hot and we would close the sliding doors that separated the living room from the rest of the house. When it came time for bed, Amy and I would race upstairs to dive underneath the covers. Later, we had a coal furnace in the basement that took things to the opposite extreme. I remember putting the butter in the refrigerator because if it sat out it would melt. Still, I never, ever felt like I went without. To this day I'm not sure how they did it, but my parents always made me feel like I was lucky because of all the things I had. For example, I don't remember ever dwelling on only getting two channels on the television. Instead, I was always excited that we got both channels, the one that showed Knight Rider and the one that showed Dukes of Hazzard. It didn't matter that I had generic tennis shoes instead of name brand, they were new and of course made me run faster. Also, it didn't matter that my pedal dirt bike wasn't a BMX, like some of the other guys, it had the wicked blue knobby tires that let me peel out like a race car. Even into seventh and eighth grade, when style was supposed to matter most, I was using my mother's old yellow 10 speed bicycle (with no back brakes, only front ones) to get to and from football practice. For some reason what was "cool" came in second to what was functional, which is one hell of an accomplishment by my parents. I don't think I could have asked for a better childhood.

May you always stay true to this
You are stronger than you know
when you face the inevitable
in life's turbulent ebb and flow

Keep your wits before you
as your journey is right now
it will mold you and shape you
but only in ways you allow

There are no ordinary moments
make sure to seize each one
they become more precious
with every setting of the sun

The most challenging times in life
are simply a chance to grow
provided you always remember
you are stronger than you know

M Kiel

Chapter 3 - High School

Main Street in Portage runs North and South with businesses and apartments, or some combination of the two, lining either side. There are a few houses along the route, but not many. From its northern tip heading into town, Main Street is a gradual hill that eases its way up for about half a mile, passing under an arch tunnel to accommodate for one set of train tracks before reaching a second set of tracks cut directly into its asphalt. From there the road steepens briefly around a bend to the right before finally leveling out just before an S-curve that marks the center of town. The next half a mile is dead straight and flat, until it passes the last side street and begins to elevate again, turning into Springhill.

Traveling South on Main Street, the side streets to the right all angle down. They are flat enough that no one would ever call it a hill, yet one or two good pushes on a pedal bike would allow you to coast the better part of the eight or nine blocks to the park or the football stadium. Above Main Street, though, the terrain climbs high and steep. Three roads rise up from the eastern side of Main Street, one from the S-curve, one in the middle and a third just before Springhill. I had spent the first eight years of school taking that first road at the S-curve, leading just two blocks to St. Joe's. I spent the next four years taking one of the others the entire seven blocks up to the high school.

The Portage school district is comprised of two buildings that sit side-by-side atop a tall hill, staring down upon a Lego patchwork of homes and businesses. On one side is the elementary school, complete with playground and wide-open grassy oval in front, around which school buses circle and inside of which children can play. To its left is the high school with far more parking than grass. Both buildings hold a view of Portage that's unrivaled by anywhere else in town except one, the practice field behind the high school.

That's where my high school life started, with football camp, somewhere in the middle of August 1987, in that big open field behind the high school. Now it's an accurately measured and chalk lined football field lying in the center of a high-end track and field development, complete with metal bleachers on one side. Used by both the track and football teams, the area has seen quite a few upgrades, including a nice fitness center in the high school and tons of resources for the athletes. However, back in 1987 there was nothing but a dirt road leading up to an empty field. When we had breaks, we hung out in the elementary school next door, using the locker room, showers and gymnasium. There were zero amenities, but we had one thing in common. That view. The one thing that hasn't changed is the view from that hill. Every day we would practice into the evening, as the sun sank down into the horizon and dipped into the stadium far below us.

For some reason, I always think of the name tags we had to wear during those first days of camp as freshmen. Everyone's helmet had a strip of athletic tape across the front bearing their name so the coaches could remember who we were. It helped us kids, though, too, because those of us that played for St. Joe's the last couple of years didn't necessarily know the kids that had been playing for Portage and vice versa. Turns out, one of those kids from Portage was "Pat," who would become my best friend through high school and beyond. My mother always called him my football friend who followed me home from camp and never left, which is fairly accurate. When I met him, the coaches all called him Pat or Patrick, so that's what I was calling him until we were hanging out at a St. Joe's dance one Friday night.

One of the first dances I went to as a ninth grader was with my friend Rick and a few others. Rick and one of the other guys were arguing with two guys named Kevin and Jason that I didn't know, so I made my way around to see who else was there. Over in the corner, surrounded by a bunch of other people I didn't know sat Pat. I called his name a few times, but he never even flinched, and the guys around him started looking at me like I was nuts. I was confused as hell because we got along pretty well earlier that week when we first met, but he wasn't even acknowledging me now. However, after a minute or two one of his friends poked him. He looked around, realizing I was talking to him and started to laugh. He told his friends I was talking to him. He then told me everyone calls him Pete. When I asked why he never corrected the coaches he just shrugged. I would find out later that Pete and authority figures weren't exactly on the same page all the time.

After talking to him for a little while, I realized Pete knew a whole lot of people at the dance. More importantly, he knew a lot of the girls. At that age, it was pretty common to have small groups of girls pocketed together in different areas. Likewise, the guys stayed in small groups; both groups staring across an often-empty dance floor while simultaneously whispering to each other. I noticed a group of really cute girls and asked Pete if he knew them. Of course he did. I asked him to hook me up and introduce me to one of them. He just looked at me and then started walking towards the girls, so I followed. He walked right up and said, "Hey Sherry - this is Mike. Go dance." I about shit. I wasn't prepared for that much of a straightforward approach. My face was probably beet red. Sherry was extremely attractive and built better than most of the girls in my grade. I would have thought she was way out of my league, but there I was walking toward the dance floor hand-in-hand thanks to Pete.

With nearly shoulder length dirty blonde hair that was frizzed out from the remnants of a cheap 80s perm, Pete looked like something right out of the movie "Dazed and Confused." I would pay good money to get my hands on a picture of that ninth-grade version of him. I also have no doubt that he would pay good money to keep that picture out of my hands. Pete was pretty tight with what most of the kids considered the rough crowd, also known as "heads" (I think it was Portage's version of "Greasers," like in the Outsiders). He had very few limits or any type of structure at home, so he did what he pleased. His parents had divorced, and he stayed with his mother, who was rarely around; when she was, she didn't exactly lay down the law with strict rules. She also moved quite frequently from place to place, which was another reason Pete ended up just staying at my place through most of high school.

The environments in which we had been raised couldn't have been more different. His, with little to no structure or support and mine with plenty of rules and regulations (often a little overboard) but also plenty of love and support from a giant family. However, the resulting 14-year-old kids that came from those two families ended up having an awful lot more in common than I would've ever imagined. My parents recognized Pete's rough upbringing, and its potential impact, pretty quickly. They also recognized the positive impact they could have on Pete. Which is why they addressed it with me early on. They told me, point blank, to pull him into my world and not get drawn into his. For our part, we decided to dip our toes into both worlds, and quite frequently. Pete ended up with his own room at my parents' house, the spare bedroom across the hall from mine. However, we also spent many a weekend night at his mother's trailer, mainly because she was never around, and we had the place to ourselves.

Pete and I ended up being pretty much inseparable; where one was found the other wasn't too far behind. We had a tight knit group of friends, calling ourselves the Righteous Brothers (yes, after the oldies musical duo). There were about 10 or 12 guys in that expanded group, but the core was comprised of six of us, or the "Righteous Six." That was Pete, Sam, and me, along with Kevin, Willie and John. Willie was the only carryover from St. Joe's that I hung out with all the time. Some of the other St. Joe's guys were still part of the big group, like Brent and Mike (a.k.a. Huey, the window jumper from first grade), but they were building their own small circles of friends. Those smaller circles would all come together for things like intramural volleyball, birthday parties and other organized events. Looking back, it was a really good crowd. Some of the guys definitely had rougher home lives while others were more privileged, but no one was into anything serious. None of those guys were into drugs or vandalism or anything like that. Aside from some underage drinking, I don't think anyone would've characterized any of us as bad kids. That being said, none of us were angels either, not by any stretch of the imagination.

As stress filled and full of angst as teenage years can be, I would characterize my high school experience as overall very positive. There were a lot of things that sucked, like growing pains, social awkwardness, insecurities and a whole lot of self-doubt. There were some broken hearts, both given and received. I was a lot more sexually active than I should have been (or was mentally prepared for); I lost my virginity when I was 14. There were plenty of clashes with parents and teachers, way too many fights just because testosterone took over to compensate for insecurities, and there were even loads of fights amongst our friends. In fact, we all chipped in to buy boxing gloves somewhere in the middle of high school. That way when we got completely pissed at each other and needed to swing, we weren't doing any serious damage to each other. Pete was the most dangerous with those things. Somehow, he could always find his opponent's solar plexus and take the wind right out of them. Didn't seem to matter if we were covered up protecting or turned half sideways and expecting it, he found a way to slip that gloved fist underneath and up to find its target. The gloves worked though. Anytime we needed to hammer on each other, we could, and then it was over and done with, friends once again.

No matter how irritated we could get at each other, we always had each others' backs, especially Pete and me. That's probably what made the rest of high school such a generally positive experience. We had our own interests that took us in different directions (which is good because we probably would've killed each other if we didn't have some time apart), but a lot of those interests intersected at different points. For example, Pete, Sam and I all played football, so in the fall we were busy with practice weekday nights and games on Friday nights. Willie, Kevin and John would hang out at the games Friday night doing their own thing, but then we all met up at the Friday night dance (known in Portage as the "Hustle") afterwards. After football season, Willie and Kevin played basketball, Pete took a break from sports, and Sam, John and I were in the Ski Club. Then, come springtime, I ran track while Pete and Sam played baseball. We were all fairly good at our respective sports and other activities.

Every Saturday morning during the winter months I shot in the Portage rifle club (which wasn't connected to the school). I was also in about a half dozen plays, mainly during my junior and senior year, that were great. I had the lead in one or two of them, but the size of the role didn't seem to matter. I had an absolute blast in the ones where my part was a little smaller as well. Our English teacher, Mr. Vrabel, wrote most of the plays. One of them was Dracula. I got to play a maestro, wear a big, funky gray wig and try out an extremely unique accent. I found out years later that he went on to rename the character "Maestro Kiel." Another was based on a Native American story that revolved around a cliff known as "lovers leap." My role was that of a warrior in love with the chief's daughter, but she was promised to another chief's son, played by Huey. We weren't allowed to wear loincloths (yes, I tried), but we wore shorts, went without shirts, and even wore some paint markings. About five minutes before one of the performances, Huey and I decided to borrow big hoop earrings from a girl we knew and each pierced one ear. We both thought it was pretty cool and were going to swap them out for a little stud and keep the earring on a permanent basis. His lasted about 3.4 seconds until his dad saw it and flipped out on him. Mine lasted a little longer. My dad didn't like mine, but he didn't take a hard-core approach. He just said he didn't like it and thought I should get rid of it. I initially took it out after bargaining for a little later curfew. However, he and my mom made me come home early one night, so I popped it right back in.

Sports and extracurricular activities were fun, and I excelled to a degree in most of them. Likewise, my classes and teachers were pretty good, for the most part. I typically got As and Bs. I had some great teachers, along with a few not-so-good ones, but my overall education went well. Especially when I started in ninth grade. I had algebra in eighth grade at St. Joe's and got straight As the whole way through. Math has always come easily to me and I rarely ever had any difficulty understanding any of it. I was even recruited to participate in a mathematics competition when I was in seventh grade despite all the other kids being eighth graders. I think it was called Math Counts. Unfortunately, I had a horrific teacher in eighth grade and the results became apparent when I started Algebra 2 in ninth grade. I failed my first test so badly that the teachers had a meeting and suggested I retake Algebra 1. I didn't put up much of an argument, even though I really didn't want to get backed up a year in math. I knew how poorly I did on that test and realized I needed a better foundation if I was going to have any type of competence in mathematics. There was one sticking point. The Algebra 1 teacher was notoriously tough. People were always talking about how hard Mrs. Schaefer was and how mean she was. One of the other parents even told my parents that I was going to hate having her. I actually loved her; she was awesome. She taught me more in that year than I think any other teacher has in my life. Don't get me wrong, she was absolutely tough. There were no easy grades, there was a lot of homework and she made little if no exceptions for anything. But by the time ninth grade was over, I knew algebra, and I knew it well. I knew it so well in fact, that I was able to take Algebra 2 and geometry at the same time the following year (my sophomore year) and aced them both, which got me back on track. I took trigonometry my junior year and then calculus my senior, which in turn allowed me to take the more advanced science classes like physics my senior year.

Pete also began taking more of the honors classes. Looking back, I think because it was expected of me, he naturally believed it was expected of him (which it was!). My sister pointed out to me years later that it wasn't just the structure and expectations of our family and environment that benefited Pete, it was Pete himself who must have been, on some level, searching for, or needing that structure. My parents had no authority to hand out consequences or place expectations on Pete. If he wanted to just walk away and say, "Nope, don't want to do that, just going to do what I want" he had every opportunity. My parents checked his report card the same as they checked mine. They gave him the same positive reinforcement for good grades (and same lecture for bad) as they did me. He could have very easily just not brought his report card to the house. He could have just bolted to his mom's house for a week or two or three and avoided my parents. He didn't. My parents had raised the bar of expectation and Pete had, knowingly or unknowingly, raised his bar of self-expectation as well. He was on a really positive path to improving his life as he grew. That path included good grades, it included graduating high school, and it included going to college afterwards. The path he was on in ninth grade could have gone in any number of directions, but I don't think college was likely one of them.

The friendship was anything but one-sided, though. I was benefiting from knowing Pete just as much as he was from knowing me and my family. I often credit him with helping me transition away from the miserable insecurities in seventh and eighth grade. Pete had this intangible charisma that was always evident. It was usually showcased in an unyielding, never-say-die perseverance in whatever he was facing and often reminded me of my dad in the way it came across as pure strength of will. I remember being about 15 and camping out in Glendale with Sam's family. There was a guy in his early 20s in the campsite next to us who was either a college wrestler or had just graduated and wrestled in college. Either way, he was older, stronger and an extremely talented wrestler. He and Pete got into a wrestling match (probably because of Pete's mouth!) for fun. Pete was no match for this grown man, but still the guy couldn't pin him. No matter what he did, no matter how many moves he pulled out of his bag of tricks, Pete wouldn't let his shoulders touch. The guy eventually tired out and we all went back to hanging out, but Pete proved his point. He never got pinned. I think that resilient, fight-with-every-ounce-of-energy attitude was somehow contagious. Of course, I think we took it a little too far because we ended up in a few nasty fights throughout high school, be it with guys from our high school or neighboring towns, just to prove we were warriors. We were definitely over-the-top knuckleheads, but I wouldn't go back and change that for anything in the world. It was far, far better than cowering in an empty train car, frightened and insecure, tears flowing into my hands.

By the time graduation was rolling around, I was preparing to go to my fourth prom. I went to three at Portage and one at Bishop Carroll, a local Catholic high school. The first prom I attended, when I was a sophomore, I was quite the unwilling participant. Pete was dating a girl who was a junior, and she wanted to go to the prom. Obviously, she wanted him to take her. Unfortunately, Pete didn't want to go by himself. He started poking at me that I needed to go as well. The problem was, it was a junior-senior prom, underclassmen weren't allowed to go unless an upperclassman asked them; which was my exact response when Pete told me I had to go. I thought it was the perfect excuse, except it opened the door for Pete to start problem-solving, which rarely ended well for me. He wound up getting one of his girlfriend's friends, who was a junior, to take me so we could go as a group. This posed another problem though, neither of the girls wanted to drive and neither of us had a license. We ended up recruiting one of my neighbors, who was a year older and going to the prom, to drive all three couples in my parents' conversion van.

Looking back, I wonder what the parents of the girls thought as they watched their daughters climb into a conversion van for prom night.

The first two proms, my sophomore and junior year, weren't a whole lot of fun. The two senior proms, one at Portage and one at Bishop Carroll, were much more enjoyable. For my senior prom at Portage, I borrowed a really nice car from my parish priest, Father Ed. He had a brand-new Chrysler New Yorker, fully loaded including a cell phone mounted on the floor. Sam and I both wore a top hat and cane outfit (just because it was fun) and we had a giant crowd gathered at my parents' house beforehand to get a group picture. We had started the trend of gathering at my parents' house my sophomore year with just Pete and me. The following year was a larger group, then my senior year an even bigger group. At my senior prom a few of us got on stage and sang Shooting Star by Bad Company and Signs by Tesla. We sounded absolutely horrible when we sang Shooting Star; not sure why they called us up again to do it a second time with the song Signs. Still, it was a blast. Then, our after-prom party was held at a chalet near a local ski resort. The parents of one of our friends had three chalets, all side-by-side, which they let us use for the night. The Bishop Carroll senior prom was also fun. Although, I didn't know nearly as many people and the after-prom party was in the basement of one girl's house and it was much, much more mellow and reserved.

Thankfully, high school was also the time when my sister Amy and I became really close. It almost seemed like it happened overnight. We got along fine as little kids, but there was always that aspect of annoying little sister that would break my toys or get in the way. When I became a teenager, that gap widened, and we clashed a little bit more because of it. Then, out of nowhere, she became one of my closest confidantes. There was no more telling on each other or deliberately trying to get each other in trouble. Well, she would occasionally have some fun at my expense. She would walk right up beside me, look me dead in the eye, and yell "MOM!" Then she would get a shitty little grin when my mother yelled from the other side of the house, "Michael! Knock it off!" Overall, we started relying on each other, and I jumped right into the protective older brother role. She was three years behind me, so we started running into each other more often in the hallways when she hit eighth grade, which is part of the high school at Portage.

During my senior year one of the other freshmen, a boy named Harry, told Amy he was going to punch her in the face. She found me in the hallway shortly after that and told me. I was livid. I found Harry in the hallway that afternoon, grabbed him by the back of his mullet and slammed his face into a locker. I let him know in no uncertain terms that he should never even talk to my sister again, let alone threaten to punch her. I think she was glad she had a big brother for things like that but wasn't quite so happy when Pete and I got into trouble. She often said how embarrassed she got walking down the hallway, hearing everyone whisper our names. Typically, she could only make out the names, Pete and Mike, before they looked at her and then lowered their voices even more. That's how she knew Pete and I got into something or caused some type of havoc, which was rather often but mostly harmless.

When graduation approached, we were preparing for a summer of work before starting college. I had been accepted to the Altoona branch campus of Penn State, but Pete had been dragging his feet. My parents kept encouraging him to pick whatever college he wanted, and they would help him with the paperwork, but he hadn't followed through. Eventually, my dad told him if he didn't get moving, he was going to fill out Pete's paperwork himself, and apply to the University of Pittsburgh's Johnstown campus, which was about 20 miles away. Pete ended up applying to, and getting accepted at, Slippery Rock University. However, before that next transition, we had a summer of work (and fun) ahead of us. I had been working with my dad's construction company since I could hold a hammer. Pete started almost immediately after we met, and then as we got older my dad started recruiting more of my friends to help on bigger jobs. The summer between my junior and senior year my dad and two of his friends bought the old junior high school, which sat right at the corner of that S turn in the middle of Portage. They were renovating it into a Mini Mall.

My mother always says that my dad kept more of my friends in college than PHEAA loans. She said that because she didn't think any of my friends would choose to work long, hard hours doing the manual labor that was required of a construction worker over an air-conditioned office job. Hence, get your butt to college or learn to work with your hands. She was partially right but working with my dad and his crew was always a blast, even if it was physically exhausting. It was also amazing to be able to take pride in a completed project. Many of my friends did both -- they went to college but took what they learned from my dad and used the knowledge to improve their own homes or even purchase fixer-upper houses to rent or flip. For a lot of my friends, that knowledge started when we began renovating that old junior high school. For Pete and me, it started way, way before!

I had always worked for my dad. To this day the biggest raise I ever got in my entire life was in elementary school when I got a 100% raise. I went from making $1 an hour to $2 an hour. When Pete came on board in high school there were two of us to do the grunt work, which was basically just the dirty gopher work. We started with all the worst jobs, but we were low men on the totem pole, so it was to be expected. We did what we were told. Interestingly enough, a lot of those dirtiest, hardest, nastiest jobs tended to coincide with the times when Pete and I got into trouble at school or elsewhere. My mother used to do the same thing. I rarely got grounded, but those lists of chores that were written out as consequences were nothing short of ruthless. You could always tell how much trouble Pete and I got into the night before by the length of the list my mom would leave on the kitchen table. On one occasion she had written our list out on computer banner paper. When I picked it up off the table it unraveled to the floor. My father was a little more subtle. It was never overt, but there were an awful lot of mornings where Pete and I were hung over as teenagers that just happened to coincide with cleaning out a sewer line or working in a cramped, hot crawlspace filled with bugs and creepy crawlies. Along with learning the ins and outs of building a house, we were also learning a whole lot of life lessons, especially that decision, action, consequence flows in that order. Always. Without exception.

Two jobs jump to mind when I think of my teenage years working with my dad. The first is when we were re-shingling my cousin's house in Virginia. It would have been between my sophomore and junior year when Pete and I were 15, going on 16. My cousin Mauvette, who we call Mets, had gotten married a few years earlier and was living in a ranch-style house in McLean, Virginia. My dad took Roger and Ron, two guys in their early- to mid-20s that worked for him, along with Pete and me down to re-shingle her roof. My dad wanted to get the job done fast for a few reasons -- first and foremost was because that's just the way he worked. All out, full speed ahead, all the time. My friends always referred to him as the energizer bunny. The second, more logical reason, was to make sure we got the old roof off and new one on while we had decent weather. It wasn't supposed to rain for the next couple of days, so we had to take advantage of the opportunity. That meant starting at first light and not stopping until dark. Unfortunately, Virginia in the dead of summer without rain means lots of sun and hot ...damn hot! I still remember the size of that roof - 6900 sq. ft. That was probably three times as big as the average house (mainly because it was one story). It was a lot of work, but that's only part of the reason I remember the job.

The main reason it's so memorable is because of how much fun we had despite how grueling the work was. Every morning Roger and Ron would climb up onto the roof before us. In the early morning dew that settled on the skylights, they would draw with their finger "Pete" on one and "Mike" on another. Then, the rest of the day they would joke about how and when we would each fall, or get thrown, through our respective skylights. My response was to wait until Mets was around and make it a point to say very loudly that they were going to throw me off the roof. Mets always knew we were joking, but there was always that hint of protectiveness that had her glare at those two every now and then. One day I needed to get at those guys good, so I waited until Mets was in one of the back rooms with a big window. Then I yelled really loudly, pretending that they were pushing me and jumped off the roof so that I flew past her window. Damn if she didn't come flying out ready to kill both of them. It was a lot of fun watching them try to explain that they didn't touch me, that I jumped off on my own accord.

Pete was having a blast needling them about Mets' fury, so they fired back. They told him at some point they were going to cut off the back of his hair, which in 1989 was a finely crafted mullet. I was dumbfounded to hear Pete's response. He told them they didn't have the balls to cut his hair. I remember watching and listening to the conversation, thinking my best friend in the world is also the stupidest person in the world. He just challenged them to cut his hair! I spent the next couple of days guarding him and watching his back. It was ridiculous, they were carrying utility knives all day every day for crying out loud! Somehow Pete's hair survived (with a whole lot of help from me, like warnings when they were sneaking up behind him). Then, one lunchtime we were sitting in Mets' kitchen getting some food. Roger and Ron almost got him earlier and were rubbing it in, telling Pete it was just a matter of time. At that point my dad had no idea what was going on, so of course he asked. Pete took the opportunity to gloat and started bragging that Roger and Ron had been after him for days, trying to cut the back of his hair. He then turned his back to everyone to get something from the counter. In one fluid (and what appeared to me as slow) motion, my dad pulled out his utility knife, grabbed the back of Pete's hair and chopped off a big chunk of his mullet. As Pete spun around in stunned silence, mouth wide open, my dad said, "That didn't seem too difficult," dropping Pete's hair in the garbage and walking out. There was never a dull moment working with my dad, and even in the hottest, most miserable conditions, there was a lot of fun to be had.

The second job is that old junior high school that we were renovating into a Mini Mall. Although that one could probably qualify as multiple jobs. We started working the same summer they bought it and continued renovating it throughout my senior year and during the following summer. After gutting the entire thing, removing everything from blackboards in the classrooms to urinals from the bathrooms, we began structuring offices. Most of the shit got thrown in the dumpster, but anything salvageable went to the basement. That basement was dark and funky, but Pete and I would often remark how cool it would be to put our own personal gym down there.

Daybreak III Enterprises Inc., the name of the company that consisted of my dad and his two friends, Dino and Denny, needed to start with a big anchor type business to build around. They got Dollar General to commit to taking the old gymnasium. From there they were able to entice smaller businesses to take up residence in the old classrooms that were becoming offices. They were looking to take advantage of the foot traffic that would come from a business like Dollar General. We began building each office to suit the needs of its tenant. There were two Home Nursing Agencies and a Medical Supply Company. There was a video rental store and a pizza joint among others. My mother and father even got in on the game, starting an ice cream shop called "Poppa's."

There was so much work to do on that plaza that my dad picked up nearly all my friends. Some of them worked out really well, others not so much. In fact, Amy, who was only 13, probably outworked more than half of them. Although, to be fair she was used to it. My dad never assigned jobs according to gender; he had her working just as hard and often. There was no sitting around or slacking off when working with my dad. You either moved or you paid a price, typically in the form of harassment. Laziness got made fun of more ruthlessly than just about anything else. A few of my friends didn't last more than a couple of weeks. The rest of us, though, were kept quite busy. Much like the Virginia roof job, even though it was hard work and we often ran nonstop, we had a blast working together. To this day we can sit around telling endless stories about those jobs -- things like Sam not paying any attention to the fact that we had ripped out most of the plumbing. He had to take a leak and ran into one of the old bathrooms. Without even thinking he started pissing in one of the urinals. Unfortunately, there was no plumbing connected to it, just open space leading to the room below where someone else was working. The screams of "What the hell?! I'm gonna kill someone…!" echoed throughout the building as Sam's urine bounced off his head. If I remember correctly, Sam spent the rest of the day hiding in fear of retaliation. Another time I had walked into the gymnasium that we were turning into Dollar General to see John lying on the floor wriggling like he couldn't get up. As I got closer, I realized some of the other guys had literally held him down and nailed his shirt and jeans to the floor. The moment he recognized I was there, and laughing, he stopped moving around and just smiled. He looked at me and said, "Go ahead, keep laughing. This is your shirt!" Damn if it wasn't one of my favorite shirts!

I spent part of that summer after graduation working with all those guys every day. We would all go out the night before, usually getting a keg and going to a field or hanging out at Pete's mom's apartment. The next morning, we would all wake up hungover, swearing we weren't going out that night. By lunchtime we started feeling a little better and by 4:30 PM we were leaving work yelling to each other that we would meet uptown at 5:00 to do it all over again. Another part of that summer I spent away from everyone. I had entered the National Guard and was in the process of going to Boot Camp. I had signed on for basic training that summer and they guaranteed to have me back in time to start college. I would then go back for AIT (Advanced Individual Training) the following summer and they would have me back for the beginning of my sophomore year.

I had gotten all the initial stuff out of the way and made it the whole way to Texas. However, before we started, they began grilling everyone that if we had any injuries or anything wrong, we needed to make them known. I was nervous and homesick to begin with, but when they started saying things like that, I got downright scared. My back often got really sore during high school and I had arthroscopic surgery on my knee, neither of which were probably a very big deal. However, they sent me to get some tests on my back and everyone else went along their way. I knew I messed up and should have just kept my mouth shut when they started asking me to sign papers that waived my guaranteed return date for college. I had already messed up once and I wasn't going to do it again, so I just said no. Eventually they sent me home without going to basics because there wasn't enough time to get me back for the start of Penn State at the end of August. It was like I never even joined. So, there I was, returning to work with my friends for the end of the summer with a lot more humility and a lot less hair.

I felt stupid for a long time after that experience. I even had a dream that summer that has stuck with me all these years. I dreamt that my parents' house, the one I grew up in, had burnt in a fire. I'm not sure if I saw the entire house in the dream or not, but the dream revolved around my old bedroom. It was burnt to a crisp and everything was ruined except one wall. When I was about 15, the only thing I asked for at Christmas were some sheets of drywall and supplies to hang them. I wanted to cover the paneling on one of my walls and graffiti it with my friends. Sure enough, Christmas morning I got a little brown bag of drywall nails. My dad said the rest of the supplies, including the drywall, were waiting in the garage. Pete and I and the rest of the guys painted (and drew) all sorts of stuff all over that wall. In my dream, that was the only wall that survived. The problem was, it didn't look anything like the graffiti that we had drawn over the last few years. It looked like a shimmering lake, reflecting a kaleidoscope of colors from the sky and just under the surface were the faces of my friends, smiling. The only other things to survive the fire were a bunch of trophies and metals, from various sports, lined up along the headboard of my bed.

That dream was so intense it stuck with me for days on end as I mulled over its meaning. Eventually, I called Aunt Gigi, my dad's sister and my godmother, who was great with everything spiritual and philosophical. Gigi was short for Regina, named after my grandmother Kiel, and she was a Roman Catholic nun. She wasn't your typical nun, though. She made jewelry for a living and loved symbolism but had no time for the church's dogma. We talked a lot about the different possibilities of what that dream may have meant. I've always been a big believer that the only person who can interpret a dream is the actual dreamer. That being said, the dreamer often needs some guidance or at least a sounding board. After a few long talks with Gigi, I decided that dream was all about self-worth. I was the room (or the house), and I had been burnt up and destroyed. Everything that I was or had grown up with, all the stuff in the room, was gone. Fire had consumed it all. Somehow, though, my friendships all survived. The bonds I had made with my group of buddies was based on something that was fireproof or could withstand and endure. In addition, those trophies, telltale signs of accomplishments, somehow survived. The proof that I was actually good at something, somewhere, at some time, managed to endure fire and chaos. The fact that I had succeeded, even excelled, could never be taken away. Once something has been accomplished, that success never gets erased. That conversation with Gigi was so awesome I wish I would have written down its specifics. It was like my subconscious telling me that there was more inside me than I recognized. I was heading into the next phase of life, college, and I had the opportunity to create the person I wanted to become, so long as I recognized what was most important -- that the bonds and friendships I had forged, and would forge, mattered most and that success would endure.

Who am I
Beyond a star lies who we are
as we search here on earth
seeking along where we belong
an elusive truth since birth

The paths we take and choices we make
unveil a journey of beauty
its main goal will shape our soul
but not our place and duty

is there a book in which we can look
to find comfort in our own skin
is it in the skies or another's eyes
that we'll finally feel we fit in

The best laid plan and strongest man
would be placed upon a shelf
pain will be brought and love will be naught
when we have no sense of self

M Kiel

Chapter 4 - PSU and Possibilities

Penn State has about 21 branch campuses, but Altoona always seems to be one of the most popular, despite being relatively small. There were only about a dozen buildings on campus, including the dorms, dining hall, and student union. The layout was simple but quite eloquent. None of the buildings was higher than two stories, except the dormitories, and they were the perfect distance apart. It didn't take long to walk from one end of campus to the other, but nothing felt cramped. There was a large athletic field behind the dining hall and gymnasium where students could play intramurals, everything from baseball to rugby to volleyball. There were no bleachers or markings on the ground; it was more like the empty lot at the edge of town where kids could play. In front of the student union was a large pond that was home to what sometimes seemed like a million ducks - they were everywhere and mean tempered! They also crapped everywhere so the pond was full of it. One of the traditions at Altoona campus was anytime someone had a birthday they got tossed into the pond. Thankfully my birthday doesn't fall in the school year. The campus had a nice small town feel to it. The classes were small, and the teachers were approachable. It was the perfect environment for someone transitioning from a small town to a large college. They could go to Altoona for a year or two, get acclimated to college life, and then move on to the main campus located in State College.

I had turned 18 just a few, short weeks prior to entering my freshman year at Penn State Altoona and I was ready to begin a new life. I had spent most of my high school existence trying to prove to everyone, including myself, that I was tough and wild, which meant tons of stupid decisions and a whole lot of unnecessary risks, like fights. I saw before me the opportunity to create a new persona, and I intended to seize it. Instead of being known as tough or wild, I wanted to be known as someone who got along with everyone, carefree, the comedian who was always smiling, laughing and embracing life. I even latched onto a new nickname, Eyeball. I had gotten hit in the eye and was complaining about my "eyeball." Whoever I was with thought it was funny that I was whining about my eyeball instead of my eye, so I ran with it. I began introducing myself as Eyeball. Since my eyes are such a dominant feature, it caught on. Eventually everyone was calling me Eyeball, including my professors.

I immediately made friends with a large group of people living in my dormitory, a few of us who lived on the third floor, several from the second floor and the first floor "Wasters" of Maple. The students of Maple dormitory had a 20 plus year tradition of designating one floor as a pseudo fraternity and referred to themselves as the Wasters. Historically, this group was comprised of students who had a desire for the fraternity atmosphere but, being nonconformists by nature, bucked the traditional Greek approach to camaraderie. They were defined by their extreme party nature and their Animal House approach to playing rugby. Ironically enough, it wouldn't be the only time in my college career that I would find myself surrounded by a group who seemed to model themselves after that epic movie.

My parents, sister, and best friend Pete moved me (and all my belongings) into my third-floor room in Maple. We made the trip, luggage and all, packed into my mother's four-door LeBaron. When my sister made the same move about three years later, it took two trucks and a full-sized van in order to transport all of her things. Ten minutes after everyone left, I was settled in and began walking around room-to-room introducing myself to my new neighbors. I immediately clicked with a group of guys who would become my best friends over the following year. Chris, Ryan, and Terry also lived on the third floor and we had more than a little in common, particularly Chris and me.

Chris and I had so much in common it was slightly scary. We clicked more than any of the others, and it showed; we were virtually inseparable. Our high school experiences were very similar. We both played football and had opportunities to play at the college level (mine at a junior college I had never heard of, and with no incentive like a scholarship), and had loved Penn State while growing up. Both of our parents owned and operated a small business and we were both die hard gym rats, hitting the free weights as often as possible. Most interestingly, though, our experiences in high school as they related to fighting and having a close-knit group of friends who were rough and tumble were nearly identical. This presented me with a significant dichotomy. My desire to reinvent myself was in direct conflict with the mindset of my new friend, as Chris had no such intentions and thoroughly enjoyed the tough guy fighter persona. I had somehow migrated towards, and was slowly becoming best friends with, someone who epitomized the lifestyle I was intent on leaving behind.

I got in very few altercations that first year, but the intimidation and ruffian style epitomized by that mindset was ever present with Chris. We began playing rugby with another friend who everyone called "Tank." The nickname was thoroughly justified as he was probably around 6 ft. 4 in., a solid 280 lbs. and, although a happy-go-lucky personality, quite intimidating. The three of us joined in with the Wasters from the first floor of the dormitory and reveled in the joy of our newfound sport. We also began throwing parties at Tank's apartment, which was just off-campus, in order to meet people. Tank and Chris were mostly interested in charging people for drinks and turning a nice profit, whereas I was truly thrilled at the opportunity to make new friends. All three of us were successful at our endeavors, and we were the life of the party. I was completely at odds with myself now. On one hand, I was assimilating with the Wasters and Tank and having a blast with a happy-go-lucky persona. Partying and having fun were all that mattered. On the other hand, my best friend was a gregarious personality that everyone flocked to but who was entrenched in that fight-for-fun philosophy.

This conflict seemed to start popping up everywhere. Aside from hanging out with these guys, I was meeting all kinds of new friends including different fraternity and sorority people. Phi Sigma Kappa was previously a local fraternity in the midst of going national and filled with a really good, albeit small, group of guys. Beta Alpha Delta, on the other hand, was known for being bad-asses and touted their initials, "BAD." They were the two that recruited me most heavily despite my insistence that I had no desire to join a fraternity. I was dating a girl, Becky, who was a sister in Beta Gamma, the sister sorority to Beta Alpha Delta. I was therefore drawn even more so to the rough crowd once again, because I really liked Becky. I even sat down for an interview and considered pledging.

I ended up not joining a fraternity at all that semester. I'm not sure why I never followed through with Beta Alpha Delta. I'm also not sure why Becky and I broke up, but we did. We remained friends though, even when she went home to Rhode Island and didn't return to PSU. We continued writing to each other way back during a time when that meant putting pen to paper, finding an envelope and a stamp, and dragging my butt the whole way to a mailbox, then waiting weeks for a response. One of the things we always swore was that I would make it up there for a visit so we could hang out on the beach. I never did make it to that beach in Rhode Island, but while I was in Atlanta, Becky brought the beach to me. She came to visit and brought with her a glass jar of sand. I still have that jar. It was one of those gestures that meant a lot, mainly because it stated triumphantly, there's more than one way to do something.

I also found a way to balance Chris's influence. While he had that tough guy, looking to throw hands mindset, not many of the others did. They were all just as interested in having fun as I was, which made it easier. That's not to say I didn't have to bail him out of sticky predicaments a few times or dig myself in a hole or two that year, but that wasn't the overwhelming theme of life. Crazy rugby games, parties, and life lessons that make being eighteen priceless was what dominated the landscape of my experience.

Overall, now that I look back, my first year or so of college was a very good learning experience, albeit in every way except that which the university intended. My grade-point average ended up being a paltry 1.78, landing me on academic probation. I had dedicated so much of my efforts toward a new type of social life, I had nearly completely neglected my academic one. At one point during that first semester about a dozen of us decided to have a drinking competition to see who could go on the longest drinking binge without classes, girlfriends, or studying. Eating, drinking, sleeping, and rugby practice were the only activities permitted. I believe I went 15 days straight; after that, I tapped out. I felt absolutely awful! Not only did I not win, I didn't even come in second. If I remember correctly, someone named Russell (who often referred to himself as Russell the Love Muscle) won the competition. Last I heard he was living in an abandoned boat yard in Maryland after failing out. Needless to say, it was activities such as this that resulted in my less-than-stellar academic achievements during that period.

I remember having a five-credit calculus course my first semester that met four days a week from 3:30 to 5, one of those days being Friday afternoon. The professor who taught the course was my academic advisor and in order to ensure attendance on those Friday afternoons, he would give a weekly quiz at the beginning of class. Fall weekends at Penn State Altoona revolved around one thing: road trips to State College for Nittany Lion football games. Most people would get organized, loaded up in vehicles and leave somewhere between three and four o'clock, which was quite problematic for me given the timetable of my calculus course. More often than not, I ended up walking into class, taking the quiz, handing it in, and then walking directly out. I was rarely there more than ten minutes. Near the end of the term when I met with my advisor to schedule my next semester's course load, I remember asking him if I would need to retake his calculus class. He was as poor an advisor as I was a student and provided me with little to no advice. He merely said that I should go ahead and schedule the next level of mathematics courses I would need. My grade wasn't very good, but it would suffice for me to proceed along with my major's requirements. He ended up giving me a D, which was pretty much the end of my engineering career. Accounting was next in line, but that didn't last long.

My second semester I put forth a much greater effort. However, I was still playing rugby and still partying like crazy. I wasn't skipping quite as many classes but was not putting much effort into them when I was present either. That semester I had my first philosophy course, and for the first time I found myself completely engaged in a class. That was the same semester I had my first psychology course as well, which I enjoyed. There were a few others that I didn't mind either. The philosophy course, however, was really sparking my interest despite being taught by a drab and monotonous instructor.

The idea of questioning life, of existence, of evaluating purpose was something I had been doing for years. I just wasn't aware that, not only do most people have the same questions to some degree, but that some of the greatest minds in human history have spent their lives exploring existential questions.

The end of that second semester my grades had improved, but not enough to get me out of academic probation. Starting out with a grade-point average of 1.78 was just too deep a hole to dig out of in one semester. I came close though. I think I was only a fraction of a point under a 2.0, or a C average. It's weird to think that I was shooting for Cs. I had spent my entire academic career getting As and Bs with relative ease. Any time my grades dipped down, I just brought them back up with a little effort. I never gave it much thought because it was never very difficult. Then again, I had the threat of my parents checking my grades every nine weeks, and that wasn't the case in college. I had to find my own motivation and put some real effort into things, which didn't dawn on me until my second semester. Still, I don't think I truly committed myself until the latter part of the spring.

There was one particular assignment that triggered me to work harder than I had been, a paper in my psychology class. We could choose the topic, so I decided to do mine on dreams and dream analysis. The dream I had discussed at such length with Gigi, about the house burning down but the wall surviving, was still resonating with me almost a year later. I called her to get some ideas on who and what I could research for my paper. She gave me a few names, like Carl Jung, and off I went to the library. I don't remember how many books I checked out, but Jung's was the one that captured my attention most. I think I read the entire book instead of just looking up parts to justify my paper, which is something I typically did. In fact, all through high school I rarely read much more than the front and back jacket of the book. I could always bullshit my way through any book report or assignment, but this was different. I was really interested in what I was writing. I incorporated Jung's philosophies and approaches to dream work along with some of the things that Gigi and I had talked about to add a personal touch. I put more effort into that paper than I had put into anything else my entire freshman year, including entire classes. I got a D.

I was absolutely floored. There was no feedback on the paper, nothing to explain what I had done wrong, just a shitty grade glaring at me from the top of the title page. It was the first time I had ever put that much effort into school and come up that short. I was really upset, and for the first time began to question whether I was cut out for college. I ended up calling Gigi. It was one of her favorite stories to tell over and over because I called her at about two or three in the morning. When she answered, the first thing I said was, "Sorry it's so late, but I couldn't call my parents. They're asleep." I don't think she ever remembered why I called or what we talked about, just that I called in the middle of the night and that I made it a point to say I couldn't call my parents because they were asleep. It never dawned on me how stupid that sounded, but she just chuckled and asked what was going on. She never even hesitated. It didn't matter that it was the middle of the night or that she was half-asleep. She was more than willing to talk, to be that sounding board, to be that voice of comfort and reassurance.

Without her and that talk, I think I may have spiraled downward. Luckily, she was always great at those talks. I definitely felt better afterwards. I wasn't great, and I still had some shitty grades, but I was ready to head into my summer, work with dad, and then return to college in the fall, hopefully recharged.

My parents had opened Poppa's Ice Cream Shop in the plaza that we had been renovating the few years prior. That meant there was another opportunity for me to work. Initially, I was looking forward to working in a nice, cool, air-conditioned environment, especially at a job that was sure to have some downtime with nothing to do but sit and wait for customers. Customers that were bound to include cute girls -- after all, it was ice cream. It didn't quite work out that easily. The summer between my freshman and sophomore years, I worked almost every day with my dad's construction company. The days I worked at the ice cream shop were typically in the evening, and usually after I finished an eight- or nine-hour day swinging a hammer. That made for some long days and I have no doubt that I grumbled about it at the time. Looking back, though, I remember it fondly, even the days I put in some absolutely ridiculous hours, like stripping and waxing the floor after closing.

A typical day involved getting up around 7 AM and driving directly to a jobsite to work until about 4 PM. My dad was never big on having a set quitting time. He was always looking for a good stopping point. That being said, he often tried to make the two coincide, finding a good stopping point around a reasonable quitting time of 4 PM. The few days I worked at the ice cream shop each week, I had to start at 5 PM. That meant I had to rush home, shower, and get cleaned up quickly to be on time. We had to clean the equipment a couple of times a week after closing at 10 PM. It didn't take very long, maybe half an hour or 45 minutes, so I was usually home by 11 PM. Every now and then, though, I needed to do some more involved upkeep and maintenance of the shop, like stripping and waxing the tile floor. That meant after cleaning the equipment, I had to take some stripping solution, apply it to the floor and run a buffer over everything until it was dull and flat, then apply some wax and use the buffer again to bring it back to a shine. The nights that needed to be done, my buddy Bill, Pete's older brother, would meet me at closing to help. He worked all day with my dad as well but was willing to pick up a few more hours at the ice cream shop. He would bring a six or 12 pack of beer, I would provide the boombox and cassette tape of Billy Joel's greatest hits, and we would have a few beers while singing, laughing, and cleaning. Those nights didn't end until about three in the morning, which probably had a little more to do with the couple of beers than it did the amount of time it took to shine the floor. We then got up at 7 AM again to head to the construction site. Like I said, it made for an extremely long day, but it was also fun, much like that entire summer.

When I returned to Penn State that fall, I was moving into the sophomore dorm, Spruce Hall, with Chris. Spruce was the third dorm on campus and had just been built a year or two earlier. It was a five-star upgrade from my freshman dorm, Maple, which was most likely as old as the campus itself -- at least that's what the 60's decor and 70's color scheme suggested. On the flipside, Spruce had a modern design and was set up in suites. Each suite had two very spacious dorm rooms and shared a bathroom, as opposed to the other dormitories and their tiny rooms that surrounded one community bathroom that was shared by the entire floor. Chris and I had a corner room on the first floor on the end closest to campus, so the sidewalk leading to the main entrance came right past our window. Oftentimes, instead of walking out of my dorm, into the hallway, out the side door, and around the corner of the building to get to the sidewalk, I simply jumped out of our window as a shortcut.

My second year had started off great. Since Chris and I knew we would be roommates, we had made all kinds of plans for what we would each bring to the dorm. Chris was a little spoiled by his parents, so he had a TV, VCR, stereo and ridiculous speaker system. It was actually the box from the trunk of his car that contained two twelve-inch subwoofers with multiple tweeters. It was the loudest system I had ever heard and could rattle the windows with ease. I had a microwave that half worked; it would only cook one side. I found it when I was cleaning one of my dad's rental apartments in the summer. The previous tenants apparently thought it wasn't worth packing up, so it was all mine. I didn't have much else to offer, so most of the "stuff" in our dorm belonged to Chris. Although, with Gigi as my godmother, I was constantly getting care packages in the mail that kept us well supplied with a range of junk food like Twizzlers and Captain's wafers. Our suitemates were nice guys as well, but they were really quiet, and their academic skills were far greater than their social skills. Chris clashed with them occasionally, but I got along well with both. Come to think of it, one of them reminds me of Sheldon from the Big Bang theory.

I was doing a lot better in my classes, probably because I was going to all of them religiously instead of ditching out. I was also actively participating and engaged in the topics when I was there. I had an accounting class that I remember putting a great deal of effort into, including recruiting two women I was friends with to help me. Jenny and Cathy helped a great deal, but more importantly became two of my most valued friends. Accounting just wasn't for me though. I was great at math and could do most of the calculations in my head, but it was mind numbingly boring. Chris and I were still playing rugby and a bunch of the friends I made in Phi Sigma Kappa were still inviting me to parties all the time. That really resonated with me, that the guys from the fraternity I decided not to pledge still wanted to hang out and be friends. The other fraternity, Beta Alpha Delta, barely talked to me after I told them I wasn't interested. The guys from Phi Sig made it a point to tell me that even though I wasn't allowed to come to some of their functions, I was always welcome at their parties. To me, it spoke volumes about their character and about the organization as a whole. Between Phi Sig's fraternity house, the rugby house, and Jenny and Cathy's (which was just at the edge of campus, a mere five-minute walk from Spruce) there was always a good party somewhere. I seemed to be finding a good balance between academic life and social life.

Chris and I got along great as roommates for about the first half of the semester. We had a good system down where we weren't annoying each other with little pet peeves, we shared just about everything we had, and even came to an easy compromise with how the room was set up. The beds in Spruce could be positioned by themselves or stacked on top of each other to create bunk beds. Chris and I chose the latter to make more room. He also had a thing about always having to sleep on the top bunk. He and his freshman roommate had fashioned bunk beds through a rigged-up chain system the previous year. It collapsed on Chris's head and we had to take him to the emergency room to get stitches. We were also good at giving each other some space when one of us was hooking up with a girl. We were good at it, but not perfect. Shortly after the semester began Chris walked right in on me and a girl I brought home from a party. He was so drunk he didn't even realize it. He just walked in, climbed up onto the top bunk and passed out. From that moment on I hung the sheet from a top bunk down the side, covering my lower bunk. It was a little like a tent, but it provided enough privacy for comfort, just in case.

On another occasion Chris and I got home from a party and were both pretty well boozed. He started drunk-calling girls left and right and eventually found someone to come over. So, being the good roommate I was, I headed to the TV lounge for an hour. When I returned, everyone was asleep, so I just crawled into my bunk and crashed. The next morning, I woke up, went to roll over, and lo and behold bumped into a naked woman. Having drunk as much as we did the night before, I started wracking my brain to remember all the events. I was sure I didn't hook up with anyone, but here she was lying beside me. Then I realized it was Chris's girl. I started kicking the bed above me and woke everyone up. Apparently, she had gotten up in the middle of the night to use the bathroom and was either too tired or too drunk to climb up onto the top bed. Luckily, we all had a good sense of humor about it. However, we did move a desk to the foot of the bunkbeds so it was easier to climb up from then on.

Chris and I were usually able to laugh off our stupid arguments or debacles with women, but eventually our friendship started to deteriorate. Looking back, I think it may have started with a girl. I was hooking up with one of the twins that lived downstairs from Jenny and Cathy, and I think Chris might have been interested in her, although he never said anything. After that, things just seemed strained. Eventually, we were hanging out at the rugby house one night when things came to a head. I was upstairs on the phone talking to a girl and Chris kept picking up the phone downstairs and interrupting. I wasn't sure if he was just drunk and messing around or if he was being an outright jackass, deliberately trying to ruin my chances with this girl. Either way, he was irritating the hell out of me. It got so bad I had to hang up and tell her I would talk to her later. I went downstairs pretty ticked off and let him know it. However, the minute I opened my mouth Chris picked up the telephone receiver and punched me square in the face with it. My immediate reflex was to swing back. That was all the longer the fight lasted, one punch each, before one of the guys that lived in the house pulled us apart. Chris's punch, with the phone, cut my eyebrow, causing it to bleed a little. My punch landed a bit more precisely, breaking his nose. It was the last night we ever spoke to one another.

One of the other guys gave me a ride to Jenny and Cathy's, where I sat fuming most of the night. I was pissed, but I think I was more hurt that my best friend would hit me with something. I could understand losing his temper and taking a swing, but to hold something in his hand like a weapon was a whole different story. The next day I went back to my dorm room. Chris never did. Later that afternoon when I came back from class there was a note written on a piece of paper.

Chris had scribbled a couple of quick sentences saying that he was moving out and that he couldn't believe I punched him, that he would have never done anything like that to me. It made absolutely no sense given the fact that not only did he strike first, but he did it with an object. Initially, I figured we needed to work some things out, but after reading that note I figured we were done. If his perception of how things went down was that skewed, he was never going to admit he was even partially at fault, let alone equally to blame. I was right. A day or so later all his stuff was gone, and I never saw him again. Rugby season was over, and he was going to State College the end of the fall semester. There wasn't even a chance we would cross each other's path on campus.

My dorm room was pretty empty with all of Chris's stuff gone. I didn't have much aside from my semi-operable microwave and a boombox, although it was a pretty nice stereo. It was even equipped with the latest technology, a CD player. I don't think I owned any CDs, they were too expensive, but I had the capability of playing them if I ever got any. I rarely saw any of the rugby guys. I don't know if they took Chris's side or if they were avoiding me so they didn't get caught in the middle, but either way the result was I didn't see them much. I didn't go out of my way to reach out to them either though. I heard Chris had moved in with a group of them living in College Park. I ended up hanging out with Jenny and Cathy a lot more. I even spent some time with my suitemates watching movies. They were both hyper organized and had this giant stack of VHS tapes with three movies on each tape (labeled and everything). I also started hanging out with the guys from Phi Sig more often.

I wasn't alone in that dorm room very long though. Shortly after Chris moved out, Stephen King moved in. He was a sophomore, like me, and had a falling out with some of his friends. He was part of a group of young black guys that had started their own underground fraternity the year before. I don't remember if he was part of the fraternity, or if he was just friends with that crowd. I knew most of them from my freshman year, mainly because they lived in the same dorm, Maple. They were really good guys, at least the ones I knew. By my sophomore year, though, they had some freshman members that weren't quite as friendly. I was walking across campus one time and one of their new members shoved their shoulder into me as I passed by. It spun me around (which is what I'm sure he intended) and he puffed out his chest like he was ready to start swinging. Then, all of a sudden, his demeanor changed. He went from tough guy attitude to shock and then to almost fear as one of the older members of his group, a guy called "Pops," came up and started joking around with me. Pops was one of the guys I had been friends with since starting college. When I didn't immediately start joking back, Pops did a double take, glancing at this other guy. I don't remember what he said or if he said anything, but I never had a problem with any of those younger guys after that. I don't think the same was true of Stephen. He would never elaborate, but I always got the feeling he didn't have the time or patience for unnecessary attitude.

Steve and I got along well from the start. He was the son of a preacher and a whole lot more organized, and reserved, than I was. One of the things I remember most about him was that he always put his cologne on his clothes the night before and hung them up to make sure the wrinkles fell out by the next day. Meanwhile, my clothes sat in two piles, dirty clothes in one corner, clean clothes in another. In my defense, the clean clothes were folded ... usually. Stephen didn't stay out late or do much partying, and he also kept his side of the room tidy. On the flipside, I was always out late, and my side of the room looked like a tornado hit it. However, I was always very conscientious about being quiet when I came in at night so I didn't wake him up and made every effort to keep the chaos on my side of the room out of his way. Likewise, he didn't get upset easily or complain about any of my bad habits. We were able to compromise and find middle ground relatively easily.

By the time December rolled around, bringing the end of my third semester with it, Stephen and I had become pretty good friends. My grades had also improved dramatically, I was dating a girl named Heather and I was hanging out with Randy, one of the guys from Phi Sig on a regular basis. I even told him that if they were still interested, I wouldn't mind joining his fraternity. It meant a lot to me that we became friends in spite of my turning down that first bid to join the fraternity. To me, that showed that the organization was based on guys connecting with each other on a real basis, not just looking to build numbers and generate money from regular dues. Randy always liked to harass me that if I would have just accepted the first bid, I would have been a founding father. They had just received their national charter in November, so all of the active guys, including those who pledged that fall (about 40 of them, including my future big brother) were all founding fathers.

The Altoona chapter of Phi Sigma Kappa (Iota Septaton) had been a local fraternity called Sigma Psi Delta, which was known for its heavy partying and hard-core hazing. In 1989, the group, led by a guy named George, decided to explore national options and move away from their hazing traditions. In 1990 Sigma Psi Delta was colonized into Phi Sigma Kappa and spent the next two years recruiting new members and redesigning their program to focus on brotherhood, scholarship and character. They also found an alumnus of Phi Sig from IUP (Indiana University of Pennsylvania) that was willing to serve as advisor. Bill, a.k.a. "Coach," was a local teacher who had pledged for the Phi Sig chapter at Indiana University of Pennsylvania (IUP) back in the 60s. He was the perfect person to guide the fledgling fraternity through its growing pains and teach them the ropes of what was required from a national fraternity. This included everything from structuring rituals and creating an executive board to identifying ways to engage, and give back to, the community, particularly through philanthropic events. The fraternity also needed to make sure it was compliant with campus regulations in order to be recognized in good standing, which was no easy task considering the guy in charge of Greek life at the time was a complete and total jackass. The overall transition was not an easy one. Luckily, the crew that pledged in the fall of 1991 contained a couple of exceptional young men like Randy, Dave, and Brian, among several others, who were up for the task. In addition to following Coach's guidance to make sure everything was in order, they began pushing national to formally initiate the new chapter. They were successful, and in November 1992 Phi Sigma Kappa Iota Septaton became a formal chapter at Penn State Altoona. I was a member of the first pledge class in the spring of 1993.

Dave was our president and the most vigilant about the chapter being a non-hazing entity. He was also the classic "Dad" of the group, always worrying and trying to keep everyone in line. If you've ever seen the movie Animal House, Dave was a great deal like the character Robert Hoover who plays the president trying to keep the likes of John Belushi in line - unsuccessfully. To be fair, as president, Dave had more on the line than anyone else. It was his name in the logbooks and he was responsible. So, legally, he would be on the hook if we did anything serious. Likewise, he also lived at the fraternity house, so it was his name on the lease. When the cops came knocking on the door because parties were too loud, or the campus representative wanted to meet with our chapter, it was Dave who had to put out the fires. To say he worried a lot is an understatement. To say we harassed him a lot about worrying is also an understatement. Still, we were lucky to have someone like Dave in a leadership position. He was dedicated, principled and a natural born leader. More importantly, he was genuine, kind, and deeply committed. He embraced the no-hazing transition not only because he thought it was the right thing to do, but because he felt there was a better way to strengthen the bond between brothers. Randy and I, and a few others, felt the same. We just had a different definition of hazing.

I've never understood how some fraternities operate. They spend three months treating a group of guys they just met like absolute shit, everything from degrading them to paddling them, all in the name of tradition. Then, after one night of formality (which typically included the height of mistreatment), the people that had just spent the past couple of months as scum or slime or the lowest of low were suddenly brothers and best friends. It just makes no sense. The only way two people become close, become bonded, become brothers is through shared experiences. Those experiences are often both good and bad, but they are always shared. When I told Randy I wanted to pledge, I told him I was up for anything, as long as it was together and had purpose. By purpose, I meant that it somehow brought me closer to the guys I would eventually call brother. He understood what I meant, and it turned out he felt the same way. Although, he and Dave had much different definitions of hazing. Funny thing was, my definition of hazing was much more in line with Randy than Dave. I had fun doing stupid, over-the-top things. I just didn't want anyone berating me while I did them.

When the spring semester started, there were probably 40 or 50 active brothers. Most of them had just been initiated about two months earlier when the chapter got initiated as a whole. After a few weeks of "rushing," which is a promotional period for fraternities and sororities to recruit new members throughout campus, they started handing out "bids" which was an invitation to pledge. Thirteen of us received and accepted our bids forming the very first pledge class of Phi Sigma Kappa, Iota Septaton chapter. There was a wide range of personalities in that group, but I hit it off quickly with Jeffrey, Nate, Ian and Rick, who liked everyone to call him "Mad Dog" after the cheap wine.

Jeffrey lived with Pete and Anthony, who were twin brothers, fraternity brothers, and Pete would become my fraternity big brother. If you think the odds are rare that my new "big brother" would have the same name as my best friend from home, try this on for size ... my new "big brother" Pete would go on to marry Amy and become my brother-in-law Pete!

I don't really remember where any of the other guys lived. I think Jeffrey and I were the only sophomores. All the others were freshmen, so they probably lived in the dorms. The first week or two was spent getting to know everyone so the brothers could choose "little brothers." When joining a fraternity, each pledge is connected to an active brother who serves as the "big brother," kind of like a mentor. The process continues each semester as big brothers and little brothers get connected and eventually form "families." I'm sure the process varies from fraternity to fraternity, but in PSK the active brothers spent a few weeks hanging out with the new pledges before meeting and discussing amongst themselves who wanted whom. The active brother would then approach the pledge and offer to serve as their big brother. I had already talked to Pete about being my big brother when I first met him. He was Randy's little brother, so consequently I was in Randy's family, which was nicknamed Jim Beam. After all of the big brothers and little brothers were sorted out, pledging was underway, and the semester was full steam ahead.

I was having an absolute blast pledging and my classes were going well. I had discovered that I didn't need to do both, study for endless hours and go to every single class to get good grades. I could either learn the material myself and study for hours on end, or go to every class religiously and actively participate, plugging into the lectures. It took far less time to just go to class and pay attention, for which I opted. However, one of the requirements of pledging, was setting aside a certain amount of time for homework and classes. My grades were reflecting it too, I was back to getting As and Bs like I had in high school. The great thing about how my study habits were structured was that my nights were open and free, which meant I could still party pretty much every night of the week. My fraternity usually had a couple of events each week, KDE (Kappa Delta Epsilon), the sorority we mingled with most, had a couple of events each week and then other fraternities, and just friends in general, would have parties peppered throughout the week. In other words, there was always a party every night of the week if I was interested, which I was. As far as pledging, there was a lot of fun stuff we were doing.

There were about a half dozen formal pledging functions in addition to a whole bunch of less formal, sometimes impromptu, get-togethers. Things ranged from serious, like education on the history and traditions of PSK, to silly or juvenile, like scavenger hunts or themed parties. All of it was fun because all of it was rooted in doing things with the other guys. Sometimes that included the entire fraternity, active brothers and pledges, sometimes it was just big brothers and little brothers or families, but it was always shared experiences. One of the more memorable, although I admit really juvenile, was "boxer night" parties, which were typically impromptu.

For one reason or another, every now and then we ended up having a boxer night party, which meant all of the pledges wore nothing but boxer shorts. Well, boxers and shoes or boots or something on our feet. I'm probably about the furthest thing in the world from a germaphobe, but the floor of a fraternity house is just nasty. There's no way anyone should ever, I mean never, walk barefoot through a fraternity house. There was no great purpose behind having us walk around a party in our underwear, other than that we were doing it together and thought it was hilarious. It may have been an attempt by one of the brothers to try and embarrass us, but if it was, it didn't work. One of the funniest boxer nights I recall is a party at Pete and Anthony's that got busted by the police. Apparently, we were making a little too much noise, which happened on occasion, and the police were responding to a complaint. I was standing in the kitchen, holding a plastic cup of beer as the door to the hallway flew open. There were a couple of officers there and the one in front said loudly, "All right everyone..." but then stopped, took his flashlight and looked at me head to toe, standing there in nothing but glow-in-the-dark Goofy (yes, the Disney character) boxer shorts and big Timberland work boots. He started shaking his head and said, "Oh just go home!" I smiled and said, "Let me get my pants." Some of the other things we did were far more planned out and with significantly more purpose behind them.

One of the best formal functions was called "Lock In," which is exactly what it sounds like. All of the active brothers and pledges went into one of the houses on a Friday afternoon after class, locked the doors behind them and no one left until Sunday afternoon. There was plenty of beer and lots of cheap food, loads of laughter and more than enough graffiti on those who fell asleep early. I always prided myself on the fact that I was the only one that survived the weekend without getting their face written on. Although, I also didn't sleep more than an hour or two the entire time. The function was representative of the semester as a whole, the purpose behind it was to bond with one another. An entire weekend with nowhere to go or nothing to do but talk to each other. Only adults had cell phones back then and there was no social media, the television only got two stations, so the movie Animal House played on VHS over and over. The only thing to do was learn about each other. Well, that and memorize the best lines from Animal House.

The semester was going exactly how I had hoped college would be when I started my freshman year. I had a great group of friends, both within the fraternity and outside, classes were flowing along with ease and there was hardly any real controversy. The occasional fight that broke out was easily broken up and it was usually only because someone had drunk too much. I was playing rugby again (Chris had gone to State College) and reconnected with guys like Tank.

Although, I did bite him on the top of the head one day after he buried my entire car under a mountain of snow and ice.

I was getting ready to go home for the weekend a few weeks before Easter, right after we had a massive snowstorm. When I went to get my car, which was parked in the parking lot in front of my girlfriend's apartment, it was missing -- or at least so I thought. As I got closer, I realized there was a mountain of snow in the middle of the parking lot, like the plow had missed an entire section. Turns out, it was my car, buried in a massive amount of snow and ice. Just then, a couple of the KDE sisters (which was my girlfriend Sharon's sorority) popped their head out of their window, laughing. I figured they had pulled the prank and buried my car. After all, we had just had a kidnapping battle back-and-forth. They kidnapped Ian, so we kidnapped a few of their pledges. It made perfect sense, but when I called them out, they denied having anything to do with my car. Regardless, I had to call home and tell my friends and family I wouldn't be in. There was no way I could dig my car out.

I figured I would walk down the hall and use Tank's phone. As I turned the corner, I saw Tank. The minute he saw me, he yelled, "Shit!" and ran into his apartment. It was pretty obvious he was the one who buried my car, not the girls. I sprinted down the hall, made my way into his apartment, jumped on his back and bit him in the head, all in good fun of course. I didn't really bite him hard. After we had a good laugh, Tank explained to me what he and a few others did. They "borrowed" a shopping cart from a local grocery store parking lot and used it to move giant blocks of ice that they chipped out of the mountain of snow and ice the plow had collected. They stacked the blocks of ice all around my car and then used a blowtorch to melt them together. Then, just for good measure, they stacked more snow on top, adding in a few beer bottles for decoration. It was actually a great prank. Lucky for me the girls of Beta Gamma had their pledges dig me out, otherwise that car would have been there until July.

Another one of my fondest memories from that semester was another prank and it epitomized just how much fun I had during my pledging experience. The active brothers were holding one of their weekly meetings in a building on campus. I think it was the library. As pledges, we had to attend, but we also had to wait outside the meeting room for the most part while they discussed all the stuff we were not yet allowed to hear. On one occasion, they were taking an awfully long time and I started to get bored. When I get bored, I tend to get in trouble. As we sat there talking amongst ourselves, we realized that one of the brothers, Steve, was not at the meeting. I suggested we pay him a visit in his dorm room. So, 13 of us walked out of the building, unbeknownst to the brothers, and crossed the campus to Oak Hall. Steve lived on the third floor, so up the stairs we went and knocked on his door. One thing led to another and we decided it would be fun to kidnap a brother. We picked Steve up, literally, and carried him down all three flights of stairs, then threw him in the trunk of Jeffrey's car. We must've had two cars, because we were all together to pull Steve out of the car at Wopsy Mountain lookout. Wopsononock (otherwise known as "Wopsy") mountain borders Altoona and boasts a classic lookout point whose panoramic view is nothing short of breathtaking.

We had no power over Steve, since we were pledges, so we would have to get creative if we wanted to have any fun with him. That's when I had quite the brilliant idea, if I do say so myself. One of the fun little things about the fraternity houses was that it's symbol, a circle with triple T's, was always on the floor somewhere. In one house it was fashioned out of tape on the carpet in the living room, in another it was painted on the concrete floor in the basement. The reason it was on the floor was that if anyone stepped inside it, they would have to finish what they were drinking. There wasn't necessarily a rush, its purpose wasn't designed to make someone chug or get them sick, but if they stepped inside the circle they had to stay put until whatever was in their hand was finished. They could have all the help they wanted if they could recruit volunteers, but they couldn't leave that circle until they were finished. It was always a lot of fun watching someone walk near the circle and then giving them a little shove. The tap dance or hop to avoid the circle was great entertainment. I was pretty good at avoiding, but one of the guys, I think it was Brian, got me good one night. As I was carrying a keg into the house he waited until I was just ready to step over the circle and then gave me a little push. I started to laugh, assuming he was joking, until he said to pull up a chair and make myself comfortable. Damn if I didn't have to sit there and serve beers all night without moving, one foot still in the circle, until the keg was empty. That taught me a lesson about the power of the circle, so when we got Steve out of the car, I took a stick, drew the circle with the triple Ts, handed him a beer and gave him a little shove. Everyone, including Steve, laughed as he had to drink a beer while we harassed him. We were out there for a little while before giving him a ride back to campus and then heading home ourselves.

My phone rang in my dorm room not too long after I got home. It was one of the brothers telling me I needed to get down to the fraternity house right away. I called Jeffrey, who said he had received the same phone call. He was going to pick me up in a couple of minutes to head down. I figured we were in trouble for kidnapping a brother, but I also figured it would be worth it from the start. As Jeffrey and I walked to the front door we got bombarded by a load of brothers. It was a professional wrestling battle royal, but there were only 13 of us pledges and we were far outnumbered. We each got an atomic wedgy to the point where our boxers got ripped. We then had to listen to the brothers rant and rave about how they were "the man." Eventually, they began leaving, one by one, but Jeffrey and I made sure all 13 of us stayed put until we were the ones that had the numbers on our side. Then, I sent Nate to lock the back door and Ian to lock the front door and we jumped on the brothers to get some payback. It was a blast, and another battle royal, but one of them got away and made it to a phone, calling the other brothers for help. They were all back again within a few minutes and our advantage was over. I remember them telling us to stay put as they went into one of the bedrooms to discuss the consequences of our rebellion. I also remember looking around at the other guys and saying that they must be out of their damn minds if they think I'm going to sit around and wait for them to think up a good revenge strategy. I found a rope somewhere in the house and tied one end of it to the banister of the staircase and the other to the doorknob of the room they were in. Then we all ran away and let them figure it out. The next day one of the brothers said one of them had to crawl out the window and down the side of the house to get out. It was a great night that we laughed about over and over and over again.

PART TWO - Storm of Change

No man, for any considerable period, can wear one face to himself and another to the multitude, without finally getting bewildered as to which may be true.
Nathaniel Hawthorne (1804 - 1864)

Contradiction

How does such a dichotomy go on that strength should permeate throughout
yet fear course in my veins so strong
I'm afraid
I'm always afraid

Where is the change from inside out when anger and sorrow dwell deep
yet happiness and joy are cast about
I hide
I always hide

Without left there is no right no matter how much it hurts
without sorrow there is no might
I stay
I always stay

M Kiel

Chapter 5 - An Earthworm and a .22

The last day of pledging was a Thursday. We were going to be initiated the following night, so all the hijinks and funny pledging stuff was finished. Everyone was scattered about doing their own thing, either at their own places or one of the three fraternity houses. In Altoona, we were not permitted to have an actual fraternity house, so we typically just used a house where only brothers lived. That year we had three of them, "Pete and Anthony's," "711," and "G spot." 711 was a house that consisted of two apartments, one upstairs and one downstairs. The upstairs was home to several members of our fraternity while downstairs housed several sorority girls. "G spot" was the main house where we typically gathered and held parties and "Pete and Anthony's" was right down the street, named after the twins who lived there. Since Pete was my big brother, that's where we were hanging out that night, relaxing and laughing about finally being finished.

Several of the brothers were outside looking for earthworms because the first day of fishing was that weekend. I remember Pete, Anthony, and Andy coming into the back door with a big can of dirt, apparently loaded with giant earthworms. I must have been either already in the kitchen, or heard them come in, because I found myself joking around with them by the kitchen table. I had a lot of fun whenever I pledged, and typically antagonized the brothers to see how far I could push. I was doing the same thing that evening, most likely flicking Anthony's ear or something irritating like that. I often did things to push everyone's buttons just to see how they would react. It was always in good-natured fun. This wasn't one of those fraternities that beat the living shit out of their pledges and degraded them for three months before a final night of initiation, after which they were automatically best friends. This was a true brotherhood that spent three months building up a kinship and a bond.

However, that's not to say that those guys didn't ever get some payback. I remember washing quite a few clean dishes. I also limited the tomfoolery with Pete after he inadvertently almost knocked out my front tooth. I had him in a bear hug, wrestling around and tried to bite him on the top of the head. I probably outweighed him at that point by about 75 pounds, so his reflex was to jerk his head straight back. I saw stars and was sure I lost my front tooth. He had a good gash on the back of his head, but to this day, twenty-one years later, my front tooth gets sensitive every now and then! I also never tried to bite him in the head again.

This time, Anthony's response was, jokingly, "You do realize you're still a pledge, right? I should make you eat one of these things!" The sound was an automatic challenge to my ears. I remember smiling and quickly grabbing the biggest earthworm I could find. I dangled it in midair in front of him and asked, "Like this?" Everyone's reaction was pretty much par for the course, knowing full well I was probably going to eat it. A few of them pointed out to Anthony he should have known better, a few yelled at me to not even think about it and a few just shook their heads before I popped the entire thing into my mouth. It was nasty and squishy but really just tasted like dirt. I chewed it up a little bit and then stuck my tongue out with a mouthful of worm. I'll admit it was pretty disgusting, but the look on Anthony's face was priceless. The reactions of everyone else in the house was just as rewarding, and it once again drove home the philosophy by which I pledged that term. I used to love to say that hazing me was impossible, because it would entail making me do something I wouldn't willingly do on my own. One of the really interesting things about this worm story though is how it evolved years later. It became something of an urban legend within my fraternity. I'll explain how and why a little later.

After I was finished irritating and grossing out the guys at Pete and Anthony's, I ended up back in my dorm room in Spruce Hall. I'm pretty sure I was asleep when my phone rang, but a girl I grew up with had called me in the middle of the night. She was calling to tell me that one of Huey's buddies from Mount Aloysius College had died. I had only met him a few times, but he was a nice guy and I felt pretty badly, especially for Huey. I couldn't fall back to sleep and didn't feel like being alone, so I called my girlfriend Sharon and asked her to bring my car and pick me up. I typically parked in the parking lot outside of her apartment complex because I had been too lazy to get a parking permit for the campus lot. She was reluctant to even answer the phone that late at night, but since I was upset, she agreed to come get me. Unfortunately, she couldn't get my car started. The 1969 Dodge Dart was a cool model, but mine was a beat-up tank. It was a little finicky and had no power anything, no power brakes, no power steering, no power windows etc., and very few people, aside from myself, liked driving it. Fortunately, there were two of her sorority sisters outside talking so she asked them if someone could give her a ride to pick me up. One of them, Jessica, agreed.

It was raining and cool, but I was waiting outside when they arrived. I was insisting that we stop at a convenience store for cigarettes before we went to her place. I initially got hooked on tobacco when I was about fourteen in the form of snuff, or dip as others refer to it. By the time I was in college I was smoking when I drank because it was more convenient and much more common. I was also smoking when I got stressed out, which was the case that night. After I was injured, I never went back to smoking, but continued with snuff until my mid-30s. When I finally quit. It was without a doubt one of the most difficult things I had ever struggled through. I remember bursting into tears many times for absolutely no reason, just melting down. Once you're addicted to nicotine, its importance surpasses just about anything else, on a regular basis, no matter what. That held true that night as Sharon tried to talk me out of running to the store. I was insistent.

When we arrived in the parking lot I jumped out of the front seat and walked past a pay phone where a guy about my age was arguing into a receiver. I was probably not very subtle when I looked at him as I walked by, but he was swearing and yelling into the phone like a wacko. I don't remember saying anything to him as I walked past, but I do remember asking someone behind the counter what was up with the guy outside. If they answered anything besides a shrug it was probably that they had no idea. So, I took my purchase and walked out the door. When I was walking past the second time, I remember him staring at me as he yelled into the phone. Looking back, I'm fairly sure it was the egocentric nature of your average nineteen-year-old, but I felt the need to ask if he was talking to me. I don't remember any other part of our conversation, but Sharon thought it looked like we exchanged a few words back and forth. The next thing I knew he had pulled out a gun. My last clear memory was of holding both hands out from my sides as a gesture that I didn't have a weapon. After that, everything went blank. There was nothing, until something began happening inside my head.

I'm fairly certain it was immediately after I was shot, and it couldn't have lasted longer than 10 seconds. Ten seconds of nothing, and it was just long enough to be fused into my soul forever. I felt as though I had dropped to my knees, my body crumbling down on top of itself into an almost fetal position, my face resting against the ground below. Yet I couldn't feel the cold hard concrete I knew was there. I couldn't hear the screeching tires of my girlfriend's car as she sped away with her sorority sister, petrified and searching for help. I couldn't smell the gunpowder that lingered in the air or taste the blood flowing down my face and drenching the cement beneath. And I couldn't see the man standing above me, holding the weapon that had driven the course of my life into that which I had always feared most.

I was surrounded by darkness; darker than any night I'd experienced before or since. Even beyond the darkness, I was surrounded by emptiness, by nothingness. I was lost in an abyss, an empty vacuum annulled of all my senses and removed from anything physical. Essentially, I was trapped inside my mind, unable to comprehend or make contact with anything outside my own body. I had no idea of the extent of my injuries nor comprehension of what was happening around me. All I could do, all I could think, all I could focus on was that I didn't want to be buried, I wasn't dead yet. I had seen a movie once where a man had been poisoned or drugged or something and was being buried alive and his screams instantly entered my mind. I wasn't sure what had happened, but I knew it was bad. The thought raged on in my head, over and over, violently and repeatedly... don't bury me, I'm not dead. A cross between the thundering, demanding voice of a drill sergeant barking orders in an empty barracks and the quiet whimper of a lost puppy hiding in a bush, this thought echoed through every corner of my dark prison. My soul, screaming to be let free, to be allowed to live on, was my only reality. And then nothing, not even thought, until the first time I remember seeing.

Chapter 6 – Sharon and Jeffrey

Meanwhile, Sharon and Jessica took off, speeding away, straight back to Pepsi (an old Pepsi plant that was renovated into an apartment complex that everyone still called Pepsi). Sharon said part of her was terrified, yet part of her wanted to get out of the car. It was a two-door and she was in the backseat, so when Jessica began driving there was no way out. Had I been able, I would've told them both to get the hell out of there. When they got back to the apartment complex, Sharon's hysterics woke up everyone in her apartment. Knowing Sharon, she probably woke up several other apartments as well. Sharon said she immediately called Jeffrey and he came and picked her up. Jeffrey told me later that before they went to the hospital, they stopped at the convenience store.

Jeffrey said he was completely smashed that night and was in a fog when he was awoken. He never even remembered it was Sharon that woke him until I told him years later. He said he did remember completely breaking down when he spoke with the cops at the convenience store, though. He was telling them who he was, who I was, and giving them some home contact information like my parents' phone number. I have no doubt he probably lost it. We were really tight, and I have no doubt that if the roles were reversed, I would have been an emotional basket case. However, years later Jeffrey used to have a field day harassing me about that conversation with the police. He always loved to exaggerate, but there were many fundamental truths about his story. Jeffrey said when he got to the convenience store, the police were taking statements but still unsure of my identity. When they had looked in my wallet, they had found two IDs. Jeffrey could never tell the story of their reaction without bursting into laughter (unless we were drinking and getting philosophical, in which case he could barely tell the story without crying). He would go on and on about the officers not knowing who I was because of my fake ID.

About a year earlier I had been walking down the hall in an apartment complex at State College and found a Pennsylvania driver's license on the floor. It was expired and the person in the picture looked nothing like me aside from having brown hair. However, the date of birth made that person over 21. If memory serves, he would've been mid-20s or around there. My first thought was that I rarely got carded if I stuck to dive bars when I wanted to get served but thought that this ID might broaden my options. I started using it, and it worked for the most part. There was one occasion where it didn't, but that was due more in part to my stupidity than the actual license. I was buying a case of beer at a distributor. The guy behind the counter asked for my ID, briefly looked at it and handed it back while he rang up my bill. Simply making small talk, he asked where in Pennsylvania Fairview is located. I had no idea. It had never dawned on me that I should look some of that information up and be prepared. When I stumbled across my own tongue, he asked for my ID again. Upon further inspection he decided not to sell me the beer.

I've never really been sure about the specifics of Jeffrey's story as far as the cop's confusion. If that guy behind the counter at the beer distributor was going to second-guess the ID, I would think that trained police officers could draw the same conclusion, probably much easier and much quicker. Especially when they had two Pennsylvania IDs to choose from, one that looked exactly like me, that wasn't expired, and another that looked nothing like me, and was expired. Granted, my real ID had a picture of me with a mullet, but that train wreck of a haircut couldn't have thrown them off that badly. For the record, I have no defense for the mullet. It was 1989.

Chapter 7 – Mom and Amy

Jeffrey and Sharon were some of the first to get to the hospital. Randy, who was my big brother Pete's big brother, was also one of the first ones there. Randy had been there when my mother got to the hospital after her chaotic ride from Portage. When she got to the hospital, the nurses greeted my mother and told her that her other son was already in with me. You can imagine this was quite a shock to my mother since she had only given birth to two children, one of whom was a girl standing right beside her. Apparently, her look of shock and confusion was obvious because the nurse quickly said, "Well, he said he was Mike's brother!" Randy had made his way into the ICU, telling them simply that he was my brother. He just never elaborated that it was a fraternity brother, not blood brother.

My mother describes the phone ringing in what she felt was the middle of the night, startling her out of a sound sleep. She said the voice on the other end simply said, "You don't know me, and I don't know you, but Mike's been shot and it's serious. They took him to the hospital." She said her initial instinct was to hope it was some sort of prank. It wasn't. She got another phone call from my aunt Judy shortly after that. Her son, my cousin Billy, had called her. He went to Penn State with me. Billy and I grew up about 7 miles apart and were in the same year. We competed against each other in some sports, like football, and ran into each other at parties now and then. We never really made deliberate plans to hang out, but we got along well when we were together. That friendship continued into college, despite joining different fraternities that were, every now and then, slightly at odds or competitive with one another.

My sister said she remembers sitting at the top of the steps, listening to the different phone calls. Asa, our foreign exchange student from Sweden, was still asleep. Most of their memories are pretty jumbled and fuzzy from that morning, but apparently, they made their way to Cresson, a neighboring town, where my Aunt Judy lived. They were picking her up on their way to the Altoona hospital. There was a torrential downpour that morning. By everyone's account, the wind and rain were about as close to a hurricane as they had seen. Amy, who was only 16, was driving and recalls the rain coming down in sheets so heavy she could barely see the road. Even at that age, there was something spectacularly strong about my little sister. She has always had this undeniable spirit and resilience. It's an aura she carries about normally, but in those moments when it's painfully obvious she's terrified, it radiates. When they finally arrived at the hospital, the first person they saw was my buddy Fritz.

Fritz came right up to my mother and gave her a hug. She said the look on his face was nothing short of devastation. He was one of my closest friends from the time I started college. He was also one of my first black friends. Growing up in a very small town, there was a lot of ethnic diversity, but just of European descent. I had friends whose grandparents still had such thick German or Italian or Hunky (Hungarian/ Slovakian) accents, I could barely understand them half the time (for the record, those were the ones who could cook like nobody's business!). However, there wasn't much -- hell, there wasn't any! -- diversity of color.

With such limited exposure, my first couple of black friends had a whole lot of ammunition with which to bust my chops. For example, Fritz asked me one time to wait while he put sunblock on his arms. I thought he was joking and said, "Yeah right, get your ass out here." When he looked at me with confusion, I responded again, "Hello! You're black!" He busted out laughing and said, "You do realize black people can get sunburned, right?" I did not, in fact, know that. My other favorite story is from stopping by Rich's dorm room, which was right down the hall from mine.

Rich was finishing getting ready and we were all going to the dining hall. I noticed a container of Vaseline sitting right beside his bed. Naturally, I started firing away masturbation jokes, one of which included, "You could at least hide your girlfriend." Rich looked at me, then at the Vaseline and then back again. I could almost see the light bulb go on inside his head. "You idiot! I use that for my hair and when my elbows get ashy!" I only dug the hole deeper when I asked, "How the hell are you getting ashes on your elbows?!" He busted out laughing and said "When black people get dry spots, we call it ashy! Now get the hell out of my room, dumb ass, I'm hungry!" Rich and

Fritz had a field day for the next couple of years with sunblock and "ashy" comments. There was always a lot of laughter with those guys, but none to be found through the rain and chaos that Friday morning as Fritz walked with my family to the hospital entrance.

Chapter 8 – First Thought – Through the Haze

I've said on many occasions that the first thing I remember seeing was a group of fraternity brothers walking past me in a single file line at the Johnstown Emergency Room. It was an amazing show of support, compassion and true friendship. However, it's not exactly my first memory. I have one other memory before this that I never felt comfortable talking about, which is probably why I wrote it. I was much more comfortable with everyone believing the happy, compassionate memory of a show of support than a depressing moment in an ambulance. The first thing I actually remember seeing was my mother in the ambulance during the ride from Altoona to Johnstown. I had initially been taken to Altoona, but they didn't have a trauma center; Johnstown did. From what I'm told, they wanted to life flight me to Johnstown, but the weather was so bad that the helicopter couldn't make the trip, so they used an ambulance.

I found out years later, actually when writing this book, that the trauma team from Johnstown met us halfway. Since they couldn't life flight me, they were doing everything else in their power to get me to the right people as fast as possible. I still don't know where the transition took place, but we left Altoona the same time the trauma team left Johnstown. We met somewhere in the middle, which by my best guess would be along the highway. My mother said that one of the trauma members, George, was an old friend of hers. When she saw him, she immediately burst into tears. I'm not sure if my first memory was from before or after that. I'm not even positive it was in the ambulance; I just know how gut wrenching the feeling was when it happened.

It's a hazy memory - like one from a night spent drowning sorrows in shots of whiskey. I don't remember any pain, sickness, or even what the blood that saturated my hair felt like. My eyes began to slowly focus in, and I saw my mother; more importantly I saw the look on her face. Throughout my life I don't ever remember seeing the slightest tinge of fear cross my mother's face until that moment.

And it seemed as though all those times when she should have been afraid and was not were forced to the surface, culminating in one agonizing moment. All I wanted to do at that moment was say I'm sorry. I tried with every fiber of my being, every ounce of energy from my body, mind and soul to just speak those two words. I couldn't. There was a tube running into my mouth and down my throat breathing for me and I couldn't speak. At that point I was fairly sure that I was going to die and the only thing I wanted to say before I went were those two words: "I'm sorry." Nothing more, nothing less, just to whisper those two words, to say something to alleviate that pain in her eyes before I died. Yet, ironically enough, that which was keeping me alive was prohibiting my last wish. Then, just as my eyes had focused in, they focused out.

Chapter 9 – Dad's Drive

Meanwhile, my father was in his truck breaking every speed limit sign he passed on his way to the hospital. He had recently accepted a supervisory position with a construction company in Virginia. He had decided to try something new, test the waters so to speak. He was planning on spending weekdays in Virginia supervising large projects for a bigger company while his crew remained busy back home. He would be staying at my Uncle Pat's place through the week and coming home on weekends.

It was definitely a time of change in my parents' world. They had resisted the temptation of moving to Virginia 20 years earlier, when they were first out of college. They liked the area in which they grew up, and because I had just been born, they needed the support of their families. Several of my dad's siblings had moved to Virginia, so they wouldn't have been alone, but it was still a far different world than that of small-town Pennsylvania. However, with me in college and my sister heading there in a few short years, the potential to make a lot more money was more tempting than ever. So, he went to try it out. It had the potential to open up a whole lot of different opportunities, including the possibility of moving there with my mother permanently. That changed the minute he answered the phone and heard I had been shot, which was four days after he had started.

He had just moved in with my Uncle Pat on Monday, but Friday morning he was in his truck, driving home, never to go back. He quit the job in Virginia, paused everything with his crew back home and spent the next four months by my side. I've struggled with writing about this for years, trying to put myself in my father's place as he drove home that morning. Despite talking to him about it countless times, I never felt like I could do justice to his experience or capture what he was thinking and feeling. I could never find the right words ... so we decided to use his:

Our nightmare began in the early hours of April 16, 1993. The phone ringing at 4:30 AM was answered by Sue. A young man's voice cracked over the wires asking if this was Mike Kiel's house and if this was Mike's mom. Upon verification, the voice continued, "You don't know me, and I don't know you, but some friends of Mike's asked me to call you. Mike was shot in the head a very short while ago." Sue got out of bed, continuing to tell herself, "This isn't right! There's a mistake. It's got to be some sick fraternity joke." Before she had a chance to call me – I was temporarily in Virginia working – the phone rang again. This time Sue was sure that the voice would be someone apologizing for the horrible fraternity joke. It was Sue's sister, Judy, whose son was Mike's first cousin who was also a student at PSU, confirming that Mike was indeed shot and had been taken to the Altoona Hospital.

The phone call came to me next. The disbelief, the shock, the horror, the anger, all rose as I tried to help calm Sue – and myself. The normal three-hour trip from the Washington, DC area to our home was completed in a much shorter span despite driving rains. My truck phone was both a lifesaver and an added disturbance as the interference continued through most of my trip. I called the Altoona Hospital first and was informed that Sue had not yet arrived, but Mike's brother Randy was there with him. Mike has no brother, but I recognized immediately that his fraternity brother Randy Lott had posed as his brother to gain access to Mike. I asked to speak with Randy who informed me that Mike was shot coming out of a convenience store. It was not a wound to his head, but rather to his neck. I asked Randy how Mike was and if he was conscious. Randy stated that he was conscious, though not breathing on his own. Then he told me the words that still haunt me: "Mr. Kiel, Mike has no feeling or movement below his neck." I just remember saying, "Oh God, no! Oh God, no!" Poor Randy tried his best to calm me down saying that they didn't know anything yet and to take it easy driving up – as well as anything else he could think of saying.

I next called Tom Cardellino, a cardiologist and personal friend. I tried frantically to get information from him without having much to give him. Tom assured me that he would call Altoona Hospital and see what he could find out.

Next I called my brother, Joe Kiel. He had already left for work, so I gave what little information I had to my sister-in-law Mary Lou. Approximately forty-five minutes passed before the reception returned to my truck phone. When it did, I called Tom again. Tom had found out that the Altoona Hospital was incapable of doing anything more and they were going to life flight Mike to Conemaugh Hospital Trauma Center in Johnstown. He had also called Johnstown informing them of Altoona's decision. He did not know how soon he would be transferred, so he could not tell me if I should head toward Johnstown or Altoona. When I was again able to reach Altoona by phone, Sue was there. She brought our sixteen-year-old daughter Amy along and had seen Mike. She said he was still in the emergency room and he looked bad. Amy was all shaken up and having a difficult time. Also, Sue still didn't know when the transfer to Conemaugh would take place, but now they were questioning the safety of the helicopter flight due to the inclement weather.

My reception was again lost, so I had to wait until I got to Breezewood, Pennsylvania, to use the pay phone. This was about the fourth or fifth time I called Tom. Mike was in the process of being transported to Conemaugh, so I needed to go directly to Johnstown.

As I began to get closer to home, the radio began to blare news than an unidentified Penn State student had been shot at a local convenience store. It somehow added to the nightmarish situation but drove home even stronger to me that this was really happening.

I finally arrived in Johnstown about 10-15 minutes after they had transported Mike. The hospital emergency room was filled with Penn State students!! The Conemaugh Hospital is approximately a one-hour drive from the Altoona campus.

After hugging and kissing Sue and Amy, we talked to the neurosurgeon, Dr. Snitzer. He was abrupt and matter of fact regarding Mike's injury at the C-3/C-4 level of the spinal cord. The bullet had gone through the back section of Mike's spinal cord and was lodged in the fleshy tissue on the other side of his neck. No surgery appeared to be necessary as the bullet was already through and the damage was finished. We went into the back room to the ER department and I saw Mike for the first time. He had a large "L" shaped cut above his left eye which was roughly sewn together – rough because there were obviously more important, life-threatening matters to deal with. He had fallen, we discovered later, onto a four-foot high cement pole in front of the convenience store. He had on a large collar to prevent further damage to his neck. He was intubated – which consisted of a plastic tube inserted through his mouth down to his lungs. This tube was hooked to a ventilator which provided the oxygen to Mike's lungs to sustain life. He lay there, completely aware of his situation and his surroundings. Also, he appeared to be frightened but not to a panic state. That would arrive numerous times in the next six weeks.

I looked down at him and my heart felt as though it had dropped to my feet. I had been praying for three hours for this not to be happening and that he would be okay. I continually asked my late mother and father, who both died in 1986, and Sue's late mother, who died in 1982 to please help him. Now I prayed even harder to anyone who would hear me to let me take Mike's place. We were told that the next 24 hours would be critical in the determination of the permanence of Mike's injuries. Doctors and nurses were coming in, using pins to determine the level of sensation Mike could feel. They would start at his hands or feet and continue. There was never a response until midway up to the chest level. There, he would begin to feel a slight sensation. The shoulders, neck and head were the only sections undisturbed in the sensation level.

Our affiliation with numerous doctors and nurses resulted in an extraordinary number of people coming into Mike's room, asking questions and doing whatever they could to help. Meanwhile, Mike's friends were still inundating the waiting room of the emergency room. We heard later that several nurses made comments such as "Who is this guy? Should we know him? Why are all of these people involved?" Believe me, they were only getting a sample of what was to come over the next two months to Conemaugh Hospital. To the staff of Conemaugh, we will always be appreciative of the sensitivity they displayed. One of the nurses, to the surprise of some others, asked Mike if he would like to see his friends before he was taken to the Intensive Care Unit on the sixth floor. He mouthed the word "Yes" and the nurse herded these teams of young men and women through the back corridors of the emergency room, two at a time, as they all bid their good wishes to their friend with tears in their eyes. Then, the social service department took this whole large group to the fourth floor with a trauma specialist and explained to them what was going on with Mike, his injury, and answered any questions.

I have only ever seen my father in that state of worry or sadness twice in my life. The first time was when his father, my grandfather, passed away. My grandmother had found him on the living room floor, dead, and called my father. By the time I got down to my grandparents' house, an ambulance was there. The moment I saw my dad he embraced me in a hug in a manner that I wasn't expecting. I could feel his hurt and sadness. I could feel his devastation and more memorable than anything else I could feel all the strength leaving his body. I was 13 years old, and at that age dads are invincible -- they're superhuman. Everyone has that moment where they see the kink in their father's armor, when they become human. That was mine. That was the first time I remember him being anything less than superhuman. Somehow though, in that moment of weakness, he became even stronger.

The second time was when my nephew Ben crawled away from my mother and rolled down an entire flight of steps. I remember my dad sitting at the kitchen table, head in his hands, waiting and worrying if the fall had done any real damage to his grandson. Luckily, Ben was a chubby little sucker who, it turns out, inherited the staircase tumble directly from his father. His other grandmother, SunAi, was a nurse so Amy and Pete called her quickly. She guided them through checking the appropriate things on Ben, who ended up being just fine. She then shared that both Pete and his twin brother Anthony used to tumble downstairs all the time. The look of relief that washed over my father's face wasn't complete, by any means, but it was obviously more relaxed. I don't remember what my father looked like when he first got to the hospital. I have a feeling that's blocked out for a reason like many things. I also don't remember much else in the emergency room with one exception.

Chapter 10 – Fury's Cost

The only thing I remember from the emergency room is extremely brief and it's in tiny splashes. It was of fraternity brothers walking past in a single file line. They, along with a significant number of other friends from college, had swarmed the emergency room and were being the typical "pains in the ass" that make me love them so much. They weren't causing problems except by their sheer number -- nearly 60 of them had packed themselves into the tiny waiting room. In order to free up room, the nurses had asked them to move to another floor and in exchange, the nurses would update them on my condition every 15 minutes and allow them to each walk quickly past me. I remember seeing several of them but none very clearly. The one that sticks in my mind the most was Ian -- short little Ian. He was a trip, that boy, and we pledged together. I had to rescue him once while pledging when a sorority kidnapped him. When I found him, he was neatly dressed in women's clothing and adorned with makeup and jewelry. He was the ugliest damn woman I'd ever seen. I remember seeing him more clearly in the emergency room than others and seeing him always brought a smile to my face, but I was lying down and they were all walking fairly quickly so I never truly saw his face. I was, and still am, thankful that I couldn't focus on his eyes. I have a feeling I might have seen the same look, at least to some degree, that I saw in the ambulance. As they finished walking by, I heard a nurse talking and then nothing again. Nothing until I awoke in the ICU room that would become my home and my hell for the next two months. That awakening brought reality, it brought physical pain, fear, numbness. It brought paralysis. But most of all it brought anger and rage… it brought a pure unadulterated hate like I had never felt before.

Like I said, when I was a child, I had a pretty volatile temper, especially by my teenage years. For some reason I had always perceived myself during my earlier childhood as very "wimpy" and I always felt the need to prove something. I had allowed that temper free reign far too often. I found myself in deep, very hot, water several times due to allowing my anger to lead my actions. I even ended up on probation after a fight in high school. I had gotten into an altercation with a neighborhood guy who had bullied me as a child and I completely lost it. I felt something snap inside me to such a degree that I nearly lost the capacity to control my actions. Despite the fact that he was several years older and quite a bit bigger, I really hurt him. He ended up going to the hospital with some pretty serious injuries. That feeling of rage from all the times he had bullied me simply took over and guided my actions, pushing my intellect and consciousness to the background. I absolutely despised that feeling, that loss of control. Up until the point when I was injured, that was always the benchmark to which I swore I would never return. That loss of control and submission to that sense of anger and hate was an unwelcome feeling, but it was nothing compared to what I felt in that ICU room.

I often joke that the only two things on my mind when I awoke in ICU were anger and sex. I wanted the man who shot me dead by my hands alone. And, could I ever have sex again? An odd combination, true, but they were the only two things that mattered at that point. Interestingly enough, since sex would entail some type of future planning, it faded into the background rather quickly. All that truly mattered, as my focus began to narrow, was that present moment, and in that moment my heart's only desire was vengeance. It began to take over every thought, and each beat of my heart seemed to pump more poisonous rage into every corner of my body, and more importantly my soul.

I remember thinking that nothing mattered except killing him. Recovery did not matter, my family did not matter, my future, my past, nothing mattered but that very moment and, in that morphine-induced moment, I wanted him dead. Whether by bullet, bat, or blade, I was going to take his life. I can still picture family members walking into the room, the epitome of love in their hearts, and I don't think I even tried to hide the fact that I was full of hate and nothing more. The same things kept echoing over and over in my head: *He didn't just take your arms and legs, he took your future, your ability to play sports, to drive, to finish college, to ever get a job or live on your own.* Even more fundamentally, that little voice screamed, *He took your ability to hug your family, to shake your father's hand, to father a child of your own or even so much as hold a niece or nephew in your arms.* He took everything and left nothing but hate, and it spread like a cancer throughout my world. The more I thought these things the angrier I became, and the angrier I became, the louder and more prominent these thoughts echoed. Ironically enough this was around the same time I was experiencing panic attacks and my body was beginning to shut down.

In those beginning days, when my survival was questionable at best, my memories seemed to fade in and out. The only consistencies I remember were the shots of morphine every hour on the hour, the sound of the ventilator compressing air into my lungs at a steady rhythm, and my father sitting beside my bed, tiny cross in hand, holding my numb fingers. He would pray while I slept and attempt to comfort me when I woke. I was not easily comforted. My waking moments were spent fixated on hate and rage, while my drug-induced sleep was ravaged with nightmares of all shapes and sizes. The nightmares were so realistic, so intensely tangible and palpable that they were more real than the waking moments. I don't know that I've ever experienced a greater horror than waking from one of these nightmares to discover that there was very little difference in my conscious life. This served only to feed that anger that was spreading through me as well as compromising my ability to recover. Marcus Aurelius, widely considered the last great Emperor of Rome, once said, "Such as are your habitual thoughts, such also shall be the character of your mind, for the soul is dyed by the thoughts." Looking back, this is exactly what was happening to me. My body seemed to be so preoccupied with my thoughts that it was neglecting any attempt to heal itself, going so far as to reject the air from the ventilator. I was dying.

There was a code in the ICU that indicated death was imminent -- Code Blue. It was reserved for those times that were so dire that doctors and nurses needed to forgo any other duties in which they were engaged. I'm not sure how many times they rushed to my room while the words "Code Blue" blared overhead, but I'm told they brought me back from oblivion at least three times, if not more. Each time that code would echo overhead, my family would gather together and wait for news, if it was me, and if so, was I going to survive. One of those times the doctors were so convinced I wouldn't make it, they brought my mother and father into "The Room" to prepare them. Dr. Miller, the Lead Trauma Specialist, explained what was happening and told them he didn't think I would make it through the night. He wanted them to prepare themselves to say goodbye. My parents immediately sent my Uncle Pat to bring my sister down to the hospital.

Amy recalls Uncle Pat picking her up from my parents' ice cream shop, where she was working, and telling her I wanted to see her. She didn't think anything out of the ordinary when one of her friends just happened to show up and say they could take over her shift. However, as they were driving down Main Street, past one of the doctor's offices, she said she looked at the speedometer and realized Uncle Pat was going 45 in a 25 mile-per-hour zone. To understand just how big of a sign that was, you would have to understand Uncle Pat and his view of rules. When a rule exists, it doesn't even get bent let alone broken, so nearly doubling the speed limit wasn't just out of character, it was extremely unusual. Amy said as soon as that registered, her heart and stomach dropped, and she sat in silent worry the entire drive to Johnstown. She knew something was really wrong if Uncle Pat was driving like that. She was 16 years old and possibly going to see her brother for the last time.

Meanwhile, my obsession with vengeance and my body's unwillingness to accept the oxygen being pumped into it became such a problem they resorted to drastic measures. They (chemically) paralyzed me the rest of the way, shutting down every bodily function not necessary for survival. Up until that point I still had control of the tops of my shoulders as well as my entire head and face. That changed instantly once they induced a coma. I could not wiggle my ears, open my mouth or even blink my eyes. Unfortunately, I was still aware, my cognitive facilities intact.

While I was on the ventilator I felt as though I was suffocating every minute of every day. No air was passing through my nasal cavity, rather it flowed freely through the tube in my neck. My only saving grace, my one solitude of sanity was that I could keep my mouth open. Feeling air circulate around my mouth, being able to even pretend I could draw a breath on my own was the only thing keeping me from a total collapse. However, after they induced me, I no longer had control over my mouth, tongue or facial features. In order to keep my lips from cracking and chapping the nurses decided to put Vaseline on my mouth, which served its purpose without fail. My lips stayed soft and supple, not a crack in sight. Unfortunately, these nurses were unaware of my compensatory trick of keeping my mouth open to avoid that suffocating feeling. They closed my mouth, probably so no flies found their way into my gullet. For the next week though, which felt like a decade, I was aware, and I felt like I was suffocating, unable to move, unable to scream, unable to even die. I could hear everything around me, my senses intact, but could not interact with the world around me. I'm sure I slept and I'm sure my brain shut down for a good part of that experience. But with my eyes closed and being unable to tell the difference between waking and sleeping, it was even more difficult to differentiate between my nightmares and the reality that was eerily similar. The band Metallica has a song titled "One" whose video gives me the willies to this day. It's exactly what I was living.

After nearly a week they brought me back around and out of the total paralysis or coma. I was even more livid having just experienced that surreal nightmare. It had worked, however, up until that point. My body had begun to accept the oxygen from the ventilator, and I was beginning to stabilize. However, I was again turning for the worse now that I was awake again. They had brought a psychologist in for some relaxation and meditation training but that was barely taking the edge off. I was still so full of spite my body just could not compensate. My father had gotten rather good at helping me use the visualization and avoid panic attacks, but overall, I was still shutting down. Then, one day, something just clicked and registered in my brain. It was a pure epiphany moment like none that I had ever had before or since.

I don't remember all the specifics during those first few weeks very clearly, mostly feelings and thoughts, but there is one thing I have remembered as though it was clairvoyant. Like I said, my father spent every minute of every hour at my bedside. His prayers and consultations were usually reserved for limiting those panic attacks and hoping some sort of miracle would begin allowing movement in some part of my body. However, for whatever reason, on that day we began talking about my state of mind. We spoke more specifically about my obsession with vengeance. His comment was short and simple, and I felt it much more than I heard it. He said, "You don't have enough room in your heart for love and hate; one will consume the other."

I remember watching his face as he said it, deep lines etched into his cheeks and forehead. I could tell he was exhausted, but he was calm and logical despite being worried and drained. I would find out later that he never went home but twice during the entire two months I remained in the ICU room. Whether it was the words he used, the look on his face or a combination of the two, something registered. An understanding of the toll anger and hate would take on the world around me. That those feelings wouldn't simply destroy me, they would burn down everything around me and inside me, began to sink in. The situation that I was in was bad enough, the fight ahead of me daunting enough, that to compound it with such an unnecessary burden would only make it worse. It was an almost instant change, like a giant weight had been lifted not from my shoulders but from within me. However, I quickly found that without vengeance and hate to occupy my mind I was forced to face what was actually going on around me, what had happened to me and what lay ahead of me. It was not something for which I was prepared, and the realization became more than I could bear. I wanted to die.

Chapter 11 – The Abyss

Meanwhile, outside of my ICU room, the rest of my friends and family were struggling with their own battles. As mentioned earlier, when he received the news of the shooting, my father had abandoned his new job. He was also ignoring his own contracting company, which he had kept going locally while he tried out the new job. All in order to sit by my side. My mother had a different struggle; she could not afford to leave her job for any real period of time. Being a college student, I was covered under her insurance. She was the office manager and responsible for all the billing at a sports medicine clinic. If she was gone too long, the company would have serious problems. On top of that, it had just changed ownership. Luckily, the new owner, Paul, gave my mother free reign to come and go as she pleased so she could visit me in the hospital anytime she wanted. In fact, he was so accommodating that my mother made it a point to tell him at her retirement party in 2017 that she never forgot his kindness. That left my sister to basically fend for herself. We were hosting an exchange student from Sweden, so at least she was not home alone all the time. Although, I have no doubt she often felt alone. She told me one time that one of the most traumatic things for her was the news coverage from that night. They played it over and over and over again. It was a video clip of the police officers standing outside the convenience store, picking up a bloodied shirt along with the rest of my things that were laying on the sidewalk. Amy said from the first time she saw the video, it was horrible. She remembered seeing that shirt in the laundry, picking it up and folding it, recalling where I bought it. She remembered the first time I came home wearing that funky belt, the tie-dyed hemp one that didn't even have a clip on the end, it just tied in a knot. Everything they were showing in that video was personal and tangible. She had felt them the last time she gave me a hug. Now they were covered in blood and being placed in an evidence bag.

My girlfriend was finding herself missing classes, exams and sorority functions in order to come down to the hospital and sit in the waiting room. Fraternity brothers and friends alike, along with cousins, aunts, uncles and my parents' friends also had a ubiquitous presence in that ICU waiting room. They would alternate visits, sometimes bringing food like a crockpot full of hot dogs and sauerkraut, and just sit in the waiting room supporting not only me but each other. Between my father, Uncle Pat and several friends, they would eat those hot dogs several days later, still cold. Sometimes I think they were trying to get the ICU room next to me! Then again, Uncle Pat was always adamant that food doesn't go bad!

One of the things that everyone who came to visit always made sure to do was sign a notebook. There were dozens of those things in various sizes and people wrote everything from several lengthy paragraphs to a single line of encouragement or support. One group of girls from a sorority that included Jenny, Cathy, Jenna, Jen (and I think a few others) decided to make a recording of themselves on a cassette tape. It was absolutely hilarious, but I never did ask them if there was alcohol involved when they made it. Everyone seemed to make a tremendous effort to just come down to the waiting room. They weren't allowing anyone in to see me other than immediate family, but still everyone came to that waiting room. I have no real memory, just what people have told me, but apparently at one point I had come out of the fog I was in from a morphine induced state and mentioned that my Uncle Joe was the only one of my aunts and uncles that had not come to visit. He had been there several times already, but when he heard that I didn't remember he was there, he came the next day.

I had several friends who went to extremes as well. One of my old high school friends, Joe, would come every day after work and just sit in the waiting room and read a book. My parents said he never even asked to come into the ICU, although it was obvious that he wanted to, he just wanted to be there. Conversely, a fraternity brother who had transferred to Old Dominion (my big brother's big brother's big brother, if you can follow that) just showed up inside the ICU room. Within hours after I was shot, word had apparently spread to other campuses as well as other towns, and anyone who was connected to me in any way, shape, or form knew the situation. That first day or so in the ICU found Jim's presence. As the story goes, my father looked up (I was still completely out of it), saw Jim standing there and asked him how he got in. When Jim replied that our fraternity brothers had contacted him immediately at Old Dominion, my father rephrased and clarified, "No, how did you get *here*?" Jim's response was shifted to a more logical answer. He described what route he took - Route 70. At this point, my father is absolutely bewildered because the doctors and nurses were even giving my dad grief for being in the room, so he still couldn't figure out how Jim got in. So he asked again, much more pointedly, "No, how did you get here in this room?" To which Jim replied, "I just asked everyone in the waiting room which room he was in, and walked in." I don't think anyone has ever told Jim where he could and could not go. Well, with the exception of the several times I told him where to go when I was pledging!

I had such an amazing show of support you would think I could have conquered any obstacle. Unfortunately, it just wasn't working that way ... or maybe it was. I was burning my way through the stages of grief at an unbearably intense but rapid pace. Anger and depression were at the forefront and were felt with a white-hot intensity. It seemed as though I had conquered the former only to be left feeling like I was hit by a sledgehammer with the latter. I was addicted to morphine by this time, receiving shots on the hour, every hour. I was also in agonizing pain between my diaphragm attempting to take over breathing responsibilities from my chest, phantom pain from my numb limbs and the general body torture that comes along with drug addiction. The doctors told my parents I was using more than a junkie. Apparently, the way people overdose on morphine (which is basically the same thing as heroin once the body breaks it down) is that it shuts down the respiratory system. Being on a ventilator, it seems, allowed me to become very efficiently addicted. All these things combined with unimaginable fear had me experiencing the depression part of grief to the point where I was ready to give up.

I remember telling my mother it was too hard, that my stomach was in too much pain from my diaphragm. I didn't think I would ever get independent from a ventilator. I remember watching my body waste away as I lost 75 pounds as if it were melting off me. I remember begging nurses for more morphine, only to be told that the hour wasn't up. I remember the quiet, dark hours between 2 AM and

5 AM. The sounds of the machines around me seemed to blend into the darkness. I had hallucinations from all the drugs and on the rare occasion that my father wasn't in the room with me the only way I could call for help from the nurses was to click my tongue. They rarely heard me. Like I said, I was in and out of consciousness and only lucid part of the time for the first several weeks, but when it all became too much, I remember very clearly hitting rock-bottom. My father was standing beside my bed and I asked him to let me go, to turn off the ventilator and let me die. The look of torture on his face as he heard those words haunts me to this day. I could see his eyes well up with tears as he walked around the foot of my bed toward the doorway, the only words he could force out were "That's not fair." Just thinking about it turns my stomach to this day. That would not have been fair, and it would have been cruel. No parent should ever have to endure that.

as I stare through the glass, thinking of a life from the past
I wonder if my future will ever hold promise
the white water tower glares back hour after hour
shrieking that life has become fruitless

where do I steer this ship full of fear
when I must be a rock for the rest
am I only smiling because I'm denying
the terror of my imminent test

I wonder what they think, as my heart begins to sink
with each solemn face that passes through the door
is this truly what's right, an insurmountable fight
or do they simply all fear the funeral roar

it would destroy their pride to see what's inside
of this hollow scared little kid
yet I force a grin from somewhere deep within
and try to keep the darkness hid

no matter what they say I'll keep these feelings at bay
for this burden is mine alone to carry
the darkness beneath shall stay in its sheath
lest it destroy all around me

M Kiel

Chapter 12 – Hope & Humor

And there it was, the very first spark or glimmer or whatever you want to call it that triggered a true survival response. There was the shadow of a reason to press forward. Maybe it was guilt, maybe it was a recognition of selfishness, or maybe, better yet, it was an understanding that giving up like that was nothing more than transferring my pain to everyone around me, especially those I loved. It was also the first time that it really registered that I wasn't the only one going through all of this. That the people around me were suffering just as much, if not more, being forced to sit idly by, unable to help. Even through the drug-induced haze I was starting to see much more clearly the anxiety and worry along with love and support that walked in and out of that ICU room on a regular basis. After I caught that first glimpse, I immediately began recognizing it every second of every day. I saw it in my father who almost never left my side, my mother and sister, my aunts and uncles, my cousins, family, friends and even in the nurses and other professionals working on me. I saw it in the notebooks that were passed around in the waiting room for people to sign and write little messages, since they couldn't see me in person. I saw how this was affecting them and felt responsible. I also felt guilty that I had not recognized it sooner, and along with that guilt and accountability came a desire to help. To do something for them as they were doing for me. I didn't realize it at the time, but looking back, I think it was a turning point; the first true step back upwards in a journey that until that point was spiraling downward.

That must be the ultimate paradox; that hope is born from despair. I'm still not quite sure I understand how that happens. It seems, at least in my case, that the absence of hope actually caused its creation. I give a lot of talks these days, ranging from colleges and high schools to professional events, and one thing I almost always include is what I call a "vicious circle." This emphasizes just how much everyone is directly affected by the people around them and vice versa. The idea that if someone has a very poor environment, or surroundings, or negative people around them, they tend to have a more negative outlook. It's only logic and makes sense - you acclimate to your surroundings. That negative outlook then causes the individual to project outward feelings of despair or anger or discomfort or a myriad of other unpleasant feelings. This has the exact effect you would expect; it drives people away or, at a bare minimum, causes them to be far less supportive. This back-and-forth cycle feeds into itself so quickly it's like an avalanche, picking up speed and strength as it goes. However, the circle can go both ways.

The exact same thing seems to happen with positive energy and support. When people are encouraging and reinforcing, I believe that feeds into an individual's desire to rise up or push forward. Likewise, when that support system sees the individual they care about succeeding in even the tiniest little thing, it fuels that fire and again, like an avalanche, the circle feeds into itself and picks up strength and speed as it goes. Unfortunately, I have no idea how either circle begins, I just know I'm eternally grateful for the one I'm in now. Mine started way back in that hospital room, of this I'm fairly sure. It could've been anything that triggered the beginning. A smile from a family member, a joke from me, whatever it was, I, and everyone around me, seemed to have latched onto it very effectively, which has made all the difference. We were choosing on which part of the journey we would place the most emphasis.

So there I was with a desire to start helping the people around me somehow, but no idea how to accomplish it. That's when it kicked in like a reflex: humor. Nurses, doctors, aides and therapists were in and out of that room constantly. I was hooked up to so many different machines they were forever checking numbers and plugs and connections. I wasn't breathing on my own, so I had a ventilator hooked up to my throat. I couldn't eat, so I had a G-tube (gastrointestinal tube) as well as a tube that ran up my nose and down into my stomach. I have no idea why they had to have both; they led to the same place. However, they tended to run the disgusting liquid nourishment through the tube in my nose, and pump medicine through the one in my stomach, if memory serves. For a while, I had a chest tube directly into my left side. An intern accidentally nicked something inside my chest or lung, causing it to collapse. I also had a pulse ox connected to my finger to measure my oxygen levels, a catheter running up my penis into my bladder and a bunch of those suction stickers connected to wires all over my chest monitoring my heart along with just about everything else. There had to have been a dozen machines in that room and I could rarely see any of them. I was lying prone on my back staring at the ceiling and couldn't turn my head very far in either direction.

The nurses had a tendency to bustle about so quickly they would trip over things or bump things when they were making their way around my bed. This was probably due to a combination of things, including my extended care along with all the other patients they needed to get to in a timely manner. Most of them had a great bedside manner and would smile often. However, this didn't prevent them from banging into something every now and then, which I could hear but not see. This was often followed up by "Oops!" For the record, when someone has a brand-new spinal cord injury and is still well hopped up on morphine the effect of "Oops" from right behind them near the machines keeping them alive is very similar to a cattle prod to the nuts. I eventually had a sign made and hung on the wall that prohibited any use of the word "Oops" outside of my field of vision.

One of my nurses, a guy named Pete, was chuckling about the sign one afternoon while checking on me. I, of course, still couldn't talk because of the ventilator hooked up to my throat, so my father was filling him in on the sign's origins. While they were laughing, Pete indicated that I needed to be slid up in the bed (having slowly worked my way down after a multitude of flips and pokes and prods from other nurses) and needed to call someone else for assistance. My father, ever the helpful one, offered to grab one side of the sheet underneath me while Pete grabbed the other side to move me toward the head of the bed. Both were men who tended to go full speed all the time, both were strong, and neither were paying attention as they spoke to each other. The result was me being catapulted up, above the top of the bed and headfirst into the wall behind me. It must have been an extremely funny sight to behold for several reasons. First, the look on their faces as I bounced off of the wall; second, the image of me launching into a "What the hell is wrong with you two?! Are you crazy?!" tirade, made even funnier by the fact that no sound was coming out of my mouth despite it moving at 100 mph; and third, the automatic response from both of them which was only to comment that I was nearly going to be charged for a second room!

Humor began getting traded back and forth quite often, but not always immediately recognized. I grew up in a family that has always required thick skin. Nothing was off-limits when it came to wisecracks and harassment. It has always been such a close-knit and loving family with an underlying bond of absolute acceptance and support that everyone has always taken free reign that a good wisecrack, regardless of how brutal, was always meant in jest. It didn't take long for a no-holds-barred approach to humor to be embraced in my ICU room. In fact, one of my little comments to a family friend had him quite worried. Tom Cardellino is a really close friend of my family who I'd known for years. He taught me how to snow ski when I was in elementary school and is one of the kindest and most genuine people I've ever known. He was a prominent cardiologist before he retired and therefore had many connections throughout the hospital. He would stop in every day, giving my parents advice and support as well as interpreting medical jargon. He was also able to get into my ICU room and see me every day. On one of these occasions he came out of my room and told my father he was worried about me getting depressed and losing hope. My dad, knowing I had turned that corner a little while back was surprised and asked what happened. Tom told him that the nurses were having some real difficulties drawing blood and that it was upsetting me. When my dad asked him what I said or did that made him think I was upset, Tom responded that I looked at him and mouthed the words "This is all in vain." Knowing me very well, my dad immediately smiled at Tom and told him to think about what I had said. I had actually told him, "This is all in vein." Hey, it amused *me* anyway.

I was getting more and more of those good moments where I could joke or smile or laugh. They never stretched into an entire day, but I could tell it was coming. My aunt and uncle had brought me a letter from someone in Pittsburgh who had a spinal cord injury. I don't remember exactly what it said, but somewhere in the mix he talked about good days popping up. The part of that letter that stuck with me was how he described having a good day that came out of nowhere, but then promptly went back to bad days again. However, a few days later another good day popped up, then another, and then another. He said that eventually those good days start occurring closer and closer together until they eventually connect. Then there will be a couple of good days mixed in with all the bad, but eventually the good days stay connected and roll along, outnumbering the bad by far. As my body began to stabilize a little, I was approaching those good days. Unfortunately, the environment I was in, the ICU room, was designed to keep me alive, not progress onward. So, since good days were popping up, it became time to look at where I was going next.

PART THREE– Atlanta

Inside Out

If I knew what was right or knew what was wrong
if I wasn't so weak, if I could only be strong
I'd have a handle on life, I'd know where to go
I'd be able to find love, I'd be able to grow

But I'm bound by my senses and questions throughout
second-guessing my faith and casting self doubt
to find a place in this world not just a façade
to find a reason in life and understand God

The more enlightenment I seek the less I know
each question gives rise to more questions below
but answers are fleeting when loss grips tight
and resilience gets tested by crushing plight

I have faced the dark and unanswered prayers
faced a deafening silence and awkward stares
found the edge of the cliff and deepest abyss
and struggled for meaning in any of this

But a search for truth and a meaning to life
results in one thing despite all its strife
if I had all the answers, the questions would cease
my journey then flat, with no search for peace

To question is right, to remedy what's wrong
acknowledging weakness defines what's strong
my reason, my place, what I comprehend
resides in the challenge, not answers or end

M Kiel

Chapter 13 - Shepherd

By the end of May, I was stable enough that the hospital wanted to move me out of the ICU and onto a different floor. It would have been a death sentence and I probably would have never gotten off the ventilator. The staff and personnel in Johnstown kept me alive, but high-level spinal cord injury rehabilitation was beyond their expertise. In fact, my parents were hesitant to keep me in Johnstown in the first place because of the severity of my injury. They briefly considered sending me to Pittsburgh once I had stabilized. However, there was so much support in Johnstown they were torn. Tom was visiting every day and knew every one of the doctors, but he wasn't the only one. Rick Schroeder, who was an orthopedic surgeon and another friend, was also visiting daily. He would test sensation levels and look for reflex responses along with deciphering a lot of the medical jargon floating around. On top of that he had a few friends who were neurologists. He would touch base with them frequently to confirm my treatment.

During one of the conversations about sending me to Pittsburgh, Rick was laying out the pros and cons, so my dad asked him point-blank what he would do if I were his son. My dad said he chuckled and said, "I had a feeling you were going to ask me that." He went on to say that he knew every doctor in Johnstown and thought they were all good, but some had limits that would cause him concern. He said Pittsburgh would have plenty of doctors with their own limits, but he didn't know them and wouldn't be able to keep watch. He recommended keeping me local and if he saw anything he wasn't comfortable with, he would stop them. Then we could start exploring places like Pittsburgh. That was probably one of the best things that could have happened for me and definitely one of the most comforting things for my parents. They had an expert set of eyes double checking and advising. It worked because I was now stable and ready to move out of the ICU. It appeared Johnstown had done all they could (under the watchful eyes of Rick and Tom); there was nothing more they could do for me.

Luckily my mother had good insurance that provided me with a few options; one of which was Shepherd Spinal Center in Atlanta, Georgia. In 1993, there were only a few places considered "Model Spinal Cord Injury Centers," which meant they provided the highest level of comprehensive treatment from injury through rehabilitation and reintegration. My choices were limited because I was still ventilator dependent and could not breathe on my own. My options were narrowed down to Craig, a rehab center in Colorado, Kessler in New Jersey, or Shepherd in Georgia. My parents had looked at a place in Pittsburgh but ruled it out immediately. When they went for a tour, they said it was dark with boxes cluttering many of the hallways. Most importantly, though, they said that they didn't see anyone out of bed. There was barely any activity. Conversely, when the representative from Georgia provided us with a videotape, Shepherd appeared as the polar opposite. There were people everywhere, activity all around and expectations appeared high. My father's Journal reflects that I chose Shepherd on June 3 and I have no doubt that decision, and the experience I had there, has played a fundamental role in my life. It could quite easily be the biggest factor, aside from my family and friends, that shaped who I am and how I live life with a spinal cord injury.

After I made that decision, there was very little time wasted. A Learjet was booked and scheduled to fly me down to Atlanta on June 8. Meanwhile, my support circle was busy organizing a "Walk for Mike" fundraiser at my old high school football stadium. On June 5 over 150 people walked around that track for hours raising money. I watched the video the next day and I think I was speechless. Well, I couldn't speak anyway with the trachea and ventilator, but even if I could have spoken, I don't think I would have been able to find the words to express my gratitude. They raised $10,000 in the span of an afternoon, but maybe more importantly I saw an amazing show of love and support from so many people.

My Uncle Pat came up from Virginia to participate and walked something like 10 miles, just enough to outdo everyone else. He was late, as usual (he always was, and still is, late for everything!), so he had to run a good portion of that ten miles in order to get it all in during the event. Unfortunately for him, he isn't the type to exercise, especially not jogging. He's an extremely hard worker and possesses a ridiculous amount of stamina, but none of that comes from jogging or any type of cardio conditioning. So, if memory serves, he was unable to walk for about a day or two afterwards because he pushed himself so far. When he came into my hospital room, he told me there was only one reason he pushed himself that far. He wanted to get the little plaque that stated he had completed the most laps. He wanted that plaque so that he could walk into my hospital room, look me in the eye and say that his mother always told him, "You can do anything you put your mind to." Then he had to sit down again because his legs were so sore! That was the mindset, though, of all of these people supporting me; they were taking the position that I could do anything. It was the type of support and reinforcement that was unbelievably valuable, because now that I was not whacked out on morphine drugs, I was scared. Really scared!

June 8 came pretty quickly, and with it came some pretty intense nerves. I wasn't sure what to expect, when to expect it, or how any of this would play out. They had weaned me off morphine by using Ativan. I remember asking for some extra as they were getting ready to transfer me from bed to gurney in preparation for the plane ride. They had to disconnect the ventilator and use what's called a bag valve mask (minus the mask, it connected directly onto the endotracheal tube), squeezed by hand, to force air into my lungs. I still couldn't breathe on my own and it was the only way to simulate ventilation. They couldn't transport the actual ventilator. Let me tell you, I was not a fan of that. I wanted knocked out or something. They didn't want to give me any more Ativan, but I think I was worked up enough that they ended up giving me Benadryl, in the hopes that it would make me sleepy. It didn't work. What did work, at least for a little bit, was seeing about thirty or forty people in the parking lot at the Johnstown airport, holding up signs and cheering me on. My cousins Colleen and Kathleen had their giant bed sheet sign with "WE LOVE YOU MIKE!!!" held up by a few people. They had hung it on the water tower outside my hospital room in Conemaugh a few weeks earlier but got yelled at and had to take it down. That sight must have been pretty comforting because I don't remember the transfer into the jet. However, what I do remember is the inside of that sucker, along with the flight down, and it wasn't pretty.

The Learjet was so small anyone over six feet tall couldn't stand up inside, and anyone much over 5 foot could easily touch both sides of the plane at the same time. There was only enough room for me (laying down on a gurney), my parents, and the two nurses. I've been stuck in tighter quarters since then, but not much. The best part of this is that the two nurses had to take turns with the bag, so I could breathe. They were making every effort to limit how often their hands would cramp up. There were two of them on the plane specifically for this reason. One person wouldn't be able to perform that repetitive motion without fatigue for that long; and if they stop, I die. They were pretty good, keeping a steady pace so that my lungs filled and emptied with air on a rhythmic schedule. I was trying to close my eyes and visualize something else, put myself anywhere but that flying coffin with my life literally in their hands. Unfortunately, every now and then they would get distracted. While I sat with my eyes closed, they were having a conversation with my parents. Trust me when I say I knew within a split second if either nurse lost track of that rhythm. My eyes popped open awfully quickly. Luckily it didn't happen very often, but from my perspective, once was too much! We ended up landing safely in Atlanta after only an hour and fifteen minutes. Those Lear Jets move really fast! Rick Abell, from the Knights of Columbus in Atlanta met us there when we landed, and my Aunt Gigi and Uncle John Plummer arrived later that night. They had driven down from Pennsylvania, bringing separate cars.

My father was planning on staying in Atlanta while I was in rehab, so Tom and Debbie Cardellino had offered their brand-new car for him to use. Gigi drove it and my Uncle John drove his own. Then, when they departed a few days later, they went together in John's car, leaving Tom's behind for my dad to use. It wasn't the first time Tom went way out of his way. When I was in the ICU in Johnstown, he had left his brand-new Lincoln Continental at the hospital for my dad to use. Despite my dad's insistence that he didn't really need it because he wasn't going anywhere, Tom left the keys there. I found out years later that he had also pulled my dad aside and told him not to worry about Amy either, offering to pay for her college. (We never took him up on it, but what an offer!) He has always been one of my favorite people … for many reasons. He and Debbie are the epitome of giving, caring, genuine people, and I'm lucky to call them my friends.

Getting off the plane, into Shepherd, and settled into an ICU room is a complete blur. I don't remember it nearly as clearly as I remember getting on that plane and passing all those people standing outside the airport. Somehow, though, I ended up settled into the new ICU room without any memorable glitches. I'm not sure if I went to the hospital first or went directly into the rehab center. There was a hospital connected to Shepherd by way of an underground tunnel. The hospital was on a busy highway, Peachtree Street, and Shepherd was next to it. Any time there were tests needed or procedures completed I think they were mainly performed in the hospital. It was a very convenient partnership.

The next day I began meeting the team that was going to work with me over the next two months. The first of these was Doctor Leslie. He was the physiatrist (a doctor specializing in the restoration of functional ability and quality of life) in charge of overseeing my case. I was still pretty nervous and wasn't sure what to expect from anything or anyone, but he really seemed nice and put me at ease somewhat. He had one of those engaging bedside manners. The only other person that jumps to mind that I met on that first day was Stacy, my physical therapist. She was unbelievably hot, with long, dark, shoulder-length hair, and a very athletic build. I found out later that rock climbing was one of her favorite hobbies. She came into my ICU room with a few other people to meet me and evaluate what shape I was in. Admittedly, I was looking pretty rough. I had lost roughly 75 pounds. My 6'2", 200-pound athletic frame, fine-tuned through rugby practice and weightlifting, had been reduced to 125 pounds of skin and bones, appearing frail at best. I was physically a shadow of my former self. After a warm smile and some pleasantries, Stacie wanted to get a look at the shape I was in. She said she understood that I had lost a lot of weight and wanted to see the condition of my muscles. However, when she drew the sheet back her first words were, "Oh my, you're just a little thing, aren't you?!" Well, I was also naked under that sheet, so her choice of words came across much differently than she intended. She caught herself quickly, I'm sure helped by the smiling expression on my face and me mouthing the words, "Are you shitting me?! Talk about kicking a guy when he's down!" Her face lit up a bright crimson red as she tried to clarify she was talking about my arms and legs and not my penis, which, quite frankly, was larger than normal due to the indwelling catheter that was causing it to swell. After the room got a good chuckle, she proceeded to move my arms and legs and evaluate my muscle tone and range of motion.

That same afternoon my lungs started sounding raspy and began to rattle again. They were collecting the mucus that had plagued me throughout Conemaugh, requiring them to suction it out every few hours. I was about to learn that the approach here would be drastically different. Both of my parents were in the room as the nurse and respiratory therapist checked my lungs. My dad told them I probably needed suctioned, and that they had been doing it nearly every day, sometimes several times a day, in Johnstown. The response was unexpected. They said they would do it once and I should be fine. What came next forced both of my parents out of the room; they couldn't even watch. One of the two hospital employees literally climbed on top of my chest and pushed on my rib cage with all of her weight, while the other one fed the suction straw down through my trachea into my lungs. The woman on top of me was hammering on the bottom of my rib cage as hard as she could to loosen up the mucus. I thought she was going to break my rib cage into smithereens. It was so aggressive that both of my parents had to turn around and walk out. They thought the same thing - that my ribs were going to splinter. As my eyes were about to pop out of my head from this violent pummeling, I could hear the amount of disgusting crap flowing through the suctioning tube. It was far more than they had ever gotten in Johnstown. By breaking everything up so much during this process they cleared out my lungs more effectively and efficiently than they had ever been cleared before. They were right, they didn't need to do it again for quite some time. Thank God because every time they did, they did it the same way, climbing on top of me and basically beating the shit out of my rib cage.

My mother and Gigi left after about two days, but my dad was busy making arrangements to stay in Atlanta for the duration. Mom had a pretty difficult time getting herself to actually leave. Apparently she tried about five or six times before I finally looked at her and said, "Mom, get going!" I wasn't a fan of her leaving, but I knew she had to go. She needed to get back to her office. Her insurance was the only thing providing me with the best resources available. My dad was still there though. He had barely ever left the ICU in Johnstown and now he was making arrangements to find an apartment close by the rehab center. My Uncle John had stuck around, and they found a place right across the street called Darlington Apartments. My dad then angled his way into a three-month lease. That's something he was always extremely good at, picking the right battles, pulling the right strings, and relentlessly going after something he wanted, or more importantly, that he needed. That was something for which I was definitely thankful, because I really needed him there!

The ICU room was sort of private. I think the rooms were set up in a straight line with an open entrance into each. The picture in my mind is one of a row of beds all lined up parallel to one another. The head of each bed against a back wall, separated by full walls on both left and right sides, but instead of a doorway entrance, the front was completely open. Each "room" was then basically a three-sided inlet providing privacy only from other patients, except mine, which was at the end and for some reason had a small extra section of wall. This gave it the appearance or feel that it was slightly more private. I'm playing it pretty free and loose with the word "private" here. Keep in mind, at this point I had been naked for over two months with tubes and wires coming out of my body in just about every way, shape, and form and more people poking and prodding at me than I could have ever imagined. Still, the fact that I had a little section in my ICU room where visitors could sit and visit much more easily than the other sections was nice.

The first week they spent a great deal of time simply trying to prevent me from getting sick and getting me to eat more. I had pneumonia twice in Johnstown and my stomach was always upset. The former was no doubt due to lying flat on my back for two months and the buildup of gunk that they were always suctioning out. The latter, though, was more difficult to figure out. I've always carried my stress in my stomach. Anytime I was upset, like getting angry, sad or almost anything, my stomach would get upset. Unfortunately, I was also getting stomach bugs and viruses, most likely due to having a feeding tube, so they were constantly trying different antibiotics. This also presented a problem with my appetite. I had wasted away to almost nothing, and without fuel my body was having a tough time fighting anything or recovering in any way. Still, I couldn't eat, my stomach was just too upset. Most of my nutrients came by way of that stomach tube in the form of the dull gray or off-white Ensure type of liquid. Eating real food became a priority, not just because it was necessary to fuel my body, but I wanted to get rid of that stomach tube as well. The nurses didn't only use it for nutrients, it was also a very effective way to administer medications or antibiotics. They simply took a syringe full of liquid meds and pushed it right through. Quick and easy. To this day though, I still think one of the funkiest feelings I've ever experienced is the burp that came after they used that stomach tube. To call it bizarre doesn't do justice to the feeling of tasting something for the first time as it comes back up!

The other big topic of that first week was how and when to start weaning me off of the ventilator. Dr. Leslie had explained the process to me. There were two settings they planned on manipulating: the number of times the ventilator forced air into my lungs each minute (BPM) and the oxygen concentration in each of those occurrences. I'm sure that's oversimplifying things but that's pretty much all I needed to understand. They were going to make it harder to breathe, plain and simple. My body needed to relearn how to breathe, and it needed to do so by using the diaphragm alone. It would no longer be aided by my chest muscles. Fortunately enough, that's an autonomic function, one that takes over on its own, like the muscles in the heart beating involuntarily. Unfortunately, it would be a physiological war to get there, completely exhausting and draining every ounce of my energy. The psychological part wouldn't be any easier.

Even back then I knew myself pretty well. I knew my brain was going to be my own worst enemy. I'm extremely resilient, but I can also be insanely stubborn, both to my benefit and detriment. If I get something stuck in my head, it's there for the long haul and that usually works to my benefit. I can channel that and use it. However, I can also fixate on things and allow them to bog me down. Getting off the ventilator was the first step in what I hoped to be a full recovery at the time. I needed to be able to breathe on my own and was praying and hoping above all else that I could get there. But I was also scared and weak; I knew I couldn't fight both the physiological and psychological battle at the same time. So my solution was simple: I told Dr. Leslie to turn the settings down as fast as he could, but I didn't want to know what he did or when he was doing it. If I could distract myself with anything else and not fixate on the ventilator, I could just let it happen. My body was still young, only 19 years old, and capable of bouncing back from an awful lot. I just needed to allow it the opportunity. The best way I could think of doing that was to turn my mind off. I was essentially trusting my body to compensate for my brain. Fortunately, my dad took some notes so I can retrace what they did.

The first recorded adjustment was June 14, about a week after I got to Shepherd. The oxygen level was turned down from 70% to 60%. The note actually says that this was an attempt to start weaning "again," so apparently it was at least attempt number two and the oxygen level may have been higher than 70% at some point. I sure don't know; I didn't *want* to know. I think it was a wise choice because the very next day they turned the breaths-per-minute (BPM) down from 8 to 7, the oxygen down from 60% to 55% and then did the same thing on the day after. June 16 the BPM went from 7 to 6 and the oxygen from 55% to 50%. They were cruising right along each day, and on the fourth day, June 17, they really pushed forward. While I was sleeping, they turned the oxygen level down to 45% and the BPM down to 4. Meanwhile, the steady rotation of family continued. My Grandpap Sweeney, also known as Moose, had come down with my dad's sister, Aunt Mauvette, and stayed for several days. As they were getting ready to leave, another of my dad's sisters, Aunt Adele, was on her way down. That was good news on the food front. Everyone wanted me to start eating better, my appetite was beginning to return a little, and Adele loved to cook.

Chapter 14 - Adele's Lasagna

It always amazed me how many people came and stayed in my father's small apartment across the street, especially considering how far away we were. They would come down for a couple of days or a weekend or even a week sometimes. Eventually, it was my Aunt Adele's turn, my dad's older sister. When I describe Aunt Adele to people, I nearly always include the terms elegant and proper. Her husband, my Uncle Chuck, got his PhD at a very early age and made a career in academia. This included positions such as Provost and President at major universities. This meant Adele was often entertaining formal gatherings and hosting both large and small get-togethers. They also traveled to many different places, both foreign and domestic. At one point, when Chuck was the President of the University of North Dakota, their hockey team won the national championship. This landed Chuck and Adele an opportunity to visit the White House and meet President Clinton. So, to say that Adele often focuses on what is appropriate is an understatement. However, she's still a part of a wacky family and by default she maintains an excellent sense of humor. It's kind of a requirement.

Adele came to visit fairly early on after I arrived in Atlanta. I was still in the ICU. At this point, I wasn't on any narcotics, but still fairly loaded up on different medicines, including blood thinners due to my lack of mobility. I was also just starting to eat regular food again and they were trying to get me to the point where I was eating enough by mouth that they could remove the stomach tube and discontinue the nutritional supplement. It didn't take long for Adele to offer to make me anything I wanted to eat. She, my Aunt Mauvette, and Aunt Mary Lou were all amazing cooks, so I jumped at the opportunity. I've always loved lasagna and she could make it with the best of them. Hers was second only to Aunt Mary Lou's (whose lasagna is legendary in my family). Adele was on it in a second. She bounced right out of my room and immediately set on task to bring me some homemade lasagna. It's my understanding that the process of cooking in my dad's tiny little apartment did not go quite so smoothly.

Apparently, it was a very tiny kitchen with very few resources, requiring Adele to go and purchase everything she needed. This included a bottle of wine that was reluctant to open. I've been told by her many times that cooking with wine adds flavor, style, and class. The fact that it also affords the opportunity to drink while cooking is just an added bonus! I'm not sure if it was when she was opening the bottle or adding wine to the ingredients, but it somehow ended up all over the wall in the kitchen. Despite several obstacles and hindrances, such as wine everywhere, she finished an excellent pan of lasagna. Then, while it was still piping hot, she brought some over to my ICU room. The nurses and other staff were encouraged that I was not only receiving such great family support, but also really good food. They figured I would eat a much larger portion of homemade lasagna than I would the drab hospital food. However, their excitement changed quickly when they realized Adele had also brought some wine for their patient, who was an immobile, ventilator-dependent quadriplegic who was loaded up with blood thinners. I was all for it, not to mention highly amused that it never dawned on any of them that aside from all of the health and hospital implications, I was still only nineteen.

Chapter 15 - Shepherd's Challenge

I was clipping along at a pretty good pace with the ventilator and had an unbelievable amount of support. Dr. Leslie was making regular visits and was always really pleased with my progress. Family and friends were a constant presence despite the distance (Atlanta was about 700 miles or about a 15-hour car ride from my home) and the walls of my room were nearly covered in cards and letters. I was getting anywhere from 15 to 30 of them each day from not just family and friends but people I had never even met. Each and every one of them found a home somewhere so they could be on display. When I ran out of room on the pinup board, we began taping them to the frame around the edge. When that was full, we progressed to the surrounding wall and eventually around the doorframe leading to the adjacent walls. The entire place was covered. My environment was enveloping me in support. Whether it was the people visiting or the written thoughts that replaced the wallpaper, I was surrounded by a positive, reinforcing energy. However, most of it was still aimed at a success that was defined by walking again - especially by me. Anything short of a 100% physical recovery was unacceptable. I wouldn't even entertain the idea.

Looking back, it seems like the most unrealistic, far-fetched idea ever conceived by man. It was almost akin to waiting for the skies to part and God to reach down, touch my head, and BAM I would be healed. Don't get me wrong, I'm very spiritual and have a great deal of faith. However, I think even my Catholic upbringing would acknowledge that such a specific individual miracle by God hasn't occurred since Jesus was walking around healing people. I highly doubt he was waiting 2000 years to return only to touch me on the head and save me from some discomfort. The doctors had told me that my spine was severed - completely. What I heard was that it was damaged and that there was swelling in my spinal column. I also latched on to a comment one of the doctors made that I had an unusually large bone structure and that there was more room for the swelling in my spinal column than he was used to seeing. To me, that meant I just had to wait until the swelling went down before we could truly get a measure of how much damage there was to my spinal cord. This is often the case when people break their neck and their spinal cord is bruised or there's pressure being applied from swelling. It is not the case when the spinal cord is actually severed. That didn't matter to me though, not in the least. I was driven in my naïveté and in retrospect I think that served me extremely well. I was facing each day with motivation and drive, looking for what's next and willing to push through the pain and discomfort (most of the time) in order to progress. Whether unrealistic or not, I had hope. To this day I think one of the smartest things the people at Shepherd did was to not squash that hope.

Every single person in that place seemed to be on the same page and hold the same philosophy, with the exception of one really shitty psychologist who I refused to speak with anyway. Everyone, from the medical director to the housekeeping staff, took the same approach when I would talk about walking. They would smile and encourage me. No one ever said it wasn't realistic and I have no doubt they knew that at the time. They knew that there was a wide gap in my spinal cord which meant there was no chance of even a partial connection that would provide the slightest degree of recovery. Yet they were still encouraging and supportive. When pressed, they were straightforward and honest. There was never any mincing of words or false hope given. My injury was complete, which meant nothing was getting through. However, when I would respond that I would be the first person to overcome that obstacle they never responded scientifically, despite science saying there's not a chance in hell. The human body just doesn't work that way. Science and logic were pretty clear that despite being amazing at their job, they didn't have the technology to fix me. Instead, they chose to respond with a giant smile and proclaim that they would stand by my side and we would do it together. I never got a sense of that arrogance that often comes from doctors who need to prove they know more than their patients. I was not only challenging but contradicting what they knew to be the truth. Still, they seemed to know that encouraging my drive was far more important than stroking their own ego. They never once stole my hope. However, they did redirect it on several occasions, and I must say they did it very eloquently.

I would often get overwhelmed and there were many, many sleepless nights. I think I've always talked in my sleep. My attendants assure me that I still do, and that I have gotten quite elaborate in what I say. This is especially true if I'm having an intense or particularly vivid dream. There was a night in Atlanta that I'm still not sure was a dream, reality, or some combination of the two. I was dreaming that I was completely paralyzed and trying, with every ounce of my being, to move something, anything, a finger or toe, flex my thigh or wiggle my foot and I couldn't. I was panicky and flooding with a hopelessness that seemed to fill the room around me. Next I was talking to a nurse who was sitting beside my bed comfortingly. I was explaining that I had such a horrible dream, that I couldn't move, and how scared I was. She simply kept repeating "I know" and "It's okay." The dream then melted into reality and I was slowly waking, in tears, talking to a nurse who was sitting by my bed. I don't know if it was her comforting me, my exhaustion, or if I simply didn't wake completely, but I fell back into a deep sleep and don't remember any other dreams from that night. My best guess is that I was having a nightmare, screaming out in my sleep and the nurse came in to see if I was okay. The way I was talking she must have thought I was awake and responded appropriately, which fed into my dream, but ultimately began waking me. Then again maybe the entire thing was a dream, or none of it was and I simply had that bad of a night. There were many of those really bad nights. Either way, when those times hit, they hit hard and made me impatient to get better. This in turn caused me to want to skip some of the things in my treatment plan that I felt I would eventually not need, like using a computer with adaptations or using a mouth stick.

There was the challenge for my therapists and the doctors. They needed to figure out a way to continue supporting my drive and not steal hope, yet they knew what I would need and had to figure out a way to get me to work on those things while I was there. They must have been well practiced because they accomplished it effectively. They never once challenged my long-term goals. Never once did they ask me to stop focusing on walking and making a 100% physical recovery. However, what they did was point out the importance of taking the right path to get there. They were extremely patient with me and for that I am truly grateful. They also seemed to know me well enough that they phrased things perfectly (then again maybe it just works for everyone). They took the very simple approach of asking me "in the meantime" to work on what was available at that point. I didn't always like the idea, but it made sense, not to sacrifice today while seeking my goals of tomorrow. That stayed with me for quite a long time, which benefited me when I got home. Instead of neglecting school, friends, social life and everything else that came along with my early 20s in order to pursue more therapy in the hopes of gaining more feeling and function, I did both. I was making sure I didn't sacrifice the life I had in the hopes of obtaining the life I wanted. In the meantime, it also helped me plug into therapy, particularly weaning off the ventilator, all the more effectively, which was important because I was tricking myself into false progress in other areas.

By the middle of June, they were moving me around a great deal more, sitting me up, putting tennis shoes on me for the first time and, most importantly getting me out of that cramped, tiny room! My first trip to the gym got my adrenaline flowing like I hadn't felt in a long time. It was a view of something else, anything else, other people and activity. I'm pretty sure I stayed sitting upright for far longer than I ever had up until that point (which was one of their goals, to build up tolerance). I was quick to point out that they had given me something to distract me from the labor of building endurance. Distraction works for me, really well. Sitting in that gym I was able to focus on other people, even have brief conversations. Not that I didn't have those things with my family in my ICU room, but it was a tiny room with nothing else going on. The gym provided plenty of stimulation to keep my brain bouncing and looking, evaluating and calculating, forgetting that the job at hand was to simply sit up. That was happening by default, which made the job much easier. However, the downside to all this activity was that I saw progress others were making as well and was finding it in myself, where it didn't truly exist. It started with sensations down my back and movement in my thumbs.

I wanted to heal so badly I think I was starting to feel and see what I was hoping for or expecting. Unfortunately, it wasn't really accurate. My body was acclimating to a new homeostasis, a comfort zone in which my muscles and nerve endings were attempting to understand the new role they would play. The tingling sensation down my back could have very easily been something like phantom pain. But I chose to give it a more profound meaning. I had met two guys, Derrick and Lamont, who were about my age. The doctors had sent them over to my room to talk, most likely as a morale boost. Both were really nice guys, and both were a good bit ahead of me in their recovery. They described having similar sensations prior to regaining feeling and function in their arms. Although, I think both of their injury levels were lower than mine, and they may have even been incomplete injuries. Looking back, I now wonder which came first, that sensation I was feeling or those guys telling me that's what they felt. I could have very well heard that, or overheard that somewhere, and then began searching for it in myself. Likewise, finding movement in my thumbs was most likely simply muscle spasms, involuntarily triggered by the way my shoulder or some part of my upper body was moving. I, however, ran with it as a sign that I was on my way to a full recovery. It's funny, a significant portion of my positive attitude and driving resilience at that time was based on progress that wasn't happening and a goal that was completely unrealistic. It was based on things that simply weren't true. Luckily, my therapists were able to channel all of that positive energy and great attitude. Even though it was based on a physical recovery that I was expecting far off in the distant future, they were able to redirect it to where it was actually useful. In the moment.

On June 22, they moved me from ICU into Room 222 in the Marcus building, which was in the unit for younger patients. I had just made the age cut off, which was 21. The new room seemed huge, but that was most likely because I had just gotten out of a tiny ICU room. The new room needed to be big enough to accommodate all the equipment along with a wheelchair since they were going to begin getting me out of bed. They started out with an operating/driving system that was most commonly used by people who had no functioning other than their head, called a sip-and-puff system. However, it was only set up for weight shifting purposes at that point. All it would do was lay down (like a recliner chair) or sit back up. While I was adjusting to sitting upright in a wheelchair, it would provide me with some control. I would be able to recline on my own. The sip-and-puff was a long straw that curled up and rested just in front of my mouth. The opposite end connected to the driving system below the chair. If I remember correctly, blowing into the straw caused the chair to recline for as long as the airflow continued. Sipping, or sucking on the straw, caused it to sit back up. I wasn't exactly a fan. The straw was always slimy because I couldn't resist chewing on it. As a result, it was rough around the edges. However, the newfound independence that I could shift my position at will and control something was a welcome change. This also allowed me to stay in a chair longer which meant I could visit with my family more. My mother, sister, and Aunt Mary Ann had gotten there just as Mauvette and Adele were leaving. Learning to shift my weight to relieve pressure was and still remains extremely important in order to avoid pressure sores/ulcers. This was one of the first things I was taught in what would become an education on how to live.

Once I had built up my tolerance to sitting upright and engaging my environment, they began to make my schedule more structured. Eventually it got to the point where I was fully engaged in a block schedule, just like college. For example, 8-8:50 might be something like physical therapy, then 10 minutes break before a 9-9:50 skincare class. Next would be 10-10:50 and occupational therapy before 11-11:50 and bladder/bowel care. After lunch I'd have another session of physical therapy and occupational therapy mixed in with recreational therapy and another class like sex ed. Everything was block-scheduled for 50 minutes, and my day filled up quickly. I often felt like they only focused on the basics with me, like getting my lungs healthy, putting some weight on and making sure I understood how to check for pressure areas and communicate that to others. They rarely talked about doing anything functional, like applying anything to a life outside of physical maintenance the way they did to the other patients. Although, to be fair, everyone else had a great deal more physical functioning than I did. I couldn't move anything below the tops of my shoulders, the others could at least use parts of their arms which meant a broader range of adaptive equipment could be explored. It's not that they weren't putting a lot of time and effort and genuine care into my progress, it's just that it felt like their expectations were far lower. They were covering the same things in the same manner, they just seemed to engage some of the other patients a little more. It could be that was just the way I was feeling. The resources were there, and they were covering the material it was up to me to take advantage of it.

Meanwhile, along with a brand-new room, I was receiving a brand-new nurse, a woman named Marilyn. Everyone began telling my family that she was going to spoil me. She did not. The only thing she spoiled me with was kindness, the rest of her was all southern attitude and she pushed me to my limits regularly. She was a heavy set, very dark-skinned black woman who just radiated warmth and kindness. However, when people talk about strong black women, she was all that and then some. She was as encouraging and supportive as the day was long, but there was no way in hell I could ever talk my way out of something or take the easy way out. The most amazing thing about her though, was the gentleness she maintained when being firm and forcing me through some of the difficult times. I always think back to one perfect example when describing her.

I had struggled with eating enough from day one, but my appetite would come and go. I'm sure there was a physiological reason I was having trouble eating. The most likely reason was that my stomach had just shrunk. I'm also sure that there was a psychological reason behind it as well. From the time I was little, I would get an upset stomach every time I would get stressed out or worried. Whatever the reason, it took a great deal of effort to eat - just like everything else seemed to take a tremendous amount of energy that I just didn't possess. Weaning off the ventilator took tremendous effort and sitting up for a very long time was like working out. I was pretty exhausted almost all the time. One day Marilyn brought in my lunch, a small little personal pizza. I wasn't hungry and I was trying to explain to her that weaning off the ventilator and sitting up at the same time was difficult enough; trying to force down food would make it an impossible trifecta. I started bargaining and asking if I could just do two out of three. Nope. With a gentle smile, but an unyielding insistence, she wanted me to do all three. I tried negotiating.

How about I lay back and eat? Nope, you'll choke.

How about I just eat later when I get in bed? Nope, you need the energy.

How about we put the ventilator back on just for a few minutes? Nope, you're on a roll. Take a

bite.

And there it was. I was eating, sitting up, and still off the ventilator. Grumpy and unhappy but doing all three with Marilyn sitting there smiling.

Overall, I had a lot of ups and downs that would change day to day and sometimes even hour to hour. My sister, mother, and Aunt Mary Ann had gotten to Atlanta shortly before I moved into the private room, right around the same time as I got the wheelchair. There were days when it was obvious I had far more energy. Then, sure enough, the next day I would be wiped out, unable to eat, or tolerate much of anything. One day my lungs would be clear and looking good, the next they were suctioning out big mucous plugs. One night I would sleep straight through and the next was riddled with nightmares and chaos. Even my mood, humor, and temperament seemed to ebb and flow. Apparently while my sister was there, she suggested naming the wheelchair when I first got it, and I had gotten rather pissy, telling her I wasn't naming it because I wasn't going to be using it.

The roller coaster ride of emotions had a whole lot of false positives mixed into it as well. I was having what I now know to be simple muscle spasms in my thumbs, for example. I was also getting a chill running down my spine and feeling like I was sweating along with having my legs spasm at the slightest touch. My family and I were all taking these things to mean I was regaining something, when in reality, it was just my nervous system adjusting and resetting to its new set point. However, all of those false positives fed into the real positives, like the success I was having weaning off the ventilator. Despite still needing mucous plugs sucked out every now and then and having bad days here and there, the oxygen levels were consistently getting turned down and everything was approaching bottom levels. This meant I was ready to get off the ventilator soon.

Chapter 16 - Pop, Pat, and the Ventilator

I had a respiratory therapist named Patty when I was in Johnstown who not only kept me alive, but actually made a little headway every now and then towards lessening the ventilator. Unfortunately, she didn't work every day. Each time she had more than one day off, by the time she returned I was battling some pretty wicked respiratory distress. I think it was a combination of a couple of things. She was extremely good at her job, and others filling in for her were either not as good or did not pay as close attention to the level of my spinal cord injury. All of the torso muscles surrounding chest, side, back and abdomen are controlled through part of the spinal cord that is much further down than where my injury resides. Many people who become paralyzed lose the ability to use those little muscles between the ribs to inhale and exhale and become dependent on their diaphragm to control their breathing. This is actually pretty common because the portion of the spinal cord responsible for controlling the diaphragm is up pretty high, the second, third and fourth cervical vertebrae.

One of the more common causes of spinal cord injuries is diving accidents. They all end up at about the same level, C5. This is because when people dive into a swimming pool or body of water that is shallow it's usually at a very similar angle. Most of these people end up on a ventilator initially due to the severity of the injury, but since the diaphragm is controlled by C3, C4, and C5, which is above the injury level, they usually regain the ability to breathe independently. Unfortunately for me, my injury level is C3-C4, smack in the middle of where the spinal cord controls the diaphragm, which made it much less likely that I would be able to regain the ability to breathe on my own. Luckily, I was 19 and in extremely good physical condition. I think it was because of my conditioning that Patty was able to make the progress she did. That, and my mother's prayers. My mom told me after the initial shock wore off, she prayed to God, really hard, to help me get off the ventilator. She promised God we could handle everything else that came along, just help get rid of the ventilator. However, each time Patty advanced, something happened that made me regress. That's why once I was stable enough to move out of the ICU in Johnstown, my parents decided to send me to a rehab center that specialized in high-level spinal cord injuries.

Trying to wean my body off the ventilator was a priority from day one. Since I was encouraging them to be aggressive without letting me know, I needed to distract myself (or rather allow the nurses and other therapists to distract me) with all kinds of other things. That way I wasn't focusing on whether I could or could not breathe, or whether I was feeling short of breath. I was regularly lightheaded due to my blood pressure dropping low from sitting upright, as I had not yet built up a tolerance after spending so many weeks lying flat in bed. So the lightheadedness typically associated with shortness of breath was always associated with a million different other things. My brain never got in my way by thinking, "I'm lightheaded. Maybe they are turning down the ventilator too quickly." Within a few weeks, the ventilator was doing very little work, my body was finally adapting and getting stronger. At that point my physiatrist, Dr. Leslie, decided it was time that I attempt to go without the ventilator completely for the first time.

He explained that the following day, when I got up in the morning, they would remove the ventilator tube that was connected to the trachea in my neck. They would replace it with a tube that simply provided a higher concentration of oxygen, but no assistance to my lungs. It was kind of like those nasal cannulas they give people in the hospital, or the masks that drop-down from above in an airplane. My body would be breathing on its own for the first time in three months. My first question was what to expect, what was I going to experience. He responded that the ventilator was doing very little work at this point, so I would mainly just fatigue easily, but other than that I would probably not notice much of anything. That prompted my next question, which was how long should I plan on doing this? Was this it? Was the next day's sunrise going to be the last time I ever relied on a ventilator's assistance? What happens if I get so fatigued, they have to reconnect the ventilator? Does that mean I'll never be able to breathe on my own? I don't think I actually asked all of those questions, and even if I did, I know I didn't rapid fire them at the same pace they fired away in my brain. Dr. Leslie was a pretty cool guy and possessed an excellent bedside manner. He always answered each of my questions and in a way that was easy to understand. He was very encouraging because he assured me that considering the progress I made up until that point he was very confident that I would be breathing on my own in no time. He also reassured me that I would definitely go back onto the ventilator the next day and that this was very common. He just said I should shoot for as long as I could, to try to go without getting hooked back onto the machine for as long as I could tolerate. Then, after a good night's sleep, I would do the same thing the following day and just aim for a little longer. That was how it worked. One day at a time.

The next morning came and around 7 AM I got all geared up and ready for my first day disconnected from that horrible Darth Vader sounding machine. My nurse Marilyn, the doctor, and several other staff along with my dad and Uncle Pat, who had come down to visit, were all energized and supporting me, encouraging me to give it my best shot. I nodded that I was ready, and they disconnected the ventilator tube, replacing it with the effortless oxygen tube. I'm not sure what I was expecting; but it was definitely not what I felt. A bizarre tingling sensation washed through my body like a low-grade electrical shock. It seemed to flow through, down, and out of my body into the bed below me. I felt like a deflating balloon. It scared the ever living shit out of me and my gut reaction was to scream for them to reconnect the ventilator. Something was wrong and felt broken inside, they needed to do something else to prepare my body for this transition. They must have forgotten something. But everyone was still smiling and looking on excitedly. The pulse ox that measured my oxygen level wasn't making any noise and was being closely monitored by the doctor and respiratory therapist, who appeared happy with the numbers they saw.

Uncle Pat and my dad were standing in the doorway, smiling and asking how I felt. The truth was, I felt a whole bunch of things all at once, beginning with terror. The last three months were so often filled with fear and weakness that every now and then a pissed off monster buried somewhere deep down in my gut would erupt with a scream of "ENOUGH! FIGHT BACK YOU PUSSY!!" That voice always seemed to show up just when I needed it most, and it exploded inside me that morning in the midst of that oncoming panic. It reverberated through my body and seemed to level me out. Then, I took a deep breath, the first on my own in over three months. The balloon filled back up and I was able to look at them, crack a grin and say, "Pretty funky, but okay, at least for now. Not sure how long I'll last, but here we go." From there, I began the process of getting dressed and transferred into my chair.

If I thought that initial feeling of disconnecting the ventilator was funky, it was nothing compared to each new thing I did that day which demanded more effort, which of course demanded more oxygen. After being transferred into my wheelchair, adjusted and lined up, I sat upright. That lasted about six seconds. By the time I got my chair up to a 90° angle, the room was damn near completely black and I was almost out. I put the chair into recline mode and went right back down muttering, "Holy shit!" while everyone else rushed over to see if I was okay. My next attempt at sitting upright was done much more slowly, but I eventually got there. After about two hours though, I was starting to feel that fatigue Dr. Leslie had told me about and began reclining more often, looking for a way to compensate. That was about the time the support team of my dad and Pat began cranking up the encouragement.

I was starting to talk about not being sure how much longer I could last off the ventilator. I asked several times, to Marilyn, to Pat and my dad, to other nurses and staff, what an average amount of time would be for a first attempt at respiratory independence. The healthcare professionals just said that everyone was different and that I should push as long as I could endure. Uncle Pat and my dad insisted that it had to be longer than a few hours. By the time lunchtime rolled around I was exhausted. I had been breathing on my own for about five hours and was not only tired but pretty uncomfortable. Marilyn had brought my lunch in and was insisting that I eat. I tried bargaining that she should hook the ventilator back up while I ate. She wouldn't budge, knowing that I was only tired, not actually at my limit. The rest of the afternoon was spent with my dad and Uncle Pat, who kept insisting that I needed to go much longer than several hours. Two o'clock came and passed, so did three o'clock, but by then I was also getting grumpy along with exhausted and lightheaded. Each time I began talking about getting back into bed and calling it a day, those two insisted I stick it out a little longer. Somewhere around 4:30 p.m. I stopped being polite and let everyone know, in less than delicate terms, that I was done. Finished. I was getting back in bed and hooked back up. I would try again tomorrow, but I had reached my limit for the day. The Bobbsey Twins, or Dumb and Dumber as I was calling them at that point, tried their hardest to guilt trip me, along with every other method, to stay in my chair and off the ventilator, but I was truly at my limit.

By five o'clock the nurses had come in and transferred me out of my chair and into bed. I never even ate dinner; I was too exhausted. Even though the ventilator was doing very little work, it was enough. I think I spent a few minutes talking to my dad and Pat after they reconnected it, but I was out almost immediately. I rarely slept well during rehab, mostly because of nightmares, hospital noises, and not being able to change positions throughout the night (I used to toss and turn and move all around before I got hurt). However, I slept straight through that evening, night, and into the morning. I was out within fifteen minutes after I got into bed at 5 o'clock and didn't wake up until the doctor and nurses came in the next morning around 6:30 or 7:00 a.m. Dr. Leslie started off by asking how I did the day before, while he picked up my chart. I told him I didn't think I did all that well, that I was back in bed before dinner. My dad and Pat were standing in the doorway looking on as Dr. Leslie raised his eyes from the chart and looked at me in confusion. He stared at me for a moment, looked back at the chart, and then looked back at me again and asked, "What time did you reconnect the ventilator?" I told him I got into bed about 5:00 p.m. He said he understood that but asked again what time I reconnected the ventilator. When I told him it was reconnected the same time I got to bed, he just stared at me for a moment. Then he looked at Marilyn, then to my dad and Pat and finally back to me and asked, "Did you reconnect it at all during the day after we disconnected it yesterday morning?" When I responded no, he looked back again at my dad and Pat, then back to me, smiled and shook his head saying, "I've never had anyone last longer than a few hours, maybe three or four at the most, but never ten!" If I could've shot daggers out of my eyes, they would have been nuclear and aimed directly at that doorway. Although that still may not have done much good, because the minute they heard Dr. Leslie's comment and saw the look on my face all I heard was "Oops!" as they took off. I was ready to kill them both!

Chapter 17 - Shepherd - Learning to Live

That first day off the ventilator, June 28, 1993, set the stage for what would be a breakneck pace in the final part of weaning off the ventilator. Since I had been so successful the first day, the goal was to never go backwards and always increase the amount of time off, which set the bar pretty damn high. The second day I stayed off the ventilator for an additional two hours, which upped the total to about 12 hours. For the next few days, it seemed to hover around that amount of time, 11 or 12 hours. By July 4th, I was maintaining my breathing off the ventilator for the majority of the day. The morning of the fourth, as they removed the ventilator and hooked up an oxygen tank, they told me I could go outside and watch the annual Peachtree Road race. The runners would be going right by the front parking lot, so it would be easy to watch the race. Even early in the day, it was really warm. Of course, it was Atlanta in July, so that was to be expected. We made our way to the edge of the parking lot as the runners were passing by and set up camp in the shade.

There were a lot more wheelchairs in the race than I expected. I also didn't expect to see them intermixed with the other runners so commonly. I'm not sure why, but I guess I just assumed they would all be lumped together in their own section. As we sat there watching all the people go by, I was getting lightheaded and uncomfortable. I was assuming it was the heat, but I was enjoying people watching, so I decided to tough it out. The air-conditioning was always cranked up inside, so I would cool down pretty quickly once we got back in. After a while, I just couldn't take it. I was really uncomfortable; my stomach was even starting to turn. We went back inside. I'm not sure if I told one of the nurses or one of my therapists, but I let them know how lightheaded and uncomfortable I was. They checked a few things to make sure I was okay, and I was. However, as they went to move the oxygen tank one of them noticed something. It wasn't turned on. I just spent the last few hours weaning off the ventilator outside, in the heat without the oxygen that I was supposed to be receiving. The upside was that I had really challenged myself, the downside was that I was pretty wiped out for the rest of the day.

My cousin Colleen and my two friends Jenny and Cathy from college came down to visit for a few days. It was right around the same time I was driving my wheelchair for the first time, along with weaning off the ventilator. They had given me the Peachtree head control system, which comprised of a motion detector in the headrest. Whichever way I move my head, the chair would follow. I was now practicing driving along with trying to increase my endurance without the ventilator. A few days after they got there, I spent my first night without using either a ventilator or extra oxygen. Making it through the night without either meant I was officially off the ventilator. Another day or two later they removed the inner cannula, which is the long tube part of the trach, replacing it with a short round plug. They removed it quickly and popped the nickel sized plug in its place. My next-door neighbor, Trey, was a young kid, maybe a year younger than me, with an injury right around my level. He was a really nice guy with a nice family. We were weaning off our respective ventilators at the same time, but I was a few days ahead of him. He drove into my room after watching them leave and asked what it was like when they took out the cannula. He was having his removed in a few days. I told him not to sweat it, I barely noticed them pulling it out. He drove away smiling and I looked at my dad and said, "He's going to kill me! It actually hurt like a mother!" I figured if I told him the truth, he would spend the next few days worrying about it. If I were him, I would have hated that.

A few days later my dad's three brothers, Joe, Pat and Mike along with my cousin Dave came down to visit. It was right around the time they were taking the button out of my neck. Within hours the remaining hole seemed to be nearly shut. By the next morning it was. With the ventilator history I was focusing more on driving the wheelchair and moving around on my own. Initially, I had someone walking with me, carrying what they called a "kill switch," which was a remote control directly connected to the chair. Whoever was walking with me often had to hit the switch to stop me from running into things like corners, chairs, walls, and, truth be told, other people. I also had some new items on my plate, like providing a statement to the detective, Tony Sassano, who was investigating the shooting. I spoke with him over the phone a few times and had to provide an audio recording of my statement. Basically, I had to describe, to the best of my memory, what I could recall from the night I was shot. I found out that Dan Moyer had shot at an apartment complex shortly before shooting me. Turns out, it was the same apartment complex where some of my friends lived. Nichele (who I knew from high school) lived next door to a couple of other people I knew. Moyer shot right at the front of their building a few hours earlier. Luckily, no one there was hurt.

My father had also gotten the ball rolling on getting a wheelchair-accessible van. A good friend of his, Carlo Falchini, had a dealership in Ebensburg, PA, a small town about ten minutes from our home in Portage. Now Carlo didn't specialize in modified vehicles, but he knew trucks and vans and had an endless number of connections. He was also one of those guys that would bend over backwards while giving you the shirt off his back, just in case you needed it. Carlo is as gregarious as he is generous, always smiling and always, *always*, actively searching for a way to help others. He was doing all the research to figure out what I would need and how to go about getting it. This was going on at the same time my mom, sister, and Aunt Ruthie had all come down to visit. It's also when they took the button out of my neck for good. Aunt Ruthie owned her own hair salon, which is where I always got my hair cut, so she brought her scissors and clippers with her. It was my first haircut in months, so there was hair everywhere, but I felt and looked a lot better.

I was now able to breathe on my own without being hooked up to some giant machine. I was also able to move a power wheelchair independently. This meant that my therapy sessions and rehab began to focus on interacting with the real world, outside of the perfectly accessible Shepherd Center. My first experience with this new challenge was when one of my therapists took me to the mall. I think it was Stacy, my physical therapist, who went with me in the van that dropped us off. The van had an elevator type lift to accommodate my large chair and floor tie-down straps to secure me in place. It ended up being almost exactly like what Carlo was finding, except the chassis (or main part of the van) that Carlo was modifying was a plush conversion van, not a commercial transport vehicle. As Stacy got me out of the van and into the parking lot she asked if I was ready to navigate some of the obstacles I'd be encountering every day. Not knowing what to expect, and frankly not really worried about it, I said sure. She said, "Okay, I'll see you inside." The next thing I knew she was walking away and into the mall without me.

As the door closed behind her, I found myself sitting in the parking lot, alone. I could see her standing, waiting, just inside the glass doors, smiling. That's when I realized her first test was simple: Find a way to get inside. I looked around and thought, "Shit, I've got to find someone to open the door." A lot of places have power doors with accessible buttons on the outside that trigger them open. Unfortunately, I had no means of pushing the button, ergo I had to wait until someone could open the door for me. It didn't take long before a few people came walking up to the doors. I don't remember if they were on their way in or out, just that they were opening the door. I grabbed my chance and politely asked if they could hold the door. Stacy smiled when I got inside and told me, "Well done!" The rest of the day was filled with similar challenges, getting in and out of stores, navigating around displays that were set up without much thought of wheelchair access in mind, and asking employees for help here and there when I needed. I was basically using my mouth and my brain in lieu of my arms and legs. It was an interesting experience, but it was just the first step in putting me into public situations where I often had to make stuff up as I went. There was no blueprint in accessing my environment; most of the time I just had to get creative.

Shortly after that, the recreational therapist got tickets for a professional baseball game (Pirates versus the Braves) so Amy and I could do something together. That was an interesting adventure. A brand-new quadriplegic and a 16-year-old were heading out into Atlanta, Georgia, on their own (more or less). Whoever had the idea, it was a good one. Even at 16 years old, Amy always had this strength and sensitivity combination that allows her to be the perfect blend of ironclad support and understanding ears. I don't remember how we got there, but I'm sure it was one of the accessible vans from Shepherd. The game was in the evening, but it was still Atlanta in July, so it was hot as balls. It wasn't long into the game before I got so hot, I needed help. I'm sure there were therapists or Shepherd staff somewhere with us, but I think they were giving us plenty of room to work things out on our own. Amy and I ended up in this little room down in the stadium, packing Ziploc baggies full of ice in my armpits, in my crotch and on top of my head to cool me down. It was a bit of a debacle, but the point of going was to learn how to navigate some of the obstacles that may pop up, even when I'm doing something fun. Luckily, I had my little sister there to make things easier.

My dad's notes indicate that we didn't get back to the rehab center until 10:15 PM, which was pretty late for me at the time. He and my mom came over to walk Amy back across the street to their apartment because it was so late. His notes also say that I spent most of the next day in bed because I was so exhausted. A day or two later we began family training, where my mom, dad, Amy, and my Aunt Mary Ann began learning about some of the things I would need and how to follow my instructions when I would direct them. They covered everything from changing my position (to avoid pressure sores) to wheelchair maintenance. Most of the focus had transitioned from my physical well-being to how I was interacting with others, everything from explaining to people what help I needed to navigating social settings with environmental barriers. Anytime I was stuck in the gym for any type of therapy other than PT or OT that focused on range of motion or problem-solving, they seemed to run out of things for me to do. One time they had me moving things around with a mouth stick, which is exactly what it sounds like. A mouth stick is just a long thin rod about the circumference of a pencil with a rubber tip on one end and a forked biter part on the other. When I complained that I could already use it efficiently, they asked me to just throw a few things around, which should help strengthen my neck muscles. One of the things they wanted me to toss were these little square blocks with Velcro on the bottom and a little plastic hook on the top. I was a little frustrated, so I used positioning, leverage and the Velcro resistance to launch those things into the ceiling. I embedded about four of them into the drop ceiling before my therapist came running over to tell me my neck was obviously strong enough; I could move on to something else.

A few days later, the staff took a handful of the patients out to a movie, both for the problem-solving of navigating environment barriers as well as a fun outing. To this day I chuckle that the movie we went to see was "Alive." It's an excellent movie based on a true story about pure survival. I'm just not sure it was the best choice for a bunch of people who recently had near-death experiences from severe spinal cord injuries. Then again, maybe it was the perfect movie. What stands out more in my memory, though, was getting into the theater. One of the other patients, a young guy named Alan, was a paraplegic whose entry level was somewhere near his waistline or stomach. That meant he had full functioning of his upper body and arms. He had a great sense of humor. On our way into the theater he zipped through the open doorways in his manual chair and then spun around to face me. He said, "Yo! Check out that chick behind the candy counter!" I, of course, trusting his judgment, turned my head quickly in his direction to look at the candy counter and see this hot chick. Unfortunately, the doorway was narrow, and I didn't think for a second about the sensitivity of my headrest, which propels the chair in whatever direction I move my head. As I spun my head to the side to look at this girl, the chair followed suit, slamming loudly into the open doorway and getting me stuck. Between the loud noise and Alan's laughter, the cute girl behind the candy counter instantly took notice of me. I'm sure my face was beet red as I swore at Alan, calling him every name in the book as I sat there stuck in the doorway embarrassed as all hell. Eventually I made my way out of the doorway and into the theater, avoiding any eye contact with the cute girl behind the counter. Alan and I laughed about it together later, but in the moment, I was not a happy camper.

A few days later I started talking about going back to college when I got home. I had declared psychology as my major a few months before I got shot and I was thinking of continuing that route, but with a twist; I felt I might do well working with other people who have disabilities. The psychologist I had at Shepherd was a train wreck. She pissed me off so many times I lost count. She seemed to be the only professional in that building who wasn't very good at her job. One of the things she did that made me blow my lid was the way she went about putting me in drug and alcohol classes. I had sat down with her one day and she began asking questions about how I socialized prior to getting shot. I told her all of the different ways I interacted with my friends ranging from playing rugby to working with my dad to being in a fraternity. When I mentioned I was in a fraternity, she actually repeated what I said as if she was shocked I would admit to such a thing (i.e. "You mean you're actually in a fraternity?!"). The minute I said that, her entire approach changed. She started talking about how badly I needed to take drug and alcohol classes. Instead of saying that as someone with a spinal injury I'm part of a demographic that has the potential to struggle with drug and alcohol abuse, and that sitting in on some of these classes may help me avoid some of the pitfalls I may not be expecting in the future, she said that as someone in a fraternity, I have a problem.

Don't get me wrong, there were many times I drank too much, but it wasn't just because I'm in a fraternity. Her indictment of this group of men who had been so supportive during everything I was going through just set my teeth on edge. She could've easily just said that she thought I would benefit from listening to others. She could've easily said that she was concerned because I already drank and if I didn't have, or develop, good coping skills that drinking could be a problem. Instead she chose to insult and degrade my support system. The number one prerequisite for a healthy therapeutic relationship is to build rapport between counselor/psychologist and client. I knew that without taking a single class. It's just common sense. Unfortunately, I think she missed that day. She came to my room on another occasion to ask what I thought about my progress. I had several family members there visiting, one of whom was my cousin Colleen. Colleen had befriended a young guy named Dunn down the hallway. Dunn didn't have any family members visit the entire time I knew him. None. Not a single visitor! Colleen spent a lot of time sitting and visiting with him, so I knew he was struggling. When the psychologist popped into my room that day, I suggested she go and talk to Dunn instead, while I visited with my family. I told her about Colleen being his only visitor. Her response was that she didn't have time to listen to his problems, that wasn't her job. I was floored. That experience stuck with me for a long time. Someone in her position, in that field, should make listening to people their main priority, if not their only priority. I ended up going to one of the drug and alcohol classes. It turned out to be geared toward people with multiple DUIs and long arrest records. It was pretty close to an Alcoholics Anonymous meeting. I didn't feel the need to go back. My dad did write several letters to the administration on my behalf to express my frustrations though.

By the end of July, I was going out of the Center without staff. The first time I did was with my dad. We went right down the street to get something to eat. On the way back things got a little hairy. The sidewalk sloped a little bit towards the road, which was a highway. I didn't notice it on the way down because I have a little more strength on one side of my neck than the other. On the way back, though, I was struggling to keep my head centered in the headrest, which would keep the chair driving straight. My body was angling to the left, and consequently my head leaned that way as well, which made the chair want to drift left toward the highway. My dad walked along beside the chair, pushing me and the chair, trying to keep it straight. We do it all the time now, anytime the terrain angles I need a little support or a boost, but that first time, right beside a busy highway was a little nerve-racking, for both of us. I was also finalizing arrangements for an accessible van through Carlo as well as getting hooked up with OVR, Pennsylvania's Office of Vocational Rehabilitation. I was lucky enough to be assigned one of the best counselors I believe the system has ever seen, Denny Hutchison.

Carlo had arranged for a full-size Chevy one-ton conversion van, the kind with four captain's chairs and a bench in the back that folds out to a bed, to be modified and equipped with an elevator-type lift. It was white with purple/plum accents on the outside and maroon interior. I was only going off some pictures I saw in magazines and color schemes that my dad dug up. Frankly, I wasn't all that concerned about the look, I just wanted the function so I could get from point A to point B, especially after my first public transportation debacle. About five of us, family and friends that were visiting, decided to use the MARTA (Atlanta's public transportation – in this case a bus) to go to a movie. Everything worked well until the ride home. As the bus stopped in front of Shepherd, and I got on the lift, it broke down. It was already pretty late at night and I was tired after a long day. We ended up sitting there for about an hour. The city had to send another bus so all the other passengers could go on about their travels. They also sent a mechanic to try and fix the lift so I could get off the damn bus. Eventually it worked, but it sure seemed like a long time.

The end of July also found me ordering my first personalized wheelchair... it was turquoise! Don't ask me where I got those colors, maybe some of the narcotics from when I was first injured were still lingering around. Then again, it was 1993; those colors were cool back then.

The beginning of August my rehab team got together and decided my discharge date would be August 18. I was going home! The next two and half weeks seemed to blur by with a revolving door of visitors and last-minute things that needed to be put in order. Jenny and Cathy came down to visit along with my sister. Then Sharon came to visit. Intermixed were aunts and uncles, cousins, and unending phone calls and letters, especially when my birthday hit on August 9. The show of support was absolutely unbelievable and humbles me to this day. Vocational rehabilitation was getting involved by being a liaison between Atlanta and back home. They said they had spoken with someone at PSU and the campus was more than happy to work with me on accessibility and accommodations. Likewise, I was exploring computer equipment and other adaptive equipment that would make me more productive, or at least more efficient in school.

A few days after my birthday they began packing Tom Cardellino's car with all of my dad's stuff from the apartment. My cousin Colleen was driving the car back a day or two later. Likewise, they began taking down all of the hangings throughout my hospital room. There were cards and letters, signs and tokens everywhere of support and well wishes. When all was said and done, I think my dad said they ended up packing up 700 cards. Afterwards, Uncle Pat, my dad and I went to the Atlanta underground, which is an entire shopping center located underground. I got a healthy dose of navigating through massive crowds in tight spaces. It was pretty good experience. I also got a chance to buy some souvenirs. I don't remember everything I bought, but it's a safe bet that I kept it small like shot glasses or things of that nature.

A day or so after Colleen left in Tom's car, Gigi arrived. She got there about two days before I was to be discharged. She came down to help with the flight home. She also came down to help me say goodbye, and thank you, to all the people who had just spent the last two months helping me. Gigi was always great at that sort of thing. She brought with her a big box of candy and some of her handcrafted jewelry, mainly earrings and necklaces, for me to distribute. The day before I was leaving my team had organized a "graduation" in the gym. Each time someone was finished with rehab everyone would gather around in the gym for about 10 minutes to say goodbye. They called it graduation. The day I was graduating some of the therapists snuck into my room to get a little payback for all the wisecracks and pranks I had pulled over the summer. While I was sleeping, they began painting my toenails hot pink. I slept right through it until they moved onto my fingernails. Apparently, the smell of nail polish, along with their giggling, triggered me awake. As I opened my eyes, they busted out laughing and took off. It was a good prank, but I had to point out that they really didn't need to wait until I was asleep. It's not like I would have been able to stop them when I was awake.

After I was up, and in my chair that day, painted fingernails and all, I rode around with a big box of candy on my lap. If memory serves, Gigi brought a five-pound box of lollipops. I think they were the ones with either Tootsie Rolls or bubblegum in the middle. I handed out lollipops to staff and patients alike, making jokes and saying brief goodbyes. Later on, Gigi walked with me to hand out some of the jewelry she had brought with her. There were a handful of staff, like Marilyn my nurse and Stacy my PT, that really seemed to go above and beyond the entire time I was there. Those were the ones to whom I wanted to give Gigi's jewelry. Eventually, I made my way to the gym where my team was gathered. They all said really nice things and wished me well. Some of them gave me little signs, like an award for getting off the ventilator faster than anyone they had ever seen, or little knickknacks as a token of good luck. Others shared a funny story that was a favorite memory of our experience together over the last two months. It was a good way to say goodbye and encourage me to take the next step. When it came time for me to say something, I think I rambled a little bit, trying to thank them for everything they did. Somewhere in the mix of my ramble, though, I think I hit the nail on the head. I told them that Johnstown, and their ICU unit, gave me a pulse, but Shepherd gave me a life -- and there's a tremendous difference between being alive and living!

On August 18th, I was getting on an airplane, preparing to return home for the first time in over four months. Shepherd had done everything in their power to strengthen my physical, mental, and emotional well-being. They had put all the pieces in place for me to continue life when I got home, most recently setting me up with a wheelchair I could take with me. It had the same drive system I had been using, but the armrests and leg rest were a little different. It definitely wasn't catered to my physique, my fingers hung over the end of the hand rests, but it did the job. They had also set me up with a company in Pittsburgh that would get me a chair designed specifically for me. They had empowered me with all the tools I needed, now it was up to me to take the next steps and move forward. The flight home would be my first challenge, and it would challenge every damn aspect I had spent the last two months focusing on, like physical endurance, problem-solving for accessibility, skin integrity and communicating what I needed to someone who had no clue what I was talking about.

St. Joe's football

Mike and Pete in high
school wearing all of
their Christmas presents.

Altoona Fraternity

Uncle Mike (l) and Uncle Pat (r) in front of
Mike's car at the Walk For Mike.

First trip to Los Angeles

Mike, Amy, and
David Hasselhoff

Danny Boy and my 1st van

Amy and Pete's wedding

Left to right: Dino, Chris (Baxter), Michael, Mike, Michael, and Matthew

Penn State's Beaver Stadium

Edinboro Fraternity

Family Cruise to Bahamas

Mike in Cancun

Family Picture
Dad, Amy, Mike, Pete, Mom

Nephews Jack (l) and Ben (r)

Moose and some of his grandkids

Maestro Kiel

Mom, aka Madre

Dad, aka Pop

Dino and the fist bump

The "Bomb"

Redneck Elevator

PART FOUR – A New Normal

All that I see is within a tree
as she reaches towards the sun
her roots below may never show
yet they strengthen where they run

Touching the skies and drinking its cries
she grows tall as nature evolves
her ragged skin protecting that within
while season after season revolves

With a cardinal's song life moves along
while leaves burst through the air
great storms may send her branches to bend
but return after all despair

A brilliant scene in the deepest green
the beating heart to nature's drum
she embraces life despite all strife
with her purest beauty yet to come

An autumn chill showcases her will
as majestic colors mark demise
yet she's steadfast for this too shall pass
and in the spring once more she'll rise

M Kiel

Chapter 18 – The Flight Home

My dad, Gigi, and I made our way to the airport. Aside from the Learjet I took to get to Shepherd, I had only flown in an airplane once when my cousin Mets and her husband took me to Utah skiing. I was in early high school, so I wasn't paying much attention to the process of checking in and boarding. I just went with the flow. Now, I had to figure out how to manage my way through that whole process with the addition of a 300-pound wheelchair. Luckily, both my dad and Gigi had flown more than once, so they knew the basic process. The accessibility part, though, was going to be something we would have to make up on the fly. We got checked in and checked our bags, taking with us one or two carry-ons, and made our way to the terminal. Gigi, who was always trying to be helpful, had picked up a couple of pieces of pizza and a soda for me. Unfortunately, with her hands preoccupied, that left my dad to try to juggle the carry-on baggage for all of us. I can only imagine what the people watching us were thinking. They would have seen a man with more bags than arms and a lady trying to balance two plates of pizza and a can of soda walking next to a kid who appeared to be moving a power wheelchair by telepathy. We definitely got some funny looks, but we made it to security.

My dad plopped the bags down on the conveyor belt and Gigi threw away the remaining food, since we couldn't take anything on the plane. Security then began directing them through the metal detectors, metal detectors that I, of course, couldn't fit my big ass wheelchair through. The result was a lot of security staring at me in confusion. It was obvious they had never seen a chair like mine and had no idea what to do with me. Likewise, I had no idea where I was supposed to go next. Then, just as I was getting ready to start explaining some of the details about my wheelchair, all hell broke loose with alarms and sirens. Everyone seemed to be jumping into frenzy mode, with more security coming over to our conveyor belt. They had stopped one of our bags after it went through the x-ray machine and began opening it up. They were calling us over and everyone looked pretty serious. With lights flashing and sirens going, someone pulled out a small pistol from my bag. Of course it wasn't an actual pistol, it was the cigarette lighter I had bought for Pete, but they didn't know that. The x-ray just showed a pistol. We spent the next 10 minutes explaining to them that it wasn't a weapon. Thankfully, they told my dad he could check my bag with the lighter and we could board the plane. Unfortunately, he had to run the bag the whole way back to the checked baggage counter. My flight was off to a brilliant start!

From there we had to figure out a way to get me out of my chair and onto the plane. Quite frankly, I have no idea how we did it. I don't remember at all. What I do remember is being propped up in the seat of the plane for what seemed like a three-day trip. I had spent the last few months building my tolerance to sit upright for longer and longer periods of time. Still, it was drilled into my head and built as a routine that I needed to do pressure shifts every 30 to 60 minutes, which meant reclining my chair to some degree. My wheelchair reclines to almost 180° flat. Airplane seats do not. It didn't take long before I was sitting in the upright airplane seat getting lightheaded and sick to my stomach, needing to lay back. Fortunately, the people near me and the other seats were very kind. My dad and Gigi began leaning me this way and that, forward and sideways and every which way you can imagine trying to get my head lower so my blood pressure would go back up. I spent a good portion of that flight sprawled across three seats, dizzy and half out of it (which is probably why there are big parts of it I don't remember). To this day my dad says that was the worst flight he has ever taken in his entire life. By the time we got home it was dark and well into the night.

Chapter 19 – First Weekend Home

I believe the plan was probably to be home earlier than midnight, but that's not how things ended up for some reason or other. We had borrowed a van from a friend, Barbie, who also had a spinal cord injury, because otherwise I would have been stranded at the Pittsburgh airport. The process of flying home was eventful enough, none of us needed the enhanced challenge of getting me from Pittsburgh to Portage without an accessible vehicle. I think there were quite a few people at my parent's house waiting for my arrival, but when we didn't get there until midnight there were only about a half dozen people left. Pete, Bill, Kevin, Jason, Steve, Shawn, and Wendy are in a picture with me from that night, which is really the only way I remember any specific details. That was a Wednesday night. I don't really recall what went on Thursday but I'm sure it entailed a lot of adjusting and moving things around in the front living room. That was the only area that could serve as a bedroom even on a temporary basis. The plans were already being drawn up to add a wing onto the side of my parent's house, but in the meantime, there weren't a whole lot of options. Nevertheless, I was pretty thankful that I could get inside at all. That was one of the first things they discussed with my family prior to my discharge from rehabilitation. Could I get into the house? Luckily, the back porch is level with the ground, so it wasn't much of an issue.

I'm not sure if it was in those first two days (if it wasn't, it was shortly after), but my mother started talking to me about my morning routine versus my evening routine. I had learned how to direct someone to give me a bed bath, do a bowel program, catheterize me, stretch out my arms and legs, feed me, transfer me, get me dressed and all other sorts of things. Some of them I did in the morning and some of them I did in the evening. My mother was going to help me in the mornings (even after I got attendant care she continued to help when needed, which was often) and she wanted me to get up and go. She didn't want me to have any self-imposed limits, so she suggested I move most of what I did for personal care to the mornings. That way, when I went out for the day I didn't have to come home at any specific time. When I went out for the day or evening, nothing about my spinal cord injury was going to cut my day or evening short. It was a tremendous amount of work for her, but it expanded my independence exponentially.

What I remember most about finally getting home was the following day, Friday. My fraternity big brother, Pete (who would later become my brother-in-law), and one of the guys I pledged with, Jeffrey, came to my parent's house to pick me up. My first adventure was about to begin. I needed to get to Altoona somehow to talk to the scheduling department in order to arrange for my classes to continue. At that point, I was still enrolled, and my previous semester had counted in full. The professors I had in the spring had turned in a grade for me, despite missing finals, instead of marking down an incomplete. I believe they simply turned in the grade I was carrying prior to finals as my end of term grade. As a result, I was still in the system the same as I would have been had I not gotten shot. The only problem was, I hadn't gotten around to scheduling the courses I was going to take the upcoming fall before I got shot and needed to do so before the term started. Now, the challenge was multidimensional, starting with how to even get from my house to campus. I didn't have an accessible vehicle.

Pete and Jeff lifted me out of my wheelchair and put me in the front seat of my dad's truck. With some help from my dad, and I'm sure a few others, they then lifted my chair into the back and secured it with bungee cords. One was going to drive while the other helped balance me in my seatbelt up front for the ride down. Once we got to Altoona, they were able to get my chair out again, lift me from the front of the truck and reposition me back in my chair. From there, I went about scheduling my classes and finalizing everything I needed to get done. Afterwards, they did the same thing again, lifting me from my chair into the front of the truck and placing the chair in back. This time to go from campus to the fraternity house, where they would repeat the process once more in order to get me inside. If I remember correctly, we got caught in a downpour at one point, getting drenched and adding to the chaos. Funny thing is, looking back I don't remember feeling nervous or anxious or scared, despite none of us having any clue what we were doing. What I do remember is laughing… a lot!

Once we were in the house, we had a couple of beers while I shared my events from the summer in Atlanta. I also gave Pete and a few guys souvenirs that I had purchased during one of my outings. One of the souvenirs was the cigarette lighter (the same one that caused the chaos at the airport) in the shape of the same type of gun used when I was shot. I gave it to Pete as my big brother. It had the exact effect that I intended; everyone briefly froze in silence but then slowly started shaking their heads. They seemed to understand that it was my way of saying nothing is off limits. That I was the exact same wise ass, seeking to push every boundary I could find, who left them four months ago and that we should be able to laugh about anything and everything. It was also my way of saying that there were a few people, like Pete and Jeff, that I did not plan on giving the option of fading away. I was going to drag them, if necessary, along the wild ride that was just beginning. The topic had come up fairly often while I was in rehab. I should expect that some of my friends would not be able to handle (or have no desire to put effort into) maintaining a close relationship with me. I had prepared myself for that and understood that it was a real possibility. However, at the same time, there were a few people in my life that I just felt were too important to risk losing. I figured I just wouldn't give them the option. It worked!

In those early days I had to perform an intermittent catheterization every 6 to 8 hours in order to empty my bladder. The wonderful process I had learned in rehab entailed directing someone to insert a tube up through my penis into my bladder in order to take a leak. I also learned that I needed to watch what I drank and how much fluid I took in so I could have a good idea about when I needed to go. My parents had also been trained so I pretty much relied on them. So after the couple of beers and extended-stay, I informed the guys that it was time for me to leave. They, of course, wanted to know why, and I, not being shy at all, didn't hesitate to tell them.

We had already been having some pretty frank conversations about my physical abilities - what I could feel and where, what the sensations felt like etc., so the conversation wasn't that far off topic. They never hesitated, didn't even bat an eye, before asking me if I was able to walk them through it. They wanted to straight cath me themselves so I didn't have to leave and could hang out for a bit longer. I figured, "Why not?" After all this is what they had taught me in rehab - how to direct others to do what I could not. Less than forty-eight hours after I got home from Atlanta I was away from home without parents, family, or any of the medically trained people that had been surrounding me 24/7 since April. I was on my own with four fraternity brothers, Pete, Jeffrey, Adam, and Mikey who were between eighteen and nineteen years old and had absolutely zero medical experience. They were looking to me for guidance just as much as I was looking to them for support. We both delivered. With a little patience, a lot of jokes and a tremendous sense of brotherhood, they catheterized me into an empty vodka bottle, and I was able to hang out for the rest of the evening.

Chapter 20 - The Pig Roast

The following weekend was my high school friends' turn to find some adventure. There was a back-to-school pig roast in a field several miles from my house that was going to generate a pretty big crowd. There were going to be a couple of kegs and a whole bunch of kids celebrating the last remaining free days of summer. Everyone was underage, so there was at least a slight attempt at keeping things quiet, unfortunately it didn't seem to work very well.

I still didn't have a van or any means of transportation other than the truck, so a few friends just decided to skip the truck altogether. They picked me up out of my wheelchair, put me in the front of Sam's car and away we went. Riding in the front seat of a car was much more comfortable than bouncing along the bench seat in the front of my dad's truck. I was much more balanced and able to enjoy the ride. To this day I don't remember if we planned ahead of time, or just thought it up on the spot out of necessity. But when we got there a few guys pulled out a big lawn chair, set it by the campfire and then carried me over and placed me on it. My gut tells me we had to come up with that idea on the spot, simply because we weren't bright enough to always think very far ahead back then. Anyway, it worked perfectly, and I was able to relax, have a few drinks and see a lot of the people I hadn't seen yet. Well, it worked perfectly for a few hours, until it got raided by the police.

I had been at a fraternity party that got raided when I first started college. There were a ton of kids there, so it required a whole bunch of police officers. They even brought city buses to transport us downtown. That was the last time I had seen that many police officers in one place at one time. This pig roast was apparently very well publicized and drew the attention of about five or six towns worth of police officers, the state police, the PLCB (PA Liquor Control Board), the fire company and ambulance. When those lights showed up flashing and illuminating the woods, all I saw were teenagers running in every direction. My immediate reaction was laughter. It was one of the funniest things I have ever seen to this day. Years later

I would learn that several of the police officers thought the same thing.

I was actually surprising myself with how little I was worried, but I honestly and truly just didn't give a shit. I had just lived through the worst experience of my life (hopefully). One of the things that kept popping in my head was the worst repercussion for underage drinking here was loss of license. Well, that was already out the window, as I sure as hell wasn't driving anymore. The officers were yelling "Nobody move," which prompted me to retort, "Okay, I'm paralyzed from the neck down... How much LESS would you like me to move?!" I had a couple of other wise-ass responses, but they were all good-natured and received with grins and shaking heads. Years later, one of the officers even told me that he had to stop, turn around, and walk back to the police car when he saw me sitting there. He was laughing too hard. Several of them kept coming over to me that night, dumbfounded how I had gotten there in the first place. After I had explained to them how the guys had lifted me into Sam's car and driven into the field, we all realized there was a new dilemma. How was I getting home?

My friends were still there; they hadn't run. Along with not wanting to abandon me, I think they were highly amused with some of my comments. Unfortunately, the police were not going to allow a bunch of twenty-year-old kids who had already been drinking to drive home - especially not with a quadriplegic balanced in the front seat. Luckily, one of the women with the ambulance was a friend of my family's. Her daughter was a very good friend of Amy's, and her niece was Barbie, whose van I had borrowed to get home from the airport. Not only did she know me and my family, but she had experienced a spinal cord injury in her family as well when Barbie was injured. She volunteered to drive Sam's car, but pointed right at us and adamantly informed us that she was not carrying me. She said, "Your friends got your ass over here and they can carry your ass back to the car!" Mrs. Huff was smiling as she said it though. She was just as amused as everyone else.

The problem was, with her driving Sam's car back to my house, she needed someone to follow us so she had a ride home. Well, about eight or nine days after I got home from rehab I came pulling into the driveway, sometime around 1 AM, followed by the ambulance. Neither one of my parents found it anywhere near as amusing as I did. We didn't all have cell phones, they didn't know where we were, and there was chaos and lights everywhere from the ambulance. The next day, there were also the small-town rumors flying everywhere that I had died or gone into shock or had some kind of drastic reaction while at the party. However, the next day my parents also ran into a friend of theirs who commented that it was really cool that I was jumping right back into life and still doing the same types of things I always did before.

I've said on many occasions that our lives can take on a vicious circle, creating a fire which fuels itself. In my case, I think the initial sparks of that fire started when I was in the ICU, like when I realized others were being affected as much if not more than I was and my father asking me to choose between love and hate. The friends and family that rallied around me through rehab then became the fire that was ignited by those few sparks. The experiences I had like this during the first few weeks I was home, were the moments that caused that fire to then take on a life of its own. My vicious circle was self-sustaining and quickly became a driving force in my life.

Chapter 21 - Back to School

With the first few weeks under my belt, I had broken in several areas of my new life. I had a bedroom, albeit a makeshift bedroom, for the time being. My parents converted the front living room, the one with the little potbelly stove that used to keep us warm as kids when the rest of the house was freezing, into a small bedroom. Aside from that potbelly stove, there was only a hospital bed and small dresser. That allowed enough room to maneuver a Hoyer lift, which was the little crane used to get me in and out of bed. Luckily, we had put a large addition onto the other side of the house when I was in seventh grade. It included a big family room, large bedroom above and finished basement below, so the front living room wasn't used quite as much anymore. More importantly than a bedroom, though, my support circle had formed. My family, friends and fraternity brothers were all introduced to the new me (which as it turned out was a hell of a lot like the old me) and were willing to jump on to the wild ride with me. I also destroyed even the tiniest of thought or expectation that I would curl up into a corner or hide away because I was paralyzed. Between already being enrolled in classes at Penn State and the events of the pig roast, the stories of which shot through my small-town like shit through a goose, there was one thing people began expecting of me: to never know what to expect next.

As the first day of classes began to approach, I needed to get a few things in order, like how the hell I was going to get there. Carlo was moving really fast in getting me the van, but it wasn't going to be ready by the end of August. That's when the guys from PSK kicked in once again. They took turns driving me down to campus the same way Pete and Jeffrey did on that first Friday, by throwing me in the front of my dad's truck and my chair in the back. Once we were there, they put me back together again and helped with whatever I needed throughout the day, including catheterization on a regular basis. They were supportive in ways I could have never imagined. I found out later that they were just as supportive of each other as they were of me. In fact, Coach told me that while I was in the ICU they would often spend the night at his house, just so they could be together. When they were together, they felt closer to me somehow. Through it all, they embodied the idea of brotherhood. Some of them even volunteered to go to class with me in case I needed anything. Most of the time I already knew someone in the class - Altoona was a relatively small campus - and other times I used the opportunity to meet new people. I figured out within the first few days that instead of trying to have someone with me taking notes, it was far easier to just copy someone else's. I also discovered that needing to copy someone's notes was an excellent way to meet women. I just looked for the cutest girl in the class and used that as an icebreaker. It was a tactic I used all through the rest of my college days. Unfortunately, the cutest girl in the class wasn't always the smartest. Sometimes I had to get two sets of notes.

I also needed to figure out a way to actually do schoolwork once I got home. That's where Denny, the Office of Vocational Rehabilitation counselor, reentered the equation. I don't remember if I met with him before the first day of class or shortly after, but he had all kinds of ideas. The biggest one was getting me computer literate, to which I was quite resistant at first. I didn't really like computers to begin with, but I conceded that I would need to use them to some degree. He began telling me about voice recognition software that would allow me to dictate text into a computer and write papers on my own. I hated the idea of using something special and what I perceived as complicated. I was rather insistent that I would just use my mouth stick. I didn't realize it then but looking back I realize he used the same approach the people at Shepherd did in convincing me to consider assistive technology. He didn't fight against my concerns or argue with my thoughts, he listened and seemed to understand my perspective. However, his experience with disabilities was pretty extensive and he was a damn good counselor. He simply took the approach of suggesting it would be better to have the technology and not need it than to need it and not have it, especially since he was paying for it. It wouldn't cost me a dime. But beyond getting me to use things like voice recognition, Denny had a bigger impact. He helped empower me. He was the first one I remember talking about my legal rights to accessibility. Without him I'm not sure I would have known what to do about accessibility issues on campus. For example, one of my first classes was on the second floor and there was no elevator. Thanks to Denny I knew to go to student services and politely talk to them about the class. They were more than happy to move it to the first floor; they never even batted an eye. Denny also said OVR could pay the people getting me to and from class, which was like winning the lottery to the guys helping me. They never expected anything in return.

After a few weeks I got my new van. Carlo had taken care of everything, and I mean everything. I found out later he told my dad he was giving it to me for 100% his cost. I wouldn't have to pay a penny more than what he paid for it. He had put in an unbelievable amount of work and effort just because he wanted to do something nice. Years later my brother-in-law's twin, Anthony, stopped at Carlo's beer distributor (which was his second business located right beside his dealership) for a case of beer. After a brief conversation with Carlo, he came back and told everyone that Carlo was so nice he wanted to move to this area just so he could live beside people like him. That was classic Carlo, he might have the biggest heart of any man I've ever met in my life. He brings a smile to my face every time I see him. Unbeknownst to either of us back then, we had just partially solved one of the biggest obstacles faced by people with disabilities - transportation. It's arguably the number one impediment to employment for someone with a disability.

Years later, when I was working, I felt the full impact of that issue. I was working 25 miles away from home and there was limited public transportation. The first couple of years I was piecing together my daily transportation with a variety of people. I typically hired high school kids or college students on break. Other times my friends would fill in when they could. I had them drive me down to my office in the morning, drive back home, and then come back for me again later in the afternoon. Seemed like I was searching for a new driver every month or two when classes changed or someone graduated. That is until Tom. Tom is retired and ran into my parents at church one Sunday. They mentioned I was looking for someone to drive and he told them I should give him a call, he loved to drive. Just like that, I had stability in getting to and from work. Tom is as reliable as the day is long and not only transports me to and from work but has taken me everywhere from day-long meetings in Pittsburgh to board meetings in Harrisburg.

My new ride from Carlo was a full-size conversion van with a raised roof and a metal lift built into the side entrance (I couldn't get a minivan converted because I'm too tall). It started off as a regular conversion van, two Captain's chairs in the front (driver and passenger), two Captain's chairs in the middle and a bench in the back that folded out into a pseudo-bed. It was almost exactly like the one my parents had when I was a teenager. The two middle Captain's chairs were removed, and four metal latches were anchored into the floor, into which a tie-down strap could be fastened and then hooked to my chair. The side doors opened up like normal, but instead of an open entrance there was a metal grate that looked like a fence folded in half. The operator controls were hanging on the inside of the door. One button unfolded the lift, the other lowered it to the ground, allowing me to drive onto it. Then, it raised me back up so the lift was flush against the floor of the van, allowing me to drive right in. There was one small problem. They were able to raise the roof enough to accommodate my height with relative ease, but the entrance was a different story. For some reason they could only raise the entrance (and side doors) a limited amount, so it was higher, but not quite high enough. At 6'3" (I grew an inch after I was shot) I sit rather high in my chair, too high in fact to drive straight in and out of the van. It wasn't that big of a deal, all I had to do was recline a little bit. However, the lift was designed to shoulder the bulk of the chair's weight on the backend, closest to the van. That meant I had to back onto the lift. Then, after I was about 4 feet in the air, I had to recline before I could back in the rest of the way. I got pretty good at it, but truth be told there were some shady moments. On one occasion, a few years after I got the van, I was parked on the lift with my attendant lowering me down to the parking lot when we realized it was about to line up with a storm drain. That meant the lift wouldn't flatten out enough for me to drive off. Instead of raising it the whole way back up, driving into the van, folding everything up, closing the doors and then driving to another parking spot, we just raised the lift a few feet off the ground and then drove to another spot in the parking lot with me still out on the lift. It was pretty sketchy, but I survived and the looks on the faces of the people looking on was priceless.

The new van made life easier for everyone, not just me. First off, no one needed to lift me in and out of my chair, which meant I only needed one person to get me from my house to campus, not two or three. That's when my cousin Kathleen's husband Rich, who was studying to be a nurse, started driving and helping me on campus a few days a week, giving the fraternity guys a break. It also meant I actually had a little privacy when I had to be catheterized. I didn't need to find one of the larger bathrooms that had multiple stalls (which I didn't fit in anyway) and always had people walking in and out. I could just recline in the van and do it there. Joel was one of the first fraternity guys to learn how to catheterize me while I was in the van. He was really nervous and probably asked 10 times if I was sure I couldn't feel it. When he started inserting the catheter, I decided to make some faces and act like it hurt, just for the fun of it. He freaked out and I laughed, which had him ready to kill me. It really was funny though, and we still laugh about it today. To be fair, I wasn't the only one having a laugh at someone else's expense, those guys did it too. Like the night my girlfriend Sharon learned how to catheterize me.

The fraternity guys didn't just get me back and forth to class. Sometimes, I would stick around all evening for a party and they would bring me back later, or my dad would bring their car down and swap vehicles. Other times, on days I didn't have class, they would drive the whole way up just to get me for a party. A few weeks into the semester I was at the KDE house for a party on a Saturday night. The guys had gotten so accustomed to catheterizing me throughout the day that it was no big deal to do it in the evenings if I stuck around for a party. I was obviously drinking more in the evenings, so on those occasions I needed to do it a little more often. That Saturday we were sitting in the living room, probably playing a drinking game or something, when the clock on the wall suggested it was time I take a leak. I don't remember if I asked Sharon, one of my brothers (there were probably two going with me) asked her, or if she volunteered, but she ended up back in the bedroom with us to learn how to catheterize me. If she was nervous, which she probably was, she didn't let on. She appeared unfazed as I started to describe the process. As I walked her through undoing my jeans and pulling out my penis, the guys were helping set up the catheter and lube, reassuring her that she was doing everything fine. Just then, my body reacted the way it was supposed to react when my girlfriend grabbed my dick -- I got wood.

Now, I was always taught that the higher up the spinal cord is injured, the more likely it is for that individual to acquire and maintain a reflex erection. Years later, after I started working, I was in my office talking about this with a rehab nurse who was helping me design a sex ed program for people with physical disabilities. As we sat around having lunch with about eight of my coworkers, they of course wanted to know how the sex ed program was coming along. Nonchalantly, she looked up from her lunch and said, "Yeah, we were just discussing spinal cord injuries, which are easy... Spinal Cord Injury 101, the higher the harder." What she meant was that the higher up the spinal cord the more likely the body would respond on its own, as a reflex. What my coworkers took from her comment was a whole lot of humor. Back at PSU in that sorority house, my fraternity brothers were responding to Sharon's impact in a very similar manner.

Despite being surprised that I could still get an erection, my fraternity brothers were not at a loss for words. They had plenty of comments, both at my expense and at Sharon's. Of course it was all in good humor, but unfortunately for me, those guys got some real mileage out of it. The following Monday, when I got to campus, I was getting out of my van and saw some of the older guys had come down from State College. They were a good hundred yards away, near the student union, but their voices carried easily as they yelled across campus "Yo Eyeball! We heard you can still get a hard on!!" It's a safe bet to say it drew the attention of every single person within earshot. Don't get me wrong, I was ecstatic that I could still get an erection, but having it broadcast from the student union is a different story. Luckily, I never did get embarrassed easily. Now, with the spinal cord injury, I think just about all humility is gone out the window, which is quite interesting considering how overly self-conscious I was about my body image.

I had always been far too critical of myself, especially when it came to appearance and body image. As a teenager, I had a pretty good build. I was skinny, but I was also muscular and well defined. If I had a little more discipline with my diet and exercise routine, my six pack abs could have been a whole lot more pronounced. Then, as a college rugby player, I was much more muscular with a relatively flat stomach, which was pretty impressive at the time considering I was drinking and eating like a bottomless pit. When I came home for my first Christmas after starting college my waist size had only gone from 32 inches to 33 inches. I remember it because Pete had put an inch or two on his waistline as well and my mother shot us a funny warning about letting ourselves go and falling out of shape. She said she wasn't buying us any bigger pants, that if we wanted to give ourselves a beer belly, we had to buy our own jeans; she wasn't buying anything bigger than 33 inches. She always had amazing beliefs when it came to body image and healthy lifestyles, beliefs I didn't even recognize she held until later on. For example, we never had a scale in the house when I was growing up. Her philosophy was that you should go by how you look in the mirror and how you feel in your clothes, not a number on the floor. Her warning was funny, but it also worked. I didn't want to pay for my own jeans, so I ran a little more often in rugby practice and added a few more sets of sit ups to my workout routine. Now, realistically, I should have felt much better about my appearance, especially by the time I put some muscle on in college, but the little voice in the back of my head yipped at me a little too often. Even on the days I liked what I saw in the mirror, that little voice would add in a little "Yeah, but...." After I got shot, lost 75 pounds and could no longer even move, let alone shape my body into something I thought would be attractive to women, that little voice got a whole lot louder and yipped at me a lot more often.

I can't think of a better example than the trach scar on my neck. After I had gotten off the ventilator, and they removed everything from my throat, one of the doctors at Shepherd said they could remove the scar as well. It wouldn't take much, a little plastic surgery and no one would ever be able to tell I had a hole in my neck. As it stood, I had what amounted to a little divot, almost like a belly button, where the tracheotomy had been. But I didn't want anything to do with someone poking around in that area any further. That trach had been there for three months and even after it came out, they had to dig around to get a few extra stitches out a few days later, so I was done. Unfortunately, when I got home, I was able to see a mirror much more frequently and the trach scar jumped out at me every time I did. It was one of those cognitive distortions, the root of which had just a hint of truth, but my perception was completely overblown.

True, it was a scar, and a doozy that was deep. It's also true that people would notice it, if they looked closely, but that's about where it ended. In reality, when people first saw me, they were probably focusing on one of two things, my eyes or my chair. I have nice eyes that jump out and brighten my appearance, at least according to the compliments I receive. They are an unusual, bright greenish-blue or bluish-green that actually change color depending on what I wear. My mother would often point out that there's no way anyone was going to notice my scar (or my hair, or my clothes or whatever else I was obsessing on) before they noticed my eyes. They're an attribute I have undervalued for too much of my life. The chair is also an attention grabber. It's large, beeps loudly when I activate it and people usually have no idea how I'm operating it. With those two prominent features, the thought that people would zero in on a little scar on my neck makes very little sense. Still, I worried about it so much that I always wore a T-shirt underneath whatever else I was wearing to cover it up. Even on ridiculously hot summer days, if I was wearing a button-down shirt, I wore a T-shirt underneath just to hide that damn scar. It took me years, and a lot of work, to force myself to stop fixating on it. The way I was successful? I found some hemp necklaces at the beach one time that covered it perfectly. They were the ones that had to be tied on so they fit snug against the skin. They then got worn until they fell off (or were cut off). With the scar covered by the necklace, I could ditch the T-shirts. However, every now and then, when they broke, I was forced to go without any cover until I got a new necklace. Eventually I was able to go without a necklace for good and now I honestly don't give a rat's ass about the scar. But that wasn't the case in the fall of 1993. That scar, along with everything else, weighed heavily on my mind, especially when it came to women.

I was still dating Sharon, but we had two very different takes on the relationship. We met early in the spring semester, while we were both pledging, because my fraternity and her sorority frequently did things together. That meant we were around each other at least a few times a week. Eventually, we started hanging out, just the two of us. The next thing I knew we were dating. I don't remember ever actually talking about it. It just kind of happened. It's not like we had one of those serious talks where we assured each other there was no one else and we were in a monogamous relationship. We were just casually dating because we had fun together. Then, I got shot. Sharon spent the next four months growing closer to my family and friends. She was always at the hospital in Johnstown, sitting with my family, hoping and praying with my friends, learning about the people closest to me. Even her parents came and met mine, our families connecting and learning about each other. Meanwhile, I wasn't really involved in the process. I wasn't actively participating in any of those relationship building moments. It was like the relationship was developing without me. Sharon even came down to Atlanta to visit, more than once, but by that point she was much further along in the relationship than I was. After I was home for a month or so, I started to realize what had happened. Sharon had been in a relationship with me for about seven or eight months straight. From my perspective, I had only been in one with her for about three months, and not consecutively.

I had a really big problem. Here was this smart, funny, beautiful young woman who wasn't just attracted to me, but committed to a relationship. It was obvious she was in it for the long haul and I have no doubt she would have stayed with me through thick and thin. She was already close to my family and appeared to understand that my new life with a spinal cord injury was going to be complicated, to say the least, and wasn't scared away. For her, our relationship had evolved into something special that was cultivated over time and through shared experiences with my family. For me, it had become more about comfort and safety. After some soul searching, I realized one of the biggest reasons I was still with her was because I was afraid I'd never find anyone else, which was completely unfair to her. It was an extraordinarily difficult decision. For one, I didn't want to hurt her, and I knew it would. But I also knew that staying in a relationship without being all in and sharing the same feelings was a train wreck waiting to happen, at which point she would be hurt a whole lot more. For another, I was very much worried I was going to spend the rest of my life alone. Still, I knew it was the right thing to do. I told her I thought we should break up.

Sharon and I remained friends after we broke up (we continue to stay in touch to this day) and the semester went on, but it was complicated. On one hand, I was just as interested in women and relationships as I was before I was shot, if not more. On the other hand, I hadn't yet figured out what life with a spinal cord injury was supposed to look like from my own perspective, let alone how to go about dating and including anyone else on an intimate level. So, women and relationships took a backseat to school and reintegrating with life, which turned out to be a mistake. I ended up not dating for a long time because of that. I felt it was more important to focus on breaking down what I believed were stereotypes people thought when they looked at me. Turns out, that was just the safer route to take. It was easy to focus on things like social discomfort, both mine and other people's, by forcing that discomfort to a ridiculous, over-the-top level. This usually resulted in everyone laughing at how absurd that initial discomfort was in the first place. Usually I didn't give a shit about things like people staring at me every time I drove past, or whispering little comments like, "That guy that can't move." In fact, I typically had fun with those things. One of my favorite examples is from a good 10 years after I was hurt, maybe 2005.

I was sitting at a table in The Olde Keg, my favorite bar in my hometown, with my buddy Chris and my leg started to spasm. Muscle spasms are pretty common for people with spinal cord injuries. The way I always explain it is that the nerve endings in my skin and muscles still work in the way they shoot messages up my body to my spine. The spinal cord then typically carries that message to the brain to be deciphered, and then shot back down. In the case of my spinal cord injury, that message only gets to the injury point and then bounces back down, unread. When that happens the muscles just contract and relax. Sometimes it's just a little twitch, other times it's a full out leg bouncing. It's kind of like making a phone call that doesn't go through, resulting in the "beep-beep-beep" sound emanating from the other end. That night, my leg was lightly tapping, and Chris leaned over and said, "The girl behind me just said, 'Oh my God, he's moving!'" So, my response was to say loudly, "Oh my God! It's a miracle! My leg's moving!" Then, as soon as it stopped (which was only about 10 seconds) I said, "Damn! That didn't last long. Oh well." After her initial shock faded, I gave her a little smile and explained it was just a muscle spasm. I've used that technique more than once over the years. I've also used it when people crossed the line with "healing prayer." Don't get me wrong, I greatly appreciate the sentiment if someone says they'd like to say a prayer for me. I always assume goodwill, and therefore assume they are praying that I will continue to have good fortune and blessings in my life. My problem is when they cross the line and decide to grab hold of me and try to "heal me." In those cases, I usually make myself spasm by taking a deep breath, over inflating my lungs usually does the job. Then, when my legs start bouncing, I'm equipped with plenty of air in my lungs to shout loudly, "Oh my God! It's working! It's working!" Several of my friends have had their drinks spew out of their nose on more than one occasion because of this one. I also believe it's one of the reasons my friend Chris is convinced I'm going to hell.

There are a whole lot of misconceptions about disabilities. They range from thinking we need some miracle cure to live a full life to assuming we can't have sex. I wrote a research paper in college once about stigmatization and disability. The results were interesting. There were two conclusions. One was that everyone surveyed agreed there was a stigmatization attached to people with disabilities. The other was that everyone thought they didn't contribute to the stigmatization. From the day I got home, I felt that stigmatization, or at least perceived it. People were looking at me differently of course, but worse than that, they were expecting less. I hated that with a passion. The fact that the bar had been lowered, that people were no longer expecting much from me because I was now in a wheelchair, irritated me. To this day I cringe at it. It's why I pushed the boundaries that first weekend home from rehab and every day since. I figured the best way I could combat those misconceptions was to live life and let people see me do it. Sometimes that was easier said than done though, especially the first year or two.

Chapter 22 - Adjusting

One of the personality traits that often got me into trouble as a kid came to my rescue after I was hurt. It's definitely one of the things that propelled me on and allowed me to make the progress I did. That trait is defiance; nothing more than obstinate, stubborn, insecure ego. That little voice in my head that always got me into trouble because it took everything as a challenge. It was a need to prove myself, to prove others wrong; to shock them and amaze them. While it may have gotten me into quite a few dilemmas as a child, it was nothing short of psychological gold when it came to pushing the boundaries of my endurance during rehab and acclimating to life afterwards. From my first mindset in Atlanta, which was nothing more than a pure drive to walk again, to today, when my gut reaction in any debate is to play devil's advocate. It's always been about the challenge. I've said many times the smartest thing everyone at Shepherd did was to not challenge my long-term desire to walk, but instead challenge me in the moment. Despite knowing full well that a complete injury like mine was a guaranteed life sentence of paralysis, they didn't force my acceptance. Rather, they chose to channel my energy and direct it appropriately. Their response was always the same. They never ruled out my hopes of recovering but encouraged me to embrace both short-term and long-term goals. I could keep my hopes of walking again, but I shouldn't sacrifice the short-term goals of the day. Work on getting off the ventilator. Work on sitting in my chair for longer periods of time. Learn how to manage skincare, bowel care, bladder care. Show you can handle the shit that is hitting you in the face right now, in the moment. They're good things to work on right now, because they're not going away, and they won't impact that long-term goal of walking in the least. I could do that -- especially when my defiant ego interpreted the objectives they put forth, like sitting longer and learning more, as a direct challenge.

That kicked in even more when I got home. People were amazed that I made it through rehab so quickly. They were amazed that I was still the same person with the same attitude and the same no-holds-barred approach to life. When I saw how people reacted to those things, it made me want to up the stakes each time. It was addicting. I wanted to do more, go faster, fly beyond anyone's expectations. This caused my first few weeks to be pretty chaotic, but it also caused me to launch right back into my life. Unfortunately, that defiant ego sometimes went overboard and became counterproductive. I remember trying cigarettes a couple of times after I got home. Not because I liked them, but because no one thought I should touch a cigarette considering my lungs were so compromised. It tasted like shit, absolutely nasty, but that wasn't the point. The point was to shock, and it did. Ironically, my stubborn desire for complete independence bailed me out. I had to rely on someone else to hold the cigarette, which completely took away from the rebellious, independent point in the first place. Unfortunately, I ended up going back to chewing snuff like I had through high school.

The first time I tried it, I was on my way to state college. I had my van, so I didn't need to go through that whole debacle of having people throw me in the front of a truck and my chair in the back. However, staying in my chair meant sitting behind the driver, which would make it difficult to interact with Jeffrey, who was driving. It was just the two of us, and I was so accustomed to transferring out of my chair anyway I decided to have a couple of people put me in the front passenger captain's chair for the hour and a half ride just to make it easier to talk to Jeffrey. I had him stop and grab a can of snuff from the store, Skoal Wintergreen. It wasn't even the long cut stuff that was easier to pinch. I had him get the fine cut.

At that point I had been nicotine free for well over four months. I had no cravings or addiction other than a strong desire to get a reaction from the people around me. It worked. Jeffrey kept calling me crazy, telling me I was nuts. That just caused me to be all the more insistent. We made an absolute mess! Jeffrey didn't necessarily chew snuff, and certainly had no idea how to put a pinch of it in someone else's mouth. It went everywhere, over my shirt, jeans and all over the seat, but eventually he got enough in my mouth that I had my dip. Then the only problem was figuring out how to spit into something. Looking back, it was still pretty disgusting, but luckily much less of a disaster than it could have been. He just held an empty can up to my mouth. I'll bet I only had that chew in my mouth for a couple of minutes, but it was enough to drive home my point in that moment. I would find a way to do whatever I wanted, and everyone needed to know that. Unfortunately, I quickly became addicted to nicotine again.

There was always such inner conflict with chewing tobacco. I was doing it in order to prove a point, to show everyone that I could do anything I wanted; yet I would never do it in front of my dad because he absolutely hated it, and always had. One night when we were teenagers, my high school buddy Pete and I were hanging out in the basement and had our cans of snuff sitting beside us. We often slept downstairs because there was a TV, the furniture was really comfortable, and in the summertime it was significantly cooler. There was a full-sized couch and oversized chair with matching ottoman. Both of them felt like you were sinking into a giant marshmallow. That night, I had tossed my can to Pete, who was sleeping on the couch, and told him to hide it, and his, under the couch. He quickly fired back, saying it would be fine where it was, on the end table by the edge of his head. If my dad did happen to see it, he would just think it was his. I told him he was an idiot and if my dad found them, we were both dogmeat. Still, I was a lazy teenager and would rather yell at him than pick my ass up out of the comfortable chair and go do it myself. The resulting consequence was exactly what I expected. When we woke up our snuff was gone, and so was my dad. All we were left with were a few hours to wait and ponder what was going to happen when we saw him next. We were working on Cardellino's vacation home at Indian Lake. Pete and I were digging a ditch to run electricity from the house to the dock when my dad finally arrived shortly before noon. He walked right up to us and got our attention. He had a 50-pound box of nails in one hand, tucked under his arm, and his weighted hammer in the other. He looked right at Pete and said in a calm, even voice, "Pete, I'm only telling you this because I love you. I want you to quit chewing today." Then he looked at me, pointed the hammer at me, and in the same calm voice said, "And you will fucking quit now." I remember both of us being shocked because he never spoke like that, at least not in front of us. It made enough of an impact that we stopped for a little while; it didn't last all that long.

So here I was doing something I knew bothered my dad and I knew I shouldn't be doing. But for some reason the attention that came from people who couldn't believe I would still chew was apparently more reinforcing. Getting addicted to the nicotine just compounded the reinforcement. The rest of that inner conflict came from the fact that it was a massive chick repellent. A lot of women, especially in their late teens and early 20s, are attracted to guys that take risks. Rowdy guys that drink too much and engage in dangerous behavior. I was pretty good at that before I got hurt and afterwards was definitely looking to recapture it in any way I could. The parties we threw were typically in old houses and I was constantly being carried up and down rickety old stairs into basements. I could still out drink most of the other fraternity brothers and I was quick witted enough to come up with great challenges when we played drinking games. Unfortunately, my brain didn't stop at that risky behavior, it added chewing snuff.

Part of my problem was that, despite the enormous amount of love and support I had, I still felt absolutely and utterly alone sometimes. I almost feel guilty saying that, but the feelings were there and unavoidable. They were there because I didn't have anyone else with a spinal cord injury that I could talk to, or bounce ideas off, or ask questions. In a way, I had no peer group. I had to make everything up on my own. The first two people I met with spinal cord injuries had some pretty warped views. One of them told me I was fucked and that I would be better off as soon as I realized I was just fucked. The other suggested that I prepare myself because I'd never be able to get a hard on again. I wanted to scream at the two of them, "How can I be fucked if I can't even get a fucking hard on?!" There didn't seem to be any "Yeah, but..." ideas or advice from them. Not "Are you fucked? Yeah, but.... only in as far as you allow yourself to be." Not "Are there going to be times when it's tough to get it up? Yeah, but... women love oral sex!" No cool ideas on how to get around obstacles or cope with things that bother them. They just seemed flat.

After the double dose of negativity, I abandoned looking for anyone who had some experience living with a spinal cord injury. I figured fuck it, I'll do it on my own. Which I have, for a long time. I was lucky enough to meet a few people at Edinboro, but I was only there for a few years. Unfortunately, I've only been able to keep in touch with a handful of those guys, and only two of them have spinal cord injuries. I have a few friends now locally that have spinal cord injuries, and I can talk to them a little bit here and there. They had wildly different experiences after getting hurt though. One guy, Chad, spent the first two years playing wheelchair basketball, meeting other people in wheelchairs, joining support groups, doing all kinds of things that gave him an opportunity to bond with other people who had shared experiences. The wildest part is that Chad is my age and was injured in September, just five months after me. He also lives in the next town over, less than 5 miles away, in the same town as my grandfather Moose. We even knew each other as kids, although we didn't discover that until later on when we became friends as adults. I still don't know how we didn't become friends sooner, especially considering we were adjusting to spinal cord injuries at the same time and in the same area. It would have been really nice to have a friend like that back then.

That first year or two seemed to be filled with ridiculous challenges around every corner; some of which were so over-the-top they were easy to laugh about, others, were mind numbingly frustrating, like how often my wheelchair broke down. Shepherd had arranged for a company in Pittsburgh to design, and then support, my wheelchair. The guy that owned the company, Bob, was awesome. He was friendly, knowledgeable and appeared to be genuinely committed to the well-being of his customers. The only problem was that Pittsburgh is 90 minutes away, on a good day. If there's traffic, the trip can easily take two hours if not more. On top of the distance, my wheelchair's operating system is a rather uncommon piece of technology, which meant if something went wrong with the Peachtree headset the only people that knew how to fix it were in Georgia. So, every time something went haywire, it would take forever to get fixed. Not to mention, it always broke down on a Friday, and not just Friday, Friday afternoon when people were leaving their offices. That meant my dad and friends were often creating homemade, patchwork remedies so I could use the chair. There were a lot of temporary fixes needed while I waited until the technician could get out and take a look at it.

On one occasion, we had to recruit a friend of the family named Enzo for his expertise in electronics. Enzo was the brother of my dad's friend Dino and he was an extremely smart guy in a few areas, luckily, one them was mechanics and electronics. I don't remember what, but something in the wiring or electronics in my chair had gone out and I was stuck lying on the couch. My dad and Enzo tore the chair apart, rewired a few things and bypassed a few others. While they were working, the chair was propped up and there were parts all over the kitchen floor. When they put everything back together it worked like a charm, except there were still a few parts left over, laying on the floor. No one knew where they went. They must not have been that important, because it got me through until the technician made it out the following week. On another occasion the recline function went out. I remember that time in much greater detail because I had to use my dad's creative solution for almost a week before the technician was able to look at it.

The recline function on my chair is just what it sounds like. When activated, everything above my waist reclines backwards and the leg rests elevate forward, exactly like a La-Z-Boy recliner. When that part of the system fails, I have a whole lot of issues, ranging from not being able to do pressure relief to not being able to get into my van. One of the times it broke, was of course on a Friday afternoon and the technician couldn't come out until later the next week. I wasn't about to go an entire week lying in bed, so my dad started to work on the electronics in an attempt to bypass the problem. He figured out that that headrest was not communicating with the computer on the back of the chair properly. In other words, the input from the headrest wasn't getting communicated to the brain of the recline system. My dad rewired the back of the chair, placing a few switches and fuses into a plastic box, that allowed someone to manually hold a switch down and recline the chair. They could also press a second switch to bring the chair back upright. However, and this was the fun part, there was a third switch that needed to be flipped when alternating between moving the chair up or down. According to my dad, this third switch reversed the polarity, which allowed the recline to function without going through the headrest. Personally, I had no flipping idea what reversing the polarity meant. All I knew was if that third switch wasn't flipped in the right direction, the system would blow a fuse.

I spent a good week explaining to people how to recline my chair when I needed to do a pressure relief and then how to sit me back upright. That meant an entire week of saying, "Can you recline my chair please? Okay, thanks. Make sure the third switch, the one on the far right is pointing toward the chair. It is? Okay good, now push the first switch so the chair reclines. Perfect! Now, before you set me back up with switch number two, in the middle, make sure the third switch on the right is flipped the opposite way, pointing away from the chair. Is it? Are you sure? Okay go ahead." (Then I would hear the inevitable POP!) "Ummm, I don't think that third switch was pointing away from the chair. Can you get one of the fuses out of my black bag? I'll describe how to replace the fuse that just blew out. Thanks." I carried around a tin of fuses that entire week. When the technician finally got to my house, he walked around behind my chair and stopped dead in his tracks. After a moment of dead silence, I heard him say, "Um, what's on the back of your chair?" I described what my dad had done so I could use the chair and his response made me laugh out loud. He said, "Would you mind calling your dad to give me a hand? It looks like a bomb and I'm afraid to touch it!"

There were other areas that, while still chaotic, began to stabilize. I had gotten the ball rolling on attendant care relatively quickly by going through a local agency called United Cerebral Palsy. It was one of the essential pieces I needed to address if I was going to have an independent life. It didn't start off all that well. The representative that came to my house didn't instill a whole lot of confidence. She was there to open up a case for me to begin receiving services, which meant evaluating my needs to determine how many hours would be appropriate and what type of person would best fill those hours. The first thing she did after entering the back door was to walk over to the basement steps, point to them, shakes her finger and says to my parents, "This here? This isn't going to work." She was talking about the entrance to the basement not having a door on it.

Both my parents and I looked at her like she was nuts and I think my sister started to giggle. I told her to rest assured I wasn't going to try and drive down the steps. I'm not sure if she was worried I would accidentally tumble down them or what, but she sure didn't come across that way. Besides, the entrance to the basement is out of the way, in the corner. It's nowhere near where I would be driving my chair, and even if I came close, it's such a narrow doorway I'm pretty sure my chair wouldn't fit anyway. She seemed to fixate on that for an awfully long time, which wasn't only irritating, it had me thinking she didn't know much about what I was going to need. I was right. The meeting was a success in that she got my case opened rather quickly, but she had no idea what I actually needed. The first person she sent was a really bad match. She was an older lady who wasn't very strong and appeared to think she was working with a two-year-old. She would say things like, "And what are we having for breakfast today, honey?" in an almost song-like tone with her voice going up and down the way a parent talks to a toddler. That was when I discovered my biggest pet peeve, people talking down to me as though I'm a child. In fact, it irritates the hell out of me when I see anyone with a disability being treated that way. Luckily, she wasn't there long and her replacement, a friend of my aunt's, was interested in the job.

Pam was from a neighboring town and a friend of my Aunt Jackie's. It turned out she was at the hospital when I was first injured. Her boyfriend was in the intensive care unit after a wicked motorcycle accident and she had been visiting him daily. She said one day, when she got to the hospital, she rode the elevator up to the ICU like she did normally, but when the doors opened there were people everywhere, mostly college kids. She said they were lined up on the floor and sitting in every corner. Eventually, as she walked past, she saw Aunt Jackie and asked what was going on. Jackie told her I had been shot and all the kids were my friends. A few months later, Pam ran into Jackie again. She asked how I was doing, and Jackie told her that I was home from rehab and looking for an attendant. It just so happened that Pam was looking for a job at the same time. Eventually, the dots got connected and Pam began working for UCP.

She was a godsend and light years different than that first lady. Pam was only about eight or 10 years older than I was and she wasn't about to treat me like I was a little kid. She had done some personal care before, so she knew a little bit, but between the two of us we were pretty much winging everything. Luckily, I was discovering I had a whole lot of excellent resources, like Kathy, who was a friend of my parents', and Tammy, who was an occupational therapist. Kathy was the deputy director of a massive vocational rehab center, Hiram G Andrews. It is a 12-acre facility under one roof, offering everything from vocational evaluation to training programs to counseling and just about every type of support service imaginable. It's like a hybrid of community college and rehabilitation and is a subsection of OVR. Kathy is the one that had hooked me up with OVR and Denny, and most likely the reason I met Tammy, who would become one of my closest friends. I believe it was at Kathy's suggestion that Tammy came to my house the first time. If memory serves, Pam started working for me not long after that. There were a couple of pieces of a puzzle coming together that I didn't even realize existed until years later.

The same year I was injured, OVR had been given a very unique suggestion from its Community Advisory Committee, or CAC. The recommendation by the group of advocates was that HGAC develop a one-stop shop for assistive technology needs. Up until that point, most OVR customers had to go to multiple places for multiple needs. If someone needed a wheelchair, they had to go to one place. If they needed computer software, they had to go to another. If they needed a reacher or splint or home modification recommendations, they had to go somewhere different. The idea that there should be one place an individual could go to have a comprehensive approach toward addressing their technology needs seemed right up HGAC's alley. It was, after all, a comprehensive rehab facility. So, the administration at HGAC began brainstorming with the University of Pittsburgh to collaborate on a new program. About the same time I was getting out of rehab and starting back to school, Tammy was getting hired by the University. They wanted her to work at HGAC and develop a program they were calling the Center for Assistive and Rehabilitative Technology, or CART.

Tammy and I laugh all the time when we try to figure out the timeline of events that cover how and when the two of us became affiliated with CART, because everything seems interwoven. After I met her at my house that first time, I began going to HGAC once or twice a week for outpatient therapy. It was primarily to do some physical therapy, strengthening my shoulders and neck along with eliminating some basic muscle pain from using my chair so often. Pam was usually with me as well, so Tammy took the opportunity to show her different range of motion exercises I could do that would be beneficial. However, with Tammy designing CART around technology, and me being such a high-level quadriplegic with a whole lot of needs, it was apparent that I was the perfect guinea pig. So, I became a test pilot for a lot of Tammy's ideas.

Tammy's specialty was always seating and mobility. She's an amazing occupational therapist overall, but she has an exceptional knack for wheelchair seating and positioning. She's got some bizarre ideas on philosophy and don't ever ask her about Plato's Allegory of the Cave!! But there's not a question on the planet she can't answer about positioning someone in a wheelchair. That became the starting point of CART, which then added everything from high-tech devices like adaptive computer equipment, software and environmental control units, to low-tech solutions like lever handles for doorknobs or wrist splints that could hold a pencil or fork. Two other women, Joan and Jeannie helped Tammy cover what was a very broad spectrum of technology. I tried out a bunch of different things during that first year, before the program was even official. I wound up returning to the center a few years later to do an undergraduate internship. That internship gave me my first taste of what it would be like to actually be employed. I would never have been able to do it without Amy who drove me to and from and even stayed during the day to be my hands as I adjusted to the demands of a real job. A good portion of which involved CART.

By that time, which was probably the summer of 1996, Tammy had things up and running really well, which meant she had all kinds of chores for me. One of which was a technology exhibit being held at a local Catholic college, Mount Aloysius (coincidentally, this is the college where my parents met). CART was going to demonstrate some of the new technology that had been recently developed and Tammy wanted me to demonstrate a new operating system for a wheelchair. It was a tongue touch system. The way it worked was the user wore a device on the roof of their mouth, basically a molded retainer, that had nine little buttons. Using nothing more than the tip of the tongue, the individual could press any one of those buttons and control the chair's movements. If synchronized correctly, the device could also connect to a computer and control mouse movement. It was a wickedly cool system, but I didn't have a whole lot of time to get accustomed to it. I also had to use an entirely different chair, one that wasn't necessarily designed specifically for me. That meant not only was I a little uncomfortable and feeling slightly crooked most of the day, I was like a brand-new driver, and not necessarily a good one. Luckily, I was able to practice for a few days. As long as I kept it slow, I could navigate my way around without running over too many toes or bouncing into too many walls.

There was a pretty good crowd at the event and a whole lot of media coverage. I was trying to make sure I stayed in a small, open area so I could safely demonstrate how the chair moved, but Tammy kept telling me to go talk to people and mingle in the crowd. She thought it was hilarious for two reasons. Not only was it a challenge to drive an unfamiliar chair through a crowd, but despite the retainer being form fitted to the roof of my mouth, I still wasn't accustomed to it. I was talking with a strong lisp. Still, it was pretty amusing to both of us, so we compromised and would call people over to our table. Unfortunately, the media realized who I was shortly after they arrived. I was the kid who just got shot three years ago. All they wanted to talk about was how I was adjusting and what was my life like. Tammy kept poking me and whispering to get them to talk about the technology. I tried my damnedest and thought I did a pretty good job of redirecting them. However, after the event about eight of us stopped at a bar to get something to eat and have a drink. While we were sitting there, the news came on and everyone's attention went to the TV to see what they would say about us. As the news anchor began giving a rundown of the upcoming stories, he said, "And coming up next, a heartwarming story of courage and survival...." Everyone at the table started grinning ear-to-ear. All I could think was, "Son of a Bitch! This is not going away anytime soon." I was right. I was a heartwarming story for the rest of my internship.

Despite all of the harassment, which don't get me wrong I completely deserved considering my propensity for pranks, I would come back to the center for a second internship. That one was for graduate school in the summer of 1999. It was even more interesting than the first. Since I was working on a Master's degree in rehab counseling, I needed to be supervised by someone who was a certified rehab counselor or had their CRC. The state had just begun encouraging (they would later require) counselors to go back to school for their Master's degree in counseling, and then get certified. Which meant very few people at HGAC had their CRC yet. One person I knew did have the certification -- Kathy, the Deputy Director. (There might have been someone in the counseling department, but I'm not sure.) Regardless, I didn't want my internship restricted to the counseling department. The center provides such a wide array of services because of its comprehensive nature, I didn't want to miss the opportunity to diversify my experience. Having Kathy as my supervisor gave me that option, since she was technically overseeing all of the departments. I designed my internship to work with the counseling department, evaluation, transitional living, psychology, recreation, life skills, CART and a few other areas. It was a really cool internship that gave me a well-rounded experience. I must have done a pretty good job during it as well, because everyone kept encouraging me to take the civil service test so I was eligible to be hired in the counseling department. I wasn't sure I'd enjoy the confines or demands of the counseling position, but I got on the list anyway. As luck would have it, a different avenue presented itself. I just had to make some decisions in college first, like whether or not I was going to continue at Penn State. I also had a trial coming up for the guy who shot me.

Chapter 23 - The Trial

Dan Moyer went on trial in December (of 1993). He was charged with criminal attempt to commit homicide, aggravated assault, simple assault, recklessly endangering another person, terroristic threats, carrying a firearm without a license and harassment. I had been talking to the assistant district attorney, David Gorman, and the lead detective on and off for the last six months or so. I remember David meeting me on campus to talk about how the trial would work. We sat in my van as he prepared me for all the questions I would receive, both from him and from the defense attorney. I kept thinking it wasn't going to be all that difficult. I didn't really remember a whole lot about actually getting shot. Each time I reminded him about that, he would respond the same way, telling me to just be honest and answer as accurately as I could. After all, I was just testifying in a case that was the Commonwealth of Pennsylvania versus Dan Moyer. I was nothing more than a witness.

I always found that rather interesting. In a manner of speaking, no crime was ever committed toward me. Instead, Moyer was on trial for breaking one -- well, actually several -- of Pennsylvania's laws. The Commonwealth of Pennsylvania was now looking at those infractions, and the coinciding evidence, to determine guilt. If he was found guilty, they had to determine two more things: the best way to ensure the safety of the rest of the Commonwealth's citizens, and the best way to penalize him to ensure he didn't break those laws again. The process didn't really seem to have anything to do with punishing him for hurting me. Oddly enough, I was okay with that. I had burned through those feelings of vengeance and retribution so intensely while I was in the hospital, I must have purged them completely out of my system for good. Even when his defense attorney started making really bizarre requests, like telling the judge I shouldn't be able to recline my chair in the courtroom because it could sway the jury, the only emotion I felt was amusement. Did he seriously think that if I didn't recline the jury would forget about the seriousness of my injury? If that's where that came from, that's funny shit.

He did win one of his requests though, I wasn't permitted in the courtroom until it was time for me to testify. After that, I was free to sit in the courtroom with everyone else. I understood that reasoning. None of the other witnesses were permitted in the courtroom until after they gave their testimony either, if I remember correctly. That included Sharon and Jessica (my girlfriend and her sorority sister) and I think Rob, the guy who was working at the convenience store who gave me CPR immediately after I was shot. There was also a bread delivery person, or someone like that. I don't remember there being a lot of people testifying, but there were enough that the trial took several days. However, there were a lot of people in attendance. It was packed with family and friends and a ton of fraternity brothers. Campus was only on the other side of town, so if they didn't have classes, most of the fraternity guys were at the Courthouse, standing vigil again.

When it came time for me to testify, I remember getting completely caught off guard by the defense attorneys first question. Not because of what he asked, I don't remember that in the least, but by the sound of his voice. I'm not sure what I had expected, but it wasn't what I heard. His voice was high and almost cartoonish. All I could think about was Mickey Mouse. That's really the only thing about testifying that has stuck with me all these years, that voice and wanting to chuckle while I was on the stand (which probably wouldn't have been the most appropriate thing to do!). I don't remember any of the questions. I don't remember getting upset or emotional in any way. I also don't remember worrying. Not about what I would say or how I would come across and not even about the outcome of the trial itself. It was a unique feeling of resolve and inner peace, but I guess those things often coincide.

After I testified, I was making my way out of the courthouse and a pile of media swarmed down on me. In retrospect, it was probably only one or two reporters and a cameraman or two, but at the time it sure felt like the paparazzi. They peppered me with a bunch of questions, but the only one I really remember is when I was asked what type of sentence I thought Moyer deserved. The answer just popped out, "I don't know and frankly it doesn't make much difference." Whatever sentence he received, or didn't receive, would have no bearing on me. It wasn't going to impact my life in the least. My fraternity advisor, Coach, told me several times over the years how much he loved that response. He said it was blatantly obvious that the reporters were hoping for some type of gut-wrenching response they could use as a headline. They were looking for outrage or anger or sadness or something. What they got was peace and calm, which wouldn't help sell their story in the least. It wasn't deliberate, it was just how I felt.

I had decided long ago, before the trial, not to fixate on it, or Moyer. I had a life ahead of me, and I wanted to live it. Not only that, but Moyer isn't the devil. He wasn't tracking me down, waiting for the perfect time to paralyze me. He was an 18-year-old kid who thought he was tough by carrying around a gun. That being said, it wasn't an accident either. He didn't trip and fall, and accidentally discharge the pistol. He pressed it against my neck and blew a hole in my spine. I don't think he planned or premeditated anything, but I also don't think that left him unaccountable. Apparently, the jury felt the same way. They found him guilty on every charge except attempted homicide and gave him 7 to 27 years in prison. If memory serves, he received a mandatory five years for committing a crime with a firearm and then another mandatory two years for something else. I would assume that meant he served seven years before being eligible for parole. I honestly don't know how much of that he did or did not serve. I never followed it, or him, again after the trial. I know the State is supposed to alert me anytime he came up for parole, but they didn't. And I never asked. That's just not where I wanted to channel my energy. I wanted to live my life, not focus on his.

PART FIVE - Gaining Momentum

The Road

As it winds and as it binds
traveling onward still
as it turns and as it yearns
reflecting what we feel

A symbol inside a thimble
embracing a setting sun
it will roll and take its toll
reducing and testing one

It takes from you all you knew
and all that's held so dear
tears a soul from its whole
then leaving only fear

yet it calls us on with each new dawn
and choices all around
a new sunrise that meets the eyes
brings options to be found

It's been said if you look ahead
this road will lead you right
looking behind you'll never find
true peace, comfort or light

M. Kiel

Chapter 24 - Finding My Voice

I decided my next step would be Edinboro University despite how much I loved Penn State and despite the amazing support system I had there with friends and fraternity. Altoona was only a two-year campus and I had already been there three. Most people either stopped at two years with an Associate degree or went to State College to complete a bachelor's degree. If I wanted to continue to complete my degree in psychology I would need to go to main campus, which compared to Altoona was, and is, simply massive. In 1994 it was also very limited in its wheelchair accessibility. My OVR counselors were encouraging me to go to a more accessible campus as well. There was one in North Carolina, one in Ohio and one in Pennsylvania that were notably wheelchair friendly and known for their disability support services. I chose Edinboro in Pennsylvania because I had heard some good things and while North Carolina would've been much better weather, it was just too far away. Looking back, if I had to do it all over again, I would have gone to State College and blazed a path of accessibility through main campus. It turns out that I typically had to do that anyway; but I was twenty years old and had only been in a wheelchair for a year. That's a lot to ask of a newly injured kid. Still, it would have been a fun adventure with a reward that would have benefited others as well.

I have never been very organized, so the decision to go to Edinboro didn't include as much planning as it should have. Luckily, the attendant I had at the time, Pam, was interested in pursuing a degree in nursing and was willing to go with me. That was a big piece of the puzzle that made things much easier. Next I needed to figure out where to live. Most people lived on the first floor of a dormitory designated for those who needed attendant care. The male dormitory was Shafer Hall, and the female one was Scranton Hall. There was assistance available 24/7 and everything was accessible including the bathrooms and showers. I had toured the campus and had gotten a firsthand look at the living arrangements. Having already had the experience of dorm life before I was injured, I wasn't very keen on doing it again. I wanted to live in a house or apartment, and when Pam agreed to go with me that became much more plausible. However, the OVR counselor that my case would be transferred to wasn't very fond of the idea. She pushed pretty hard for me to just live in the dorm. It would turn out to be a huge headache, but a great learning experience.

Pam and I looked at several different places while we were up there; mostly houses because the apartments were already rented out. It was well into the Summer and most people's living arrangements had been finalized ahead of time. The first house we found was pretty rough. It had a shale driveway with a sloped pathway through the yard leading to the front door. The path had several pieces of concrete and stone for a makeshift sidewalk, but overall it was a wheelchair nightmare. Even the actual entrance to the house was a train wreck. The first door opened into a screened-in porch, but the threshold was set up about six inches from ground level and dropped back down six inches on the other side. It was a nice little sitting area, but the front door was level with the screen door. This meant another six-inch step up into the house. Eventually, we found a little one-story house that was about as close to accessible as we could have hoped. It had about two small steps up to the front door, but nothing a small removable ramp couldn't fix. Pam looked in through the windows and got a good feel for the layout. It appeared very manageable as long as we could figure out something for those front two steps. Having a father who owns his own contracting company could remedy that easily, so we got the number off the sign in the window and brought it home to contact the owner.

Pam called first and spoke to the owner, whose name I decided not to use. I'll instead refer to him as "the Owner." She told him that there were two of us, looking for a place to rent for the upcoming school year. After a minute or two of pleasantries and back and forth discussions about rent, keeping the property neat and clean, the need for a security deposit, and a timetable for when we could enter the house and look around, Pam mentioned she was a caregiver. This prompted the Owner to ask whether Pam or I were handicapped, to which Pam responded that I was a quadriplegic and I used a wheelchair. His demeanor completely shifted, and he launched into all sorts of reasons why he couldn't rent to someone in a wheelchair.

He said aside from the two steps in the front, the doorways were standard width, the hallways were too narrow, and his insurance wouldn't cover renting to someone with a disability. I was completely floored. This guy was an absolute jackass. I wasn't quite sure how to handle this. Up until this point everyone I had encountered after my injury had been relatively nice. I had gotten used to the awkward stares, side whispers, and occasional wacko, but this guy was overtly being a dickhead. Pam had already hung up, but I wanted to call him back and flip out, tell him he was a fucking idiot. The 6'2", 200-pound rugby player still buried inside was ready to throw some fists and fight, but that wasn't really an option. I didn't know what to do, so I called my father, who launched.

He didn't call back screaming and yelling vulgarities; that's not my father's style. He was pissed, that's for sure, but a rational person with an airtight argument is far more dangerous than a screaming loose cannon. While talking to the Owner, he went step-by-step, nullifying each of his excuses. The front steps could be easily bypassed with a ramp that would be put up and removed at our expense. My chair fits through standard doorways with ease and plenty of clearance. Likewise, the hallways were standard width and could easily accommodate my wheelchair. When he insisted that his insurance company wouldn't cover him renting to someone with a disability my father asked for the number of his insurance agent. He then proceeded to hang up and immediately call the insurance company and spoke with the agent, who of course said that made no sense whatsoever. His insurance would absolutely cover renting to someone with a disability.

When my father called the Owner back, he spoke to him for eight minutes. I know this because my dad saved his phone records. He was always looking at the big picture, and like a good chess player, consistently several moves ahead. He was going to use every resource available, including the legal system which quite plainly says it's illegal to discriminate. He had the foresight to expect that the Owner, at some point, might claim that the unit was already rented. If that happened, he had an eight-minute conversation documented with the question ready to go, "Why did he continue to have an eight-minute conversation if the house was unavailable?" He had also documented the conversation with the insurance company. It turns out that's exactly what happened. During that eight-minute conversation every other aspect of the debate was dissected, leading up to my father flat-out asking him if he would not rent to me because I was in a wheelchair. The Owner responded with a blunt "Yes." When my dad asked him if he was aware that was illegal, he responded that if he couldn't rent to whom he wanted, he wouldn't rent it at all. My dad assured him that he would see to it that he didn't rent it at all.

The stupidity involved baffles me to this day. If he really didn't want to rent to me, he could have simply said no to the ramp. He could've easily used that as an excuse. It was his property, he had every right to say no, he didn't want a ramp placed over top of the front steps. Instead, he revealed the ugliest side of humanity -- the side that discriminates and holds prejudices. The upside was the opportunity for me to learn, and it was a truly valuable lesson. I had learned from a young age to always pick my battles. My parents implemented that approach to parenting, and I learned it from them. But for most of my youth, I was your typical teenager that allowed emotions to run rampant and the battles I picked usually entailed screaming, ranting or actual fighting. Here, though, I watched my father lead by example. He was showing me exactly how to pick a real battle, and then to go at it full force. It was obvious that I was not going to be renting that house, but the situation was far from over. Before the end of that eight-minute phone call, the Owner was well aware that he would hear from us again through legal channels. We were contacting the Pennsylvania Human Relations Commission.

In the meantime, I still needed a place to live. I ended up taking the house over by Lakeside that had the piecemeal sidewalk (that wasn't really a sidewalk) and the screened in porch. I don't remember who owned it, but they had no problem with us placing some strategically designed boards and ramps so I could get in and out. First, my dad built a removable wooden ramp leading up to the screen door. Next, he built a catwalk from the screen door to the front door. It was as wide as a piece of plywood and supported with 2x6 planks underneath. It made for a perfect bridge from the front screen door to the inside main door. Finally, he also added two side ramps on either end, so I could take advantage of the screened in porch and sit out there if I wanted.

Once I was inside, the living room and kitchen were one open space and there were two bedrooms, only one of which I could fit into. Unfortunately, the bedroom wasn't big enough to accommodate a bed, my chair and the lift I use to transfer at the same time. So, my bed was set up in the living room and my dad built a workstation/desk for my computer in the bedroom. I couldn't even fit into the bathroom, let alone access the shower. That meant coming home every weekend for a shower. After a week of bed baths, that shower always felt glorious. There were very few luxuries, but the place worked and allowed me to be on my own. Fortunately, I only had to endure it for a year. While I was there, some accessible apartments were being built on the other side of town.

Over the next couple of years my dad continued to take the lead in the housing case with the Human Relations Commission. I was definitely an active participant, but I allowed him to take the lead in order to learn. Meanwhile, I had an ongoing conflict with my OVR counselor that I was refusing to let him anywhere near. She wasn't very friendly and often picked little, petty battles. My guess is that she needed some way of exacting control in a case where she had very little. She had wanted me to live in the dormitories, and I had refused, opting instead to live off-campus. From then on, she made things difficult. Typically, it was little passive aggressive things like allowing my attendant Pam's timesheet to set on her desk without processing because it was filled out in the wrong color ink. Instead of calling me and encouraging me to take responsibility for managing my attendant's timesheet correctly, which would promote independence and empowerment, she chose to simply let the timesheet set there. Eventually, when Pam didn't receive a paycheck, it would prompt me to contact her office in order to determine the problem.

It would drive Pam crazy, not to mention throw her finances out of whack. She was having a difficult time managing her money as it was. She wasn't making a lot and had her own bills, including tuition, so when an expected paycheck just never showed up things turned into chaos. This also had both of my parents, especially my dad, livid. Every time something would come up, he was ready to launch, but I would never let him. I needed to find my own voice, and this was a perfect opportunity. As pissed off as I was each and every time, and I was definitely pissed when she pulled her little antics, I needed to find a way to manage my emotions and remedy the problem. I needed to learn how to deal with an idiot. There's an old saying that the epitome of diplomacy is the ability to tell someone to go to hell and have them look forward to the trip. My dad had that ability and I needed to find it. I also needed to practice that relentlessness with which he was approaching the situation with the Owner.

It took a few years, but just as I was finishing my master's degree and getting ready to leave Edinboro, the case against the Owner was finally taken before a judge. My dad and I had both spoken with lawyers for the commission and had been in constant contact the entire time. It seemed to have taken forever, but there was finally a hearing in Pittsburgh. I had made it very clear from the beginning when speaking with the people representing me that I didn't want any money from this guy. If there was any type of compensation or monetary award, I wanted it to be given directly to the Office for Students with Disabilities at Edinboro. That way it could be put to good use. The hearing was an interesting experience. At one point he did in fact try to say that the house had already been rented, going so far as to give the lawyers the name of a woman who was supposed to have been renting it. However, while testifying under oath, the girl said that she had been considering renting the house but decided against it. She testified that at the end of her initial conversation with the Owner, he had one last question. He asked if any of her roommates were "n------."

It truly was shocking how much of a jackass this guy was. At one point during the hearing, he leaned over to his lawyer and whispered something. The look on her face was one of absolute disgust. She had leaned away, mouth dropped open and eyes opened wide. It was apparent that she was completely appalled at whatever he had just whispered to her. I would have given just about anything to be privileged to what he had said. The judge ended up ruling in favor of the human relations commission (and me). He was prohibited from renting the unit and had to pay about $10,000. Part of that was my travel expenses along with pain-and-suffering and all the other jazz that goes along with a judgment. I had no desire to separate it out in any way; I just opted to have him send any and all money to the Office for Students with Disabilities. It was pretty satisfying when all was said and done. I had never thought to follow up on the issue. But as I was looking things up online, to refresh my memory for this book, I stumbled across an appeal he filed later that year. According to documents I found online, the appeal was heard by J Kelly, J McGinley and Senior Judge Jiuliante in January 2000. Judge Kelly reversed the decision based on an argument that the house was a personal residence and that the Owner never truly vacated it. This determination was made based on the fact that he didn't remove all of his personal property from the house, choosing instead to keep some personal items locked in a room that could not be accessed by tenants.

I think I actually laughed out loud when I read that rationale. The bottom of the page indicated that Judge McGinley dissented, but however that works, the ruling was reversed based on Judge Kelly's opinion that he had some pictures and sheets locked away in a tiny room. I still think I won that battle, though. From 1994 through 2000, he was bombarded with the headaches of retaining a lawyer, doing interviews, and defending a ridiculous argument time and time again. I was a thorn in his side for six years. I have no doubt that he was nothing but irritated the entire time, whereas I learned some of the most valuable lessons (and techniques) about picking the good fight. I learned how to be relentless when necessary but compromise when appropriate, be meticulous in an argument, never be intimidated, and always to be nice... until it's time to not be nice. Those lessons served me really well dealing with my OVR counselor and have carried through and been invaluable over the past twenty plus years. When I left Edinboro in 1999, I have no doubt she was glad to see me go. I know I was pretty excited never to have to deal with her again. Ironically enough, I ran into her again several years later.

Somewhere around 2007, I was appointed by Governor Rendell to the Pennsylvania State Board of Vocational Rehabilitation. The Hiram

G Andrews Center, where I had been working since my graduate internship, had its 50th anniversary the year before. Our director, Don, asked if I would join him and a few others on stage for the event and speak a little about the importance of taking a comprehensive approach to rehabilitation. I enjoy speaking to crowds, although I'm horrible at preparing beforehand. I function much better off the cuff. I gave a quick speech on rehab, independence and empowerment to about a hundred people or so and apparently there were some there that were impressed. Don told me a few months later that they wanted my resume for the State Board. There were some openings, and the next thing I knew I got a letter from Governor Rendell informing me that it was his pleasure to appoint me to the O.V.R. State Board for the next six years (and on which I continue to serve under Governor Tom Wolf).

I was a good twenty years younger than anyone else on the Board, but I had some ideas and more importantly I really wanted to learn. The State Board is in charge of setting policy and procedure for the entire Commonwealth's rehab program. There's definitely a lot involved that permeates throughout our entire system. As such, there was a good bit I needed to learn. My first meeting was in Erie and I was given a heads up beforehand that it was going to be a lively one. There were several topics that were going to be discussed that elicited some very strong opinions. It wasn't until I actually entered the room that I realized our meetings were held in a public forum. I was going to be sitting at a table at the head of the room in front of an audience of about fifty. I don't get stage fright, at least not very easily, so that didn't rattle me in the least. As I made my way around the crowd, a woman stood up and greeted me. She called out, "Hey, I recognize you!" It was the OVR counselor with whom I had so many problems in college. I just smiled and said hello as she asked how I was and what I had been up to. I informed her that I was working at a rehab center as a counselor. Her niceties really appeared phony, but I remained pleasant, nonetheless.

One of the other things I learned throughout the years is that ego is best checked at the door. It's never beneficial. Make no mistake, I thoroughly enjoy joking around about how great I am, but when it comes to real life and real interaction, ego actually irritates me. I could have puffed up my chest and threw it in her face that I was sitting on the Board of Directors that sets the parameters for her job. But it was far more appropriate to keep ego in check. Eventually, I had to cut our conversation short, informing her that I needed to go. As I drove away from her and toward the front table, I could see her face change. The dawning comprehension that my name was sitting at the front table designating a place on the Board really was a cool site. As much as she irritated me during college, I learned a lot. As disgusting as the experience with the Owner was, I learned a lot. Following my father's example, it was through those times that I found my own voice. However, finding my own voice wasn't the only thing that was important. Knowing when to use it, how to use it, and where to direct it, wound up being just as important. Sometimes, I even fire that voice directly at the mirror!

My Father's Eyes
in my father's eyes a strength resides
like nothing I've ever seen
developed through life, fortified by strife
they're windows to his true being

they reflect passion of youth, the beauty of truth
yet they hold the wisdom of time
determination and will, like trademarks of steel
have touched more lives than just mine

these eyes have shown, while I have grown
teaching more than wrong from right
they taught to achieve, and how to believe
and to persevere with all of my might

what my future holds, and how it unfolds
I'll discover around the bend
but I hope someday, I'll look in a mirror and say
I see my father's eyes again

M. Kiel

Chapter 25 - Edinboro

There was a whole lot more to my Edinboro experience than an ignorant idiot and an inflexible counselor though. To begin with, moving up there in the first place was like leaving the nest all over again. After having all those friends and family near me when I was in ICU and rehab, not to mention the entire first year home, I was heading three hours away, and none of them were coming with me (at least not in person). I don't remember being nervous or scared, although I probably was and justifiably so, but I do remember being excited. It was, after all, another adventure. But, like all adventures it brought challenges. One of which was living in that first little house with hardly any accessibility. It made me truly appreciate what I had at my parents' house and what I would later have at the apartment. I could only access one of the bedrooms and the living room. I couldn't fit anywhere else.

I had my bed in the living room and my dad's makeshift desk in the bedroom. I also couldn't come and go as I pleased. I couldn't open the door and even if I could, there was nowhere to go other than the front porch. I didn't have fraternity brothers to hang out with; I checked the campus registry and Phi Sigma Kappa wasn't listed. The result was I sat at the desk and worked. I worked hard. My dad had designed a perfect table/desk that I could drive my chair underneath. The computer and keyboard, along with trackball mouse, were at the perfect height for me to reach with a mouth stick. A microphone mounted on a gooseneck and secured to the desk with a C-clamp was also at the perfect height. With all that in place, I found myself focusing on schoolwork more than I ever had in my entire life.

I was immersing myself in homework and projects, which helped because I had some really challenging classes. I remember one, experimental psychology, that required more writing than I had ever imagined. I think one of my papers was about 40 or 50 pages. Luckily, by then I was using voice recognition, like Denny recommended. Unfortunately at that time, voice recognition software called DragonDictate had some glaring limitations. I think they called it "discrete speech." That meant that I could only type one word at a time. Saying anything longer than one word and the software interpreted it as a command, like opening or closing a document, clicking the file tab or controlling the mouse. Today, Dragon is called Dragon NaturallySpeaking. That means it will type out text just as fast as I can speak. I can dictate full sentences. There are even settings that can have it automatically add punctuation. Back then though, I was limited to one word at a time. Little did I know it would get even worse. In graduate school I had to write a research thesis that was almost 130 pages. One. Word. At. A. Time.

It paid off though, my grades were really good, just as good as they were in high school. Classes became easy again. There were other challenges though. Since I couldn't get into the bathroom, I had to take bed baths every day. You would think I would have become accustomed to them considering that was par for the course all through ICU, rehab and then the first six or eight months I was home. I did not get used to them. They were miserable. And they were even worse by the time I was in Edinboro because I had started growing my hair long. My dad made it a point to finish the accessible bathroom before anything else in the addition, just so I could get a shower. When the bathroom was finished, it was nothing short of heavenly. After getting wiped down with a damp washcloth for months on end, the feel of a nice hot shower cascading over me was absolutely glorious. Unfortunately, a couple of months after the shower was finished, I moved to Edinboro and had to take bed baths again. The irony was not lost on me. I had moved three hours away from home, specifically to go to a more accessible college. In doing so I had gone from those nice hot showers back to the lukewarm damp washcloth. Pam and I came home every single weekend, just so I could get a shower.

Despite lacking some of the comforts of home, that first year in that first little house was a success. I studied hard and learned a lot. My main reward was pizza and wings almost every Thursday, while Pam and I watched Friends and ER, which had premiered that fall. I learned a little bit about the Office for Students with Disabilities, but more importantly I learned even more problem-solving techniques. The OSD provided lots of resources, like someone to write for me when I needed to take a test. It also provided van transportation, but I didn't realize that until the following year. The professors I had were great as well. They were super friendly and always willing to work with me. I had a college algebra class, I think it was the first semester, that the professor loved giving pop quizzes. She made it clear from day one that she would be giving multiple surprise quizzes throughout the term. I approached her after class and told her I had a dilemma.

I was never shy to begin with, but after the previous two years I was becoming straight up blunt (although still polite). I described how OSD requested notice ahead of time to provide a writer for test taking and how that wouldn't be possible if I didn't know about the test until the last minute. I don't remember the professor's name, but she was great. She never even hesitated before offering to write for me, as long as I didn't mind. That was absolutely fine by me, it was one less thing I had to worry about. When it came time for her first pop quiz, she passed out the test to everyone else before giving me one and sitting down beside me. She said, "Just tell me what to write." I thanked her and started looking at the five small algebra problems. After about 30 seconds of silence, I started telling her numbers to write down. I gave her five of them. She looked at me a little confused and asked where I wanted to write the numbers. I told her each of the numbers was the answer to each of the questions, the first number was the answer to the first question, the second number the answer to the second etc. She just stared at me for a second and said, "Don't you want to show your work?" I looked back and said, "Um...are they wrong?" She said, "Hang on..." and proceeded to look at the test. After a few minutes she just shook her head, smiled, and said nope, it looks like you're good.

Even though I wasn't going out a lot, I still had some fun. Like when Pam and I decided to go to my cousin Danny's for Halloween. He was going to school at Kent State University in Ohio, which was only about two hours away, and every year he had a big Halloween party. Kent State was also known for blocking off at least a street or two and having a Halloween street party. It was a blast and I ended up going back almost every year for the next few years. However, I don't think any of them topped the very first year, when I met his crazy neighbor. Now, I've met a lot of interesting people over the years. I've traveled quite a bit and met people from all walks of life.

Unfortunately, or fortunately depending on your sense of humor, a certain percentage of them are just wackos. I mean, they are characters that are just so far out there and over the top that they make having a sense of humor a prerequisite for having a spinal cord injury and using a wheelchair. Don't get me wrong, I love meeting new people and most of them are your average, genuine, everyday people who are kind and compassionate, interesting and fun. But the ones who aren't, the ones who have neither filter nor common sense, man they are just out there, and they are story worthy. They are the few, the proud, the moronic -- and they are the ones who often have me referring to my wheelchair as an "idiot magnet." Ninety percent of the time I find it amusing, since they often provide an entire evening's worth of entertainment. However, most of them reach that point where I just have to say okay go away, you've crossed into the idiot zone and my head is going to explode shortly if you don't crawl back under whatever "stupid rock" you crawled out from under. Some of these characters take their time, slowly and efficiently pushing their way to the idiot zone... others just seem to have a natural, God-given talent to jump there at warp speed. To this day, Danny's neighbor ranks as one of the most memorable of these characters.

Danny had a house full of people, everyone dressed up and having fun, and it was getting warm despite being the end of October. I had gone out onto the front porch to get some air and talk to the other 12 or 15 people who were out there doing the same. That's when I met him: "Dan's neighbor." The ultimate hillbilly, and he wasn't wearing a costume. He had the ratty baseball hat on crooked, equipped with several buttons and pins, the half a cigar hanging out of his mouth with about three days of stubble on his cheeks. He had a shirt on that was two sizes too small and didn't quite cover his beer belly, along with a partially crunched can of Budweiser, and he topped off the look with some baggy pants, plumber's crack, and neatly rolled copy of Playboy in his back pocket. He was a walking cartoon. Of course, the minute he walked onto the front porch my idiot magnet kicked into high gear and pulled him right in.

If I remember correctly, he had instilled a sense of fear and loathing in every female at the party and had been banished to the front porch. He proceeded to ask me every question in the book about my life, my injury, and my chair, which I don't mind in the least. In fact, I prefer when people ask questions instead of assuming or being so concerned with political correctness that they're afraid of offending me. But he was smelly, far too close to my face and frankly, just irritating. I was very polite though, as usual, during my penance that was this conversation, but after he almost burned my arm a third time with his cigar stub, I decided to have a little fun. By this time, the other 15 people on the porch had stop talking and were focused on our conversation. When he began asking how I operated my wheelchair I... well... I lied. Someone else had asked me the same question literally five minutes earlier and I had just finished answering in great detail … and he was standing right there, staring at me, not 2 feet away! I had told everyone about the motion detector in my headrest that operates very simply; whichever way I move my head, the chair follows. How he did not hear me explain it the first time, I have no clue. So, when he asked, I told him I had a microchip surgically implanted into the frontal lobe of my brain and that whenever I wanted to move the chair, I simply had to think about how I wanted it to move. (It's actually not that far-fetched nowadays with all the trials and research but remember this is in the mid-90s.)

I lost about five or six of the front porch crowd right away. They politely took their laughter into the house so as not to ruin my fun. After he bit hook, line, and sinker on the microchip portion I decided to take it a step further. I told him that because it was such new technology there were still several glitches … the main one being that if someone else were to place a hand on top of mine and concentrate extremely hard, the synapses and neurotransmitters in their brain would transfer through our skin and that person could then also control the wheelchair. I lost another six or seven people before I finished the sentence. The look on his face was priceless, he was in complete awe. Then, he asked if he could try it. Of course, I let him.

I told him he had to concentrate really hard, otherwise it wouldn't work. This guy actually held my hand and stared directly at my face. It was obvious he was trying like hell to move the chair. I didn't move and told him he must not be concentrating hard enough. He proceeded to close both eyes, scrunch up his face and concentrate with every fiber of his being. He looked like he was going to either blow his head off or take a crap... so I moved my chair a few inches. His eyes snapped back open and he looked as excited as a kid on Christmas morning. I stopped moving and told him he must have stopped concentrating. His eyes clamped shut and his face scrunched up and he was focused again. So I moved again. Every time he would open his eyes I would stop moving and tell him it stopped because he wasn't concentrating hard enough. Like any genius, he decided to keep his eyes pinched shut and occasionally try and peek through with one eye. He looked like a 9-year-old girl watching a scary movie. Each time he tried to peek, I would stop moving and tell him he wasn't concentrating. He would say, "I'm sorry! I'm sorry!" and clamp his eyes shut again. That's when I realized that everyone was gone from the porch.

I looked over and noticed that the entire house was peeking out from the windows and the doorway, people lying on the floor inside laughing. I, however, am very good at keeping a straight face and had done so the entire time. It was right about then that he stood up straight (did I mention he was so focused he was partially leaning over his hand?). I figured he had finally caught on. I was wrong. He picked his hand away and said, "You know, my dog could really help you. He is really smart. You could put him on your lap and just tell him where you wanted to go. He really knows his way all around town. All you'd have to do is tell him where you want to go, then he could think, just like I was, and get you where you wanted to go." Even I couldn't keep a straight face for that one. I told him I needed to go inside. Despite that bizarre encounter, the trip was fun and, more importantly, it made me want to take more trips.

Over the next couple of years, while I was still in college, I made a bunch of road trips. I went back to Ohio for Halloween parties or just to hang out. I went to Rehoboth Beach with my family almost every summer. I went to Virginia to visit family and countless other places that were just a few hours' drive. We even drove to Florida twice for spring break. The spring break trips were really interesting. The first time we went it was Pam, one of her friends, and two of my buddies, Bill and Bobby. We drove home from Edinboro on a Friday night, planning to leave the next morning and drive straight through. When

Pam and I got home, we realized I left my battery charger for my wheelchair in Edinboro. I couldn't go an entire week without charging my chair, and my wheelchair company was in Pittsburgh, which wasn't going to be open until Monday. My dad came to the rescue like he always did. He drove three hours to Edinboro, picked up my charger, and drove straight back home. He drove all night just so I could go on vacation.

Sometime during that first year, a man named Lester contacted me about building accessible apartments. One of the things my OVR counselor did that was really helpful was put Lester in contact with me. He was the contractor that was building the accessible apartments on the other side of town. He had a general floor plan and some good ideas but needed a little bit of help. My counselor knew I grew up in construction and knew I was looking for a place that was accessible, so she sent him my way. We met a couple of times and brainstormed ideas for the apartment building. There were four units, three of them were two-bedroom and the fourth a single bedroom. All four of them had roll-in showers, wide-open floor plans, radiant heat in the floor and height adjustable desks in each bedroom. The front door was even automatic, with a large square power button. One of the most creative things we came up with was what I was calling the bumper rails along the floor. Even the best drivers are going to bounce their chair into the wall a little bit here and there. Foot plates can be sharp, wheels can be dirty, and accidents happen. One of Lester's concerns was how damaged the walls would get over time from simple accidents like a footplate scratching the wall. We came up with an idea to place a 1 inch thick and 12-inch-tall board all along the floor against the wall. It was nailed into the drywall and then covered with carpeting. The appearance was seamless, like the carpeting on the floor rose up the wall about a foot. It was pretty slick and provided a good shock absorber for any time a footplate rubbed up against the wall. It didn't even remotely damage the carpet covered board. By the time the first year was winding down, Lester was pretty well on his way. He said the apartments would be finished by the end of the summer and I could have first pick. I chose the back, left apartment with two bedrooms that had a nice view of the woods.

Before leaving for the summer, Pam and I decided to go out for a drink. We hadn't really gone out to the bars much but wanted to celebrate a successful year. The town of Edinboro was pretty small and only had three bars -- The Hotel, the Boro Bar, and the Copper Coin. I think we went to the Copper Coin. While we were there, I noticed a group of about six people who were getting rowdy and having fun. Then, one of them turned around and I saw my fraternity letters emboldened across his chest. I had checked the fraternity listings thoroughly; Phi Sigma Kappa was not listed on the campus registry. I wasn't sure where they were from, but I was sure as hell going to talk to them. I went over and introduced myself. The guy told me his name was Roland and introduced me to his little brother, Ben, who had just been initiated. The two of them introduced me to Shannon, Lisa and a few others. They told me there is an entire chapter of PSK, but it wasn't recognized by campus. It was underground. They told me they have parties all the time and a good group of people that are really close. I was welcome anytime. I was pretty excited to come back in the fall. Between an accessible apartment, with a roll in shower, and an entire chapter of my fraternity, my second year was bound to be much more eventful than my first.

When Pam and I first moved into the apartment complex we clicked immediately with our three other neighbors. It was almost like an instant second family. Pat and Bob lived on the same side of the building, John and Mike were across the hall from them and Rick was across the hall from us, in the one-bedroom apartment. Pat always had a lot of really cute attendants, one of which was his girlfriend Jenny. She didn't live with Pat but spent enough time there that she may as well have. It was a great environment. Everyone would hang out in each other's apartments, almost like it was one giant house. We even left our doors open most of the time, at least when we were home. I was also happy to finally have some people around me who knew what it was like to use a wheelchair. Pat, Bob and John all used power chairs and Rick, who had a spinal cord injury, used a manual chair. Mike was able-bodied but a personal care attendant. They also knew what it was like to rely on others for things like attendant care. At the same time, I was getting to know my neighbors, I was also trying to find those fraternity brothers, but wasn't having any luck. Then, one day I stumbled across another guy wearing letters outside one of my classes. He had this giant, full beard and he was the epitome of the image that pops to mind when I hear the words "Grateful Dead." He said they had a house right down the road from my new apartment, barely more than 100 yards away.

I had the perfect little community coming together between the accessible apartment and the fraternity house down the road. I brought both groups together for the first of what would be many parties, and everyone got along great. Pam still harasses me about that first party though. I spent most of the night hitting on Lisa, the tall, cute blonde, who was one of the little sisters I had met at the bar the previous spring. When some of the girls were leaving at the end of the night, I went with them, trying to get Lisa to come back and hang out longer. I struck out, and even worse I wasn't paying attention and ended up driving into a ditch and getting stuck. I have to say, getting a wheelchair stuck in muck along the side of the road is not the best way to impress a woman.

I continued to work hard in school, but I was in such a good groove I was able to take time to go out and party without it negatively impacting my grades. My apartment was probably a little under a mile away from town, so driving my chair to campus or to a bar was relatively easy. The world was opening up and becoming a little more accessible. I had my own vehicle, but I was also able to use campus transportation if needed. That made it a little easier on Pam, she didn't have to drive me back and forth all the time. In using the campus vans, I was meeting a lot more people with disabilities too. The vans could hold several wheelchairs, so they often stopped at other buildings, including the dormitories, to take people from place to place. If memory serves, that's how I met several of the guys who lived in the dorms. Chad, Ben, Dan and John (John had a spinal cord injury very close to my level) were some of the ones that I often invited to the parties I was throwing at my apartment. Not to brag, but I did throw some pretty good parties. I would pick up different bottles of booze and we would try out different cocktails, everything from Alabama slammers to margaritas. When a lot of those guys from the dorms came over, the apartment looked like a roller derby. It was hilarious.

I still went home pretty often, but definitely not every weekend. It was more like once a month, which was fine by me. That three-hour drive was not something I ever looked forward to. I also made it a point to visit Penn State every now and then as well. I kept in touch with the active brothers through the occasional phone call, so I always knew what was going on with the new pledge classes. It was fun being the alumni brother that they heard stories about for a couple of weeks before finally meeting. One of my favorite things to do was give each new class a song to memorize. It was always something really silly, like "Do - A Deer" from The Sound of Music, or "I'm a Little Teapot." I also told them they had to choreograph a little dance. It was one of those things that was technically hazing, but to me, and I hoped to the guys pledging, it felt more like a fun, bonding experience than it did a hazing ritual. They always had a blast doing it. The absolute coolest part, though, was how the circle of brotherhood just continued to revolve.

It was during one of these trips back to visit the new brothers that I discovered the extent to which the earthworm story had evolved. Remember when I said it became something of an urban legend? Well, I learned that each new pledge class heard about that story, but they also heard about what happened a few hours later in the hospital. It was only a few hours after I ate the earthworm that I was injured and needed rushed to the emergency room. The ER staff had to do several things to keep me alive, one of which was intubate me. After that, they removed the tube from my mouth and cut a tracheotomy through my neck. Now I've heard two versions of the worm story, the first being that when the doctor performed the tracheotomy, he discovered a black disgusting sludge like substance in my neck. The second was that the doctor pumped my stomach and somehow this same substance got lodged into my throat. In both scenarios, what followed was the doctor going out into the waiting room and asking fraternity brothers what I may have eaten that night. When the doctor further explained what he found and why he was asking, he was greeted with a unanimous, "That would be an earthworm," to which his response was to open his mouth to say something, stop, shake his head, turn around and walk directly back out. I'm not sure where that came from or if any part of it is true, but I'm fairly certain that worm was not lying in my throat for five hours.

Eventually all of the guys that were there when I got shot, and began telling that story, had obviously moved on. The new guys picked up right where the old ones left off though. When I wanted to go down to campus and visit for a party or function, some of the brothers would drive to my parent's house, leave their vehicle, and drive my van to Altoona, just like we did in the beginning. Then, my dad would always bring their vehicle down, often at one or two in the morning, and swap vehicles to bring me home. God love my dad, most of the cars my fraternity brothers left him were pretty beat up, smelly, piece-of-shit vehicles. They were, after all, poor college kids. That also meant the gas tank was usually near empty. But my dad wouldn't just put gas in the tank, he would fill it up, every time. The younger brothers often brought one or two of the pledges with them. They would sit in the back and we would talk the entire ride down. That was one of the best ways I got to know the newer, younger guys. It became a tradition that at some point each semester, I would visit and gather all the pledges (and new brothers) around to tell my story. I would explain what happened when I got shot and how the fraternity reacted, coming together the way they did. I'm pretty good at talking, so when I tell the story it can be captivating, especially in that atmosphere. These young guys, the new pledges, would gather around as I described how my brothers went above and beyond, everything from driving my van to straight catheterizing me. As the years went on, I wasn't able to make it down to Altoona as often as I would have liked. Fortunately, I was almost always able to make it at least once a semester. I would get to see the new class sing something like "I Want to be Like You" from the movie The Jungle Book and then tell them the story of true brotherhood and what it means to be a part of something special in Phi Sigma Kappa, Iota Septaton.

Back at Edinboro, I had become really close with a few of the fraternity guys, like Ben, Matt and Danny, who everyone called Junior. Ben had long black hair and looked like a shady biker. Matt was short and scrappy, but often thought of other people before himself. Junior had a thick goatee and only one kidney. On top of that, it wasn't even his. His brother Scott had donated it to him when Junior got sick a few years earlier. All of the guys were really friendly, but something just seemed to click with those guys. All the guys had gotten together and built a ramp to the side entrance of the house. There were only one or two steps, but the ramp made things a whole lot easier. The doorway led to the kitchen, but from the kitchen there were three steps up into the living room, so I typically stayed in the kitchen. I had a little spot right by the back corner where I could face the crowd. Junior always stood beside me, I think he liked being out-of-the-way.

Junior was also a lot of fun to harass, but to be fair, he often brought it on himself. He typically stood on my left side, so he could easily reach my drink holder (which is mounted right under my arm rest below my hand) when we were at parties or went out. Anytime I needed a drink, or if he just intermittently felt like I could use one, he would grab my glass and hold it up in front of me. Unfortunately, he had a really bad habit of not paying attention to what he was doing, especially after a couple of mixed drinks. He would grab my glass, begin holding it up toward my face, but then get distracted and look away. This always resulted in the straw being too far away for me to reach. I'd politely draw his attention back. Well, as politely as two really good friends are when they're drinking, which is to say, it didn't take long for insults to be hurled in both directions. I'd usually give him one freebie and then I would start making fun of him. I would start firing away comments, but he paid so little attention that when he realized I was talking he thought I was simply saying I was done. So, he put the glass back down, never having given me a drink! It was an endless cycle, happening multiple times throughout the night every time we were together. It became a running joke. I typically only went to the house for a function or a party, otherwise, those guys came to the apartment or sometimes I would drive my chair and meet them at the bar in town. There were always a lot of laughs to be had with those guys.

Over the years I lived in that apartment, there was a little turnover in its residency. The first person to move out was Bob. He had a few issues and wasn't always the nicest to Pat and Jenny. When he left, it was probably for the best. Pat got a new roommate shortly after that,

Ken, who was a little older and used a scooter because he had a stroke. John and Mike moved out when they graduated, and Dan and Catrina moved into their apartment. Dan had a spinal cord injury and Catrina was his girlfriend/attendant. Rick moved out and an older gentleman, Mel, moved into his single bedroom apartment across the hall from mine. The open community atmosphere remained the same, with the exception of Mel. He wasn't the friendliest, and a little uptight. He lived there for about a year before Shane moved in. Shane had cerebral palsy and had to use an augmentative communication device 90% of the time because he was extremely difficult to understand. He had an attendant, though, who could understand just about every word. It was quite impressive. They were both much friendlier than Mel.

In 1997, I finished my undergraduate degree in psychology and decided to apply for the Master's program. I had done really well in my classes, particularly a couple of the toughest ones, experimental psychology and statistics. My advisor, though, suggested I pursue the rehab counseling program instead. When I didn't get into the psychology program, I didn't have much choice if I wanted to go to grad school. So, I met with Dr. McHenry in the rehab counseling department. Much like when I decided to go to Edinboro in the first place, everything was happening last-minute. Dr. McHenry told me I needed to take the GREs (graduate record exam) to apply. That meant going through a ton of red tape to arrange for someone to write for me. I wasn't very keen on that idea, considering I didn't have a whole lot of time to get stuff done. He thought of another idea. He said that they also accept the Miller Analogies Test as a qualifying exam, and he could administer that. He even volunteered to write for me. I took him up on it. I don't remember what score I needed, only that I made it by the skin of my teeth. Seriously. I think I was one question away from disqualification. But I made it. When I returned in the fall, I would be returning to graduate school.

When Pam and I returned in the fall, she wasn't enrolled in classes anymore. She had been struggling with some of the required courses, like college algebra. I felt bad for her because she was working really hard. She was trying to get her degree in nursing, but some of her academics just weren't at the level they needed to be for a degree.

What made matters worse was she was an excellent caregiver. She was working a whole lot more hours than a full-time job in caring for me on top of taking some tough classes. She got me ready every morning, in bed every evening, handled meals in between and even had to get up in the middle of the night if I needed something. She needed the money that the hours provided, so she didn't want me to hire anyone else. On top of everything else, she often got really bad test anxiety. That meant even when she knew the material, she struggled with getting the grade. That was probably a very difficult time for her when I returned to grad school. She really enjoyed living in Edinboro. The open countryside was beautiful, the apartment was great, and she had become close with the little sisters in my fraternity. On the flipside, she couldn't handle classes anymore and didn't want to waste the money, yet she was willing to stay up there so I could continue my education. She had her moments and had a temper that would unleash a tirade occasionally, but I'm not perfect either. I'm sure I provoked a couple of those rants. Bottom line was, I was really lucky. She had enabled me to get through undergrad living on my own and then begin graduate school.

We got back to Edinboro about a week or two early, before classes started. I went home every summer, despite signing a year's lease for a few reasons. First and foremost, Pam needed a break from being a full-time live-in caregiver, but there also wasn't much to do there in the summer anyway. I don't ever remember having to get much organized to move back in, but then again, I wasn't the one who had to do anything. Since we didn't have anything to do, we spent our time hanging out with our neighbors and a few other friends. Some of them had stayed for the summer, either because it was their full-time home or because they were taking summer classes. Junior was one of those people that lived there year-round. In fact, he grew up there.

Several days before classes started, Junior and I decided to go out for a little while. The Copper Coin had the best food, so that's where we started. There weren't a lot of people back yet, so the crowd was fairly small. After a while we struck up a conversation with two girls and spent most of the night just hanging out with them. One of them was short with long blonde hair and kept flirting with me pretty heavily so I directed most of my attention to her. By the end of the night we were all pretty loaded and it was last call. The girls asked if we wanted to go back to their apartment, which was right down the street. I don't think they even finished talking before I was agreeing and ready to go. Junior was no different. I guess drunk and horny doesn't help with thinking ahead, because I didn't even ask if their apartment was on the first floor, let alone wheelchair accessible. She was on my lap riding down the street at 2:30 in the morning. I wasn't even remotely thinking about whether I could get my wheelchair into her apartment or not. I probably should have been though, because when we got there, I saw three steps that were ready to end my night. The girls hadn't thought about it either and seemed to be just as caught off guard as we were.

The girl on my lap kissed me several more times and apologized. She said halfway through the night she completely forgot about the wheelchair. It never even dawned on her when she invited me back to her place. She got off my lap and looked around, asking if I had any ideas. Junior was a little wobbly, but he was laughing nonetheless. Apparently, I had quite the look on my face. She kissed me again, long, and whispered in my ear that she really wanted to figure out a way for me to get inside. That's all it took. I looked at Junior and the wheels started turning. I looked around for a few minutes and eventually decided all we needed was a screwdriver. She had one inside, so we took the door off the hinges and laid it on the steps. There were only three and they weren't very high, so I drove right up. I've always been proud of my ingenuity and creativity, but never more so than that night. Then again, drunk and horny is also a giant motivator!

Graduate school was going to be a lot of work, but it didn't seem as hard as I was expecting. The classes were all in the evening and typically only met once a week. They were obviously geared toward people who had full-time jobs. That meant I could sleep in and do schoolwork at my leisure throughout the day, since I wasn't one of those unlucky ones that was working on top of having school. What was getting difficult was the living arrangement with Pam. We were going in two different directions and it was becoming obvious that she wasn't really happy. I couldn't blame her; I think she was still feeling the sting of doing poorly in some of her classes. But it felt like she was taking it out on me sometimes, which I'm sure caused me to lash out on my end, making matters worse. The bottom line was, we would both be better off if we made a change. It's not like we were dating, it was a working relationship that was mutually beneficial, or at least was while she was going to school. When she didn't have classes anymore, the arrangement was a little lopsided, with everything focused on me. We talked and decided that she was going to move back home. I was lucky again in that she said she would stick around until I found some good attendants and got some structure in place.

Somehow, I always seemed to get lucky in my support systems. After only about a week or two of advertising and posting flyers, I got some interest from some really good people. Mike, one of my original neighbors, said he would move in as my roommate on a temporary basis. He could throw me in bed in the evenings and be there in case I needed something in exchange for free rent. Bernadette, one of Pat's attendants was willing to pick up some of my meals and cook for me. When she realized I needed pretty much everything, she said she was interested in picking up weekend mornings as well. The cornerstone though, the anchor that allowed me to stay there without Pam, was Mimi. One of the van drivers put me in touch with his wife who was interested in picking up some hours in the morning. She was phenomenal. Absolutely reliable, friendly and was able to throw me around with relative ease. When Pam moved out, it was definitely a transition, but we were both better off for it. She continued to work with me when I came back home for holidays and summer break though.

I interviewed a few people for the roommate position over the next month or two, while Mike hung out and helped me in the evenings. There were some really shady characters that applied. The deal was free room and board in exchange for putting me in bed in the evenings and being there at night. Throwing me in bed isn't all that involved. All I do at night is brush my teeth, take some pills and use a Hoyer lift to transfer from my chair to bed. Then I get undressed and positioned. It doesn't take long and it's not that difficult, but some of the people that applied just gave me the willies. One guy was coming from New York. His girlfriend lived nearby, and he wanted to be closer. The minute I met him I cringed. He smelled like ass and when he smiled, I don't think he had more than four teeth. All I kept thinking was I can't even imagine him brushing my teeth, let alone relying on him to put me in bed and trusting him throughout the night. I was starting to get worried, because Mike was getting antsy. He was talking about moving out soon. Somehow, I got lucky again. Bernadette and her boyfriend needed some space from each other, and she asked if she could move in. I very happily said yes.

Bernadette was a great roommate and excellent caregiver as well. She was a lot of fun to hang out with and had a great sense of humor. She was also really, really cute. Like I said, Pat always had really attractive attendants. She was a self-proclaimed hippie chick. She even had a pair of wooden shoes; I think they were from Holland. You could hear her from a mile away when she wore those things. She was also all about eating healthy and taking care of herself. I, on the other hand, always had a cupboard in the kitchen that was loaded with all the junk that Aunt Gigi sent. It had everything from Pringles and chocolate to Twizzlers and crackers. Bernadette used to yell at me every time we would get a care package from Gigi, asking if we were trying to make her fat. It was all in good nature though. What was even funnier was when Bernadette started putting pictures of Victoria's Secret models inside the junk food. It was her thought that if she opened up the cabinet to break her diet, she would see the models and remember she wanted to keep her figure. I always told her I thought it was backfiring because those pictures made me want to open the cabinet more often, and she was the one that had to open it for me.

Bernadette continued to work for Pat at the same time as living with me and working for me on weekend mornings. She also took care of meals, while Mimi came in every weekday morning to get me ready. Bernadette and Jenny became best friends and our ecosystem rolled right along. Everything had stabilized after Pam moved home, although it was an interesting transition. The new system I had in place was working well. I even felt comfortable enough taking on a new endeavor. My buddy Pete, from high school, had just graduated from Slippery Rock and asked if I wanted to go in as a 50-50 partner on a health and fitness center. His degree was in exercise physiology and he couldn't stop thinking of all our conversations when we were working on that old junior high school. How we talked about renovating the basement into a gym. His one sticking point was that he didn't want to make a gym, he wanted a health and fitness center. He made some really good points, that there were plenty of ratty gyms and the way to make any real money was to target people interested in a healthy lifestyle, not just muscle heads and gym rats. So we went for it. He came up a couple of times during my first year in graduate school and we started laying out the foundation for what became "The Underground" health and fitness center. It was quite the undertaking, but we did it. We renovated the basement we had talked about years ago. We bartered with my dad and his two friends. We would renovate everything at our expense, which would give them more usable real estate, in exchange for no rent. We put everything else in place and opened the doors in 1999. We went on to run it for the next nine years, until we began getting pulled in too many directions. Pete had gone back to graduate school for his Master's Degree in special education (he would later achieve his superintendent papers and is currently a principal in the Portage School District, not bad for someone who in high school never even considered going to college) and I was working at the Hiram G. Andrews Center about 30 minutes from The Underground. We decided to focus more on our chosen professions and sold the business. It's still there though; now it's called "No Excuses."

When my first year of graduate school was over, I had a 4.0 grade point average. I left for the summer, but Bernadette was taking summer classes, so she remained in the apartment. Like I said, my lease was for the entire year, so it was there anyway. I was really happy with how life was going. My grades, my friends, my living arrangement, everything had just fallen into place perfectly. While I was home that summer, I called the apartment to talk to Bernadette and our answer machine picked up. It was the weirdest thing. It was Bernadette's voice and she was saying that the two of us weren't home. I knew what it said, I was there when she recorded it. But there was something about hearing it. I left a message and told her to give me a buzz. Then I remembered she had gone home for a week. I found myself calling the number again anyway, just to hear the sound of her voice. That's when it hit me. I had some serious feelings for Bernadette. The realization came down on my head like a ton of bricks. I had never been in love before and wouldn't find myself feeling that way again for more than a decade, when I fell in love with Krista, who I dated for well over a year. But the way everything inside me got ratcheted up by a simple recording spoke volumes. I mean, of course I love my family and all my friends, but that "in love" feeling was brand new and man was it intense. I had no idea what to do with it. Not to mention, I hadn't been in any kind of real relationship since Sharon.

In retrospect, I should have seen it coming. I had fun with Bernadette no matter what we were doing, who we were with, or where we were. I could talk to her about anything and I felt stronger anytime she was near, like I didn't need anything else when I was with her. She had an awesome sense of humor and never really seemed fazed by the chaos that always seemed to follow me. We went to dinner and a movie one time that turned into a train wreck. Come to think of it, maybe that's why it felt like a date, because of how badly it went. Sadly, that's been a trademark of many of my dates, that they went off the rails. Dinner went fine, but when we got to the theater, the accessible seating was in the last row, flush against the back wall. My wheelchair is pretty big, so it was tight to begin with. If I wanted to recline at all, either for a pressure relief, to stretch or even just to lean down to talk to Bernadette, there wasn't much room. I was only able to recline a few inches, because along with my head rest approaching the wall, when my feet elevated, they were pushing into the seats in front of us. To make matters worse, there were two buttons and one toggle switch on the back of the head rest I had to worry about.

The buttons allowed someone else to control the recline function. The top button, when pressed, brought the chair down, and the bottom button brought it back up. The toggle switch was the on-off for the entire chair's power. As you can imagine, my friends loved that part of my chair. They would randomly walk past and push the button, startling the hell out of me. The worst (or best in their opinion) was when I was taking a bite or taking a drink of something and the chair would lurch backward. They also love to walk past and flip the toggle switch down, cutting off all power. Granted, I have to admit that I usually deserved it. I really am a wise ass, but in my defense I'm also really good at it, so it's a lot of fun. Anyway, I had to be careful those buttons didn't touch the wall behind me, otherwise the chair would continue reclining against my will. I obviously didn't try hard enough, because that's exactly what happened about three quarters of the way through the movie. That little button touched the wall and that was all she wrote. The headrest was forced into the wall and my feet were forced into the seat in front of me. The toggle switch ended up getting ripped off and I was wedged in between the wall and the seat. It made quite the scene. Luckily, Bernadette was able to find the emergency switch that bypassed the headrest. She sat me back up, but the headrest was broken and hanging, not to mention the toggle switch broke in the "off" mode. I couldn't use the headrest anymore. After the movie was over, she had to take me out of gear and push me out to the van. I remember her laughing and poking fun at me, saying, "Boy, you're one helluva date!" I was laughing as well. She even made that chaos fun.

I wasn't sure how I was going to handle all of those emotions when I returned in August. On one hand, Bernadette had drifted away from her old boyfriend and was pretty much single. On the other hand, if I let her know my feelings, I was risking her not feeling the same way and then ruining a friendship not to mention living arrangement that I relied on to stay in college. If knowing I had romantic feelings made her uncomfortable and she wanted to move out, I was in trouble. Somehow, I pulled off a magic trick when Pam moved home. I was lucky enough to get everything in place to stay in college. I was pretty sure the odds were highly against getting that lucky twice.

On top of all that, I hadn't been dating much. I went out with a girl named Elan, who was from Malaysia, briefly but nothing of substance. I had placed dating on the back burner because I was reluctant to put myself out there. As it turned out, I didn't have to worry about it much when I got back. Things were already upside down. Jenny and Pat had broken up, and Pat was moving home. Jenny had also started dating Pat's roommate Ken (who she would go on to marry), and Bernadette was really upset because she was so close to both of them. Things had definitely gotten turned on their ear. I told myself there was too much chaos to tell Bernadette how I felt, and then later, I convinced myself that I couldn't risk making her uncomfortable and losing my roommate/attendant. I had to make sure I finished graduate school. In reality, there's no way Bernadette would've ever left me stranded. I think I used that as an excuse to play it safe. I never said anything to her. It's one of the greatest regrets in my life, but it taught me one of the most valuable and enduring lessons. I used to have a bumper sticker on my wall as a teenager that had a picture of a black diamond and a skier with the phrase "No guts, no glory." It was simple and to the point. I allowed that moment to slip through my fingers because I had no guts. But it taught me that great rewards are only achieved through great endeavors, and in a life of such endeavors, the only regrets we'll have are the risks we never dared to chance.

It was a difficult lesson to learn, but one I'm thankful I learned. When I fell in love with Krista, a decade later, I made sure to tell her. That was a little different though, I saw that one coming. I knew I was falling in love with her from the start, it didn't hit me out of nowhere. That relationship lasted well over a year, but I think I knew within a few weeks, after the first time one of our dates went completely haywire. I had set up what I thought was the perfect romantic day. An afternoon that included the cherry blossoms in Washington DC, a visit to a museum and then dinner on the terrace of the Kennedy Center as the sun went down. I had my uncle Mike set up to play chauffeur since he's only a few miles away from the monuments. That way Krista didn't have to drive through the city. It was the perfect day, sunny and 75°. Unfortunately, everyone else on the East Coast seem to have the same idea. Traffic was horrendous, by the time we actually got to the monuments we were easily two hours behind my schedule. We decided to eliminate the museum and have my uncle drop us off instead of finding a parking spot. That way we had some time to walk around before dinner. Unfortunately, when uncle Mike drove back around to pick us up, he pulled too close to the curb. My new minivan had a fold-out ramp anchored just inside the sliding door on the passenger side. After the side door slid open, the van's kneeling system lowered the chassis while the ramp deployed so it wouldn't be too steep. Mike parked so close to the curb, when the van lowered the sliding door caught the edge of the cement. Everything got wedged. We ended up recruiting strangers to help rock the van side-to-side as Krista tried to drag the door closed. It looked like a mini riot in the street. Luckily it worked and we got the van back together and working condition. Unfortunately, by the time we got to the Kennedy Center, the terrace was closed due to high winds. Lucky for me, Krista has a great sense of humor, so we laughed a lot that day. Not all of my train wreck dates worked out that well, but they all have one thing in common: they're really funny to look back on.

Meanwhile, despite forcing myself to keep my feelings about Bernadette tucked away, the rest of my final year at Edinboro went well. There were definitely some memorable moments. One that sticks in my head is when one of the fraternity brothers was in a play up in Erie, I think it was Tennessee Williams Arsenic and Old Lace. Bernadette and I, along with a bunch of the brothers and little sisters all went. It was a really good play, and everyone did an excellent job. Afterwards, we were allowed to join the cast for the wrap up party in back. They had a jazz band playing as everyone mingled. Bernadette especially enjoyed the evening because I wound up with a new friend. One of the women involved in the play came up and introduced herself, planting a big kiss right on my lips. I didn't mind that much, she was pretty cute, but throughout the rest of the night she kept sneaking up behind me. It seemed like every time I wasn't paying attention, I would feel these hands come out of nowhere, grab my face and turn my head. There she was, planting another kiss on me. After about an hour or two of these sneak attack kisses, this woman had her arm around my shoulder, having just kissed me again, and looked irritated. Frowning, as she held her cheek next to mine, she said, rather loudly, "You're really cute - better than that jerk that keeps staring at me." I looked around and asked who, to which she responded, "My stupid husband." I thought Bernadette was going to wet her pants she was laughing so hard. I told her it was time to go.

On another occasion, I was meeting Matt and a few fraternity brothers along with Chad and a few guys from the dorms at the Boro Bar. A few minutes after I got there, Chad came in with some stranger. This guy was literally carrying the battery from the back of

Chad's chair. Apparently, it had come loose somehow as he was driving down the sidewalk. Matt helped this other guy put everything back together so that it would last for the night. After they got it fixed, Chad bought them both a beer to say thank you. We all sat at the table for a few minutes talking when out of nowhere the stranger stands up, walks over to Matt, whispered something to him, and then dumped his beer on top of Matt's head. He then proceeded to walk out the front door. None of us had any idea why he dumped the beer, but I was livid and spun my chair around, following him out. I had just made it outside before the door closed behind me and yelled to him, asking him what the hell he thought he was doing. He just looked back at me, paused and said, "Do you think I was wrong?" I said I thought he was an asshole. Without blinking he said, "I think you look like Jesus. Do you think you look like Jesus?" My long hair was hanging down just below my shoulders and I had several days' worth of stubble on my face from not shaving. In retrospect, yeah, I kind of looked a little bit like Jesus, but when that was his response after the whole back-and-forth, I had no idea what to say. He jumped on his bicycle and pedaled away as I stared at him. That's when it dawned on me. I was no longer a 6'2", 200-pound rugby player. I was confronting some nut job skinhead by myself outside of a bar with the door closed. I thought to myself, "Okay, I probably shouldn't do this kind of stuff anymore without other people around!"

I wrapped up all my classes and finished with a 4.0 GPA. I had arranged for my graduate internship to be at the Hiram G Andrews Center and made sure it was diversified throughout the building. The Underground Health and Fitness Center was up and running and I was ready to head home. We had one final big blowout party at the apartment. I still remember Jenny walking around with a tray of Jell-O shots telling everyone they had to take one in honor of graduation. I was talking to one of my professors who had stopped by when Jenny came over pushing her Jell-O shots. She had no idea this woman was my professor but wouldn't take no for an answer. I let her ramble for a little bit and then introduced them. I said, "Jenny, this is Dr. Cowher, Chairman of the Rehab Counseling Program." Jenny's face turned beet red and she ran down the hall. Dr. Cowher and I both got a good chuckle. When things wound down at the apartment, we went downtown to the bar, then ended up back at the apartment again. After only about two hours of sleep, I had to get up the next morning and start getting things together to go home. That made for a long, sleepy drive home, but it was a great way to say goodbye, for the time being, to all of those great people that had made the last several years so much fun and so fulfilling.

Chapter 26 - New Job

That summer I had my graduate internship that was supervised by Kathy and included a lot of the assistive technology stuff with Tammy. After that, I was offered a contract position with the Center for Independent Living. I had already registered for a conference in DC, so I was planning on taking a few days before starting. As luck would have it, my new boss said she'd be more than happy to pay for me to go to the conference. It was, after all, a National Spinal Cord Injury Association conference. I remember riding the elevator down from my hotel room with a guy a few years older than me in a manual wheelchair. He was obviously in excellent physical shape and his wife was drop dead gorgeous. We talked for the whole ride down, as people got on and off and on again. He and his wife were both really nice people. As we got off the elevator, I headed toward the back entrance to the ballroom and he headed toward the front. Turns out, he was giving the keynote speech. He had won a couple of Olympic medals in the Paralympics and was even on a box of Wheaties. You would think his name would have stuck in my head forever, but it didn't. The one name I do remember from that night is Mitch Tepper, who I met right after the introductory ceremony. As the crowd made its way out of the ballroom, he told everyone within earshot, "Anyone that wants to talk about sex, we'll be at the bar, follow me!"

Turns out, Mitch specialized in sexuality, relationships and disabilities. His main focus was to break down the stereotype and stigmatization that people with disabilities are either uninterested or unable to have intimate sexual relationships. It's a ridiculously underserved topic considering its importance. It's also ironic because everyone is always interested in the topic even if they are uncomfortable talking about it. That was pretty apparent that night because while I and about a half-dozen other people joined him at the bar, another 25 people followed us in. They didn't sit with us, but they sure as hell weren't talking among themselves. They sat far enough away that they wouldn't be part of "that group" yet they were definitely close enough to hear every word. It was a great conversation that I'm sure opened a lot of minds that were listening from the outskirts. Mitch had a real knack for normalizing the conversation. I tell that story all the time when I'm giving guest lectures. The big thing I point out is how much more of an impact Mitch had, talking about sex, than the guy from the box of Wheaties, who it turned out was the president of the National Spinal Cord Injury Association. I've also told that story many times at work, which is probably how I got picked to develop the sexuality and relationships group. I've always thought that was ironic considering my own struggle in becoming comfortable with women, sex, and relationships after I was injured.

As I said earlier, I had two internships at the vocational rehab center, Hiram G Andrews Center (HGAC). Just as the second internship, the one for graduate school, was ending, the Center for Independent Living (CIL) representative that worked in CART was leaving. She worked as a contract employee at HGAC, providing peer counseling in CART. That meant she was cataloguing equipment, vendors, and customer satisfaction, then providing that information to new customers. She was basically documenting which equipment worked well and for whom, along with which companies were preferred and why. Her boss, the Executive Director of CIL, offered me the job. I had spent quite a few years learning about counseling and wasn't really interested in cataloguing equipment and reviews, but the contract had a line at the end that said, "… and other duties that may apply." I ran it by the administrators, suggesting I could take the job and basically just continue the responsibilities I had during my internship, filing it under "other duties that apply." They liked the idea, so I took the job.

A few years later HGA asked the University of Pittsburgh to develop another program, this one to address cognitive rehab. A neuropsychologist named Mike began developing what he called PASS, Promoting Abilities for Student Success, which was like a cognitive support program for students already enrolled in classes. Mike recruited Jamie, who had previously been working with life skills in the evening, to run PASS with help from me. Jamie would pull the students out of their classes for about an hour at a time, and then have them participate in groups that focused on cognitive goals. I got them for an hour to process everything they were learning with

Jamie. My very first group was hilarious. It was initially designed for Jamie and me to co-lead, but Jamie only lasted one session. During that session there must've been about six or eight times when the participants became really quiet, which I'm fine with. I actually like using silence; it's really effective. I also have a whole lot of patience, I had 12 minutes of dead silence one time during a group. Jamie, on the other hand, couldn't stand it. As soon as there was a moment of silence, she started asking another question or encouraging a participant to speak. After the group was over, I told her that if we were going to work together in that group she had to relax during those moments of silence. Without hesitating, she said, "Nope! That's all you then. I can't stand that silence!" As the program evolved over a few terms, it became apparent that pulling students out of their classes for cognitive support a couple of times a week was only minimally effective.

Therefore, Mike hired a woman named Deb, who also became one of my dearest friends, to redesign it to be a full-time program. Under Mike's direction, Deb went on to create a really cool program called the Cognitive Skills Enhancement Program, or CSEP. I was lucky enough to be there at the beginning to help design it. Instead of getting pulled out of their programming, the students would be participating in CSEP all day, 8 AM to 3 PM. This turned out to be much more effective. I ended up spending a lot of time bouncing between two university programs, CART and CSEP, along with all the other things I was doing like transitional living, outreach, and advocacy. A puzzle that began merely months after I was injured - that I never knew was being built - was nearing completion. The Center for Independent Living (CIL) contract was eliminated and I got folded into the University of Pittsburgh contract. Mike told me to write up my own job description that included everything I was already doing, anything else I wanted to do, and send it to him so he could sign it. So, after about 12 years, two internships and two contracts, I ended up helping to design, and working within, two different programs spearheaded by the University of Pittsburgh at HGA. I think the most interesting part about that is those two programs created the perfect balance of addressing someone's needs, and not just someone with a disability.

Everyone has strengths and weaknesses, things they are good at and things they are not so good at, with the things they're not so good at creating obstacles. That's everyone. Not just someone with a disability -- everyone. CSEP and CART were designed to figure out ways around those obstacles. CSEP uses self-awareness to figure out the right strategies. CART uses technology to figure out the right tool. Think of it this way: if you can't do something the way you want to do it or are unsuccessful, what do you change or do differently? If there's something in our way, we either use a tool to make it easier or we try a different approach. That's CART and CSEP and I would be lucky enough to take part in both programs from their inception.

After going to a couple of conferences that first year, I decided to start looking a little further out. I had done quite a few road trips, so I had some traveling under my belt. Those were interesting endeavors to say the least; none of us had any idea what we were doing, friends and family alike. I think the primary concern about accessibility was simply whether or not there were steps and if so, how many. Granted, steps were a rather significant aspect that needed to be considered, but it wasn't the only aspect. In fact, back then it was quite frankly of very little importance. The first things asked, anytime I went anywhere, were "Can I get in? Are there any steps?" The first answer was always yes, because the second answer didn't really matter. I would get carried up and down steps on a regular basis, both in and out of my chair.

Chapter 27 - Traveling - Lessons Learned in LA

In 2001, Los Angeles was hosting a conference promoting all the newest assistive technology and I got my boss's approval to go. It was an opportunity to expand my knowledge base as well as begin really traveling. In addition, my cousin Dan had moved out there from Ohio to see just how far he could take a music career. He got a job in the copy department at Disney and spent nights and weekends working on his band, Dumfinger. He had nearly lost two of his fingers when a power saw he was using got away from him. After they were surgically reattached, he had some difficulty with fine motor movements. Apparently while he was playing guitar he would often yell, "Stupid dumb fingers!" Thus, Dumfinger was born. Since Dan and I had virtually grown up together, I had wanted to visit him since he moved out west. This conference gave me the opportunity to accomplish several things at once -- learn more about assistive technology, begin traveling, and visit my cousin that I hadn't seen in quite some time. The only problem was I had no idea how to go about any of it, so I just made it up as I went, which is the way I've done most things since my injury.

First, I made sure my attendant was able to go with me. I knew enough that I had to start there at least. Then I completed a registration for the conference, called the hotel and reserved a room. I don't remember how in depth I got during that phone call about accessibility, but I did point out that it needed to be big enough to accommodate my large wheelchair. Next, I booked the flights for Pam and me and made sure they were nonstop direct flights. I had no idea how I was getting onto the plane. My dad had helped carry me when I flew home from Atlanta, but he wouldn't be there this time. I decided I'd cross that bridge when I came to it. I've always been rather good at leaping before I look and begging forgiveness rather than asking permission. However, I did want some type of understanding about what to expect when traveling with a disability, so I started digging online. One of the most helpful websites I came across was gimponthego.com. It's a website run by someone who uses a chin control power wheelchair and appears to have traveled quite extensively. His site also collects information from other sources and includes loads of travel tips. One of the most valuable things I came across was the procedural manual for handling wheelchairs used by the ground crew at airports. It was the perfect resource! Most people have very limited knowledge of assistive technology, specifically the types that are more involved and complicated. This is simply due to a lack of exposure, nothing more. I already knew that anyone trying to handle my wheelchair was going to be confused as all hell. It was almost a guarantee that they would have never seen a chair like mine. Knowing the guidelines they were going to reference when they saw a piece of equipment they didn't understand was priceless.

The instructions clearly stated that the first thing the ground crew needed to evaluate was whether the chair could be stored upright or needed to be turned on its side. This was determined by the dimensions of the cargo compartment and cargo compartment access door as relates to the size of the wheelchair. This was important for several reasons, first and foremost was whether the battery needed to be removed or not. If the battery was gel-based it did not. If it was anything else, then it would need to be removed and packed in sand as a safety precaution. The instructions get ridiculously involved when directing the crew how to remove the battery, so thankfully my chair is gel-based. The other thing I was able to do was ask the ground crew directly about the height of the access door. My wheelchair reclines to almost 180°, or in other words can lay down almost completely flat. That gave me the option of adjusting it to accommodate the height of the cargo compartment, which alleviated any concern about placing it on its side. With all of that, I had covered just about every aspect of the flight. My dad even used air miles to upgrade my seats to first class. Next up was figuring out how I would manage once I was in Los Angeles. The two biggest things I needed were a Hoyer lift (in order to get in and out of bed) and an accessible vehicle, which I was thinking would have to be like my own full-sized conversion van with the elevator type lift and raised roof. They modified minivans to be wheelchair accessible, but even those with the most clearance were too small. Fortunately, just before this trip I got a very lucky surprise.

Tim is a friend of mine who, at the time, did all the driver's evaluation and driver's training in our office. Being one of the most knowledgeable people in his field that I've ever met, Tim was always keeping up to date with the latest advances in vehicle modifications. When something particularly groundbreaking or new became available he would often hold an in-service so the rest of our team could be kept up to speed. As luck would have it, he had organized one of these in-services shortly before my trip. It was to discuss a new van modification package that had been recently released. It was a minivan with the most recent modification system available, which included a custom-lowered floor system that had an additional two or three inches of clearance.

While we were all listening to the vendor give his sales pitch, Tim and I began to mainly focus on the door, particularly its height. I remember looking at him and asking, "Is the clearance inside greater than the side door opening where the ramp deploys?" When he replied that it was, I told him I thought I could fit. He pulled out his tape measure, looked at my chair and then inside the van and said, "You just might." I wasted no time, and may have even interrupted the presenter, going directly to the ramp and lining my chair up. I had to recline quite a bit, but with some guidance I was able to direct my chair up the ramp and into the van. Once inside, it was the moment of truth. I obviously can't see above my head, so I relied on Tim and the others who could. I began to sit back up, very slowly. I made it to an upright sitting position and from there, could tell much more easily how much room I had around my head. Next I slowly started to angle my chair forward toward where the front passenger seat had been removed. Not only could I fit inside, I was able to pull my chair right into the empty space where the passenger usually sits. It was absolutely unbelievable!

The full-sized van to which I had become accustomed could only accommodate my height in the middle. The two front captain seats remained in place while the middle ones were taken out, which is where I parked my chair. The long bench in the back that could be transitioned into a pseudo-bed also remained intact. While this setup allowed me to get back and forth from one place to another, it was far from perfect. One of the biggest problems was that I could never see where I was going. The raised roof accommodated my height, but my head was above the front windshield. I did, however, have a TV in the ceiling which was positioned right in front of my face. Unfortunately, my sense of direction was absolutely screwed after eight years of not being able to see anything. It was also bumpy as hell and during the winter there was usually a climate battle that occurred between whoever drove and me. The heat was not sectioned off into climate control like today's vehicles, it had to come from the front. When I was freezing, which was most of the time, and needed the heat turned up whoever drove was typically dying in a sauna. All that on top of not being able to talk to the driver very easily. Sitting several feet behind and not being able to talk very loudly, made a huge difference in the amount, and quality, of conversations held. The content of a good conversation decreases significantly once there's more than an arm length or two between people. However, now I was sitting as if I was in a regular passenger seat. The driver a mere foot or two away.

I could see where I was going. I could see the person in the driver seat. I could speak without yelling and we could see each other's face. Not to mention there was climate control, access to the radio and a very obvious feeling that the ride would be much smoother. The one thing I hadn't expected, that I had completely forgotten about, was the side window. It was down. That's when I realized traveling in a van like that I would once again be able to feel the wind on my face. I was downright elated. It must've been pretty obvious because they took about 20 pictures of me sitting in the front of that van. As soon as I got back to my office, I began looking for rental companies in Los Angeles that had one of these conversions in their fleet. Luckily enough Wheelchair Getaways did. It was expensive, but it was available. I never even looked for a full-size model. I made my reservation and discussed all of the specifics with the company including drop-off and pickup. To this day I'm not quite sure what excited me more, the trip itself, or the opportunity to ride in that van. Next in line was figuring out how to manage the hotel room, primarily getting in and out of bed. So I called my friend John for some guidance on a Hoyer lift.

There was no way in hell I was going to try and take my lift with me across the country. I figured the easiest thing to do would be to rent one from a local medical supply company. Unfortunately, I had no idea where to start looking for someone reliable. Then I remembered that John, who owns his own medical supply company, is part of a national organization of reputable companies. I asked him if he could search through his list and find someplace reliable. He not only found a good company, but he made the arrangements, had the lift delivered to the hotel and even paid for it (over the years, he ended up doing that several times, just out of kindness). He has always been one of those guys that goes way above and beyond. He definitely took one headache away from that first trip. After that was figured out, all that was left was to wait until the day of the flight.

There were several things that made me anxious as our departure date approached. What would I do if my chair broke down while I was in California? Or if the airline broke it? Where would they put me after they carried me off the plane if the chair was broken and inoperable? What would I do if the external catheter leaked while I was sitting on the airplane seat? What if I were to have an accident like diarrhea?! It's not like my attendant can get me cleaned up. I would be stuck in a seat, with nowhere to go and no means to move around for quite a long time. It's a four-hour flight not counting the amount of time it takes to get everyone on and off the plane during loading and unloading. Would I get a pressure sore from sitting that long in one spot? About half of the things on my mind I expressed outwardly, to my parents, to Danny, and to my friends. They were able to help me process through contingency plans, but more importantly they helped me look at some of those things more realistically.

If my chair broke or the airline broke it, I would just need to find someone to fix it. Just like any other time. It had broken countless times before, usually on a Friday evening just after 5 PM when everyone closed for the weekend, and I had survived so far. Lots of things could go wrong, things that were out of my control, but worrying about them before they happened was useless. It was really helpful to hear it from those guys. However, the other things were just too overwhelming to even speak out loud. If I ended up wet because the external catheter leaked or a mess because my bowels moved involuntarily, I was just screwed. Catastrophically screwed. Fortunately, those fears were disproportionate to their likelihood. What I mean by that, and the way I worked through those fears, is that none of those things happen very often. The likelihood that they would occur just because I was flying made no sense. The external catheter never leaked unless it wasn't put on right or the bag got twisted because it was moved around. As long as I made sure it was good before I got on the plane there was no way for it to twist on its own or come off. The same logic held true for my bowels. They never just moved on their own. There's no reason to think they would just because I was flying. My skin would be fine as well, as long as I moved around a little bit, leaned forward or had my attendant shift me slightly, there's no reason I would get a pressure area. I had never even had one at that point, my skin integrity was excellent. I would often sit in one position in my chair for far longer than five or six hours without having an issue. Still, those fears and that anxiety would constantly creep into my brain. It took a lot of work to force myself out of that mindset. I had to either repeatedly talk myself out of negative thinking or shift my focus to something else. The latter was probably the most effective. Just thinking about something else, working on something else, doing something else, anything but letting my mind race into that worst-case scenario mode. Sometimes it was much easier than other times, but eventually it got me to the day of my flight.

One of the things that really helped on that first trip was the support from my Uncle Tom in the Pittsburgh airport and Danny in LAX. The personnel in both airports, at both terminals, were extraordinarily friendly and helpful, not to mention flexible. It was prior to 9/11, so they allowed both Tom and Danny onto the plane despite not having a boarding pass. Tom came on in Pittsburgh, helping carry me from my wheelchair directly into the plane and onto my seat. Likewise, they allowed Danny onto the plane after everyone else had departed. He was able to help carry me from my seat out of the plane and directly to my wheelchair. It was still nerve-racking and very obviously a first for everyone involved. No one in either airport had ever seen a wheelchair like mine, and they all said they had never been asked to carry someone like I was asking, yet they were ready and willing. Seeing how I had never traveled before either, it was very much a case of the blind leading the blind. Everyone was looking to me for directions and instructions about how to get me out of my chair, how to carry me, and how to position me in the airplane seat. Unfortunately, I had absolutely no clue what I was doing, so I did what I've always done best. I smiled, made a few jokes to put everyone else at ease, and just made shit up as I went. It worked and we arrived in LA just fine. Then, playing off our newfound experience in Pittsburgh, I told the flight crew we had my cousin Danny waiting for us at the gate if they were willing to let us do the same thing. They were more than happy to help. Everything else fell into place neatly. The rental van was just outside, which Danny drove to the hotel since he knew his way around, and once we checked in the lift was waiting for me. We threw everything in the room and went downstairs where there was a Champs restaurant connected to the lobby. Aside from one ear that was clogged and needed to pop, both my chair and I were no worse for wear. It was a tremendously successful trip out, but that damned ear didn't pop for several days!

I had arrived on Monday, I think, and the conference started the following day. I made plans to meet up with Dan once or twice in the evening through the week but couldn't do much. I had a lot going on with the various seminars and he was still working all week. We were able to meet up one night and took a walk down the street. We found a really cool cigar lounge. I was thrilled because there was a chessboard right in the middle the booth, Danny was excited because it was someplace he could actually smoke. California had enacted the ban on smoking in public places long before anyone else. He got me up to speed on what it was like living in LA and I filled him in on what I was doing at work and what the conference was about. We played chess and had a few drinks, laughing and reminiscing. We didn't stay out too late though, that was the plan for Saturday. After the cigar lounge, we made our way back to the hotel. I had to get up early for the conference and he had to work the next day.

The conference ended up being great, I saw some really cool stuff demonstrated, ranging from technology like eye gaze computers that could type based off of nothing more than tracking someone's eye movement to presentations like Eric Weihenmayer who described what it was like to use JAWS (screen reading software for people with visual impairments) at 10,000 feet. Erik is completely blind and had climbed some of the highest peaks on the planet. He was a really good speaker with an excellent sense of humor. He was also spending some time at the technology booth after his presentation. He encouraged everyone to stop by and he would sign posters.

I have to admit, I was pretty impressed that he had found a way to successfully climb mountains. I decided to stop by his booth, grab a poster and have him sign it. It was all sorts of crowded and noisy, but there was someone standing at the edge of his booth, near where I was sitting, handing him posters. I can't talk very loudly, so I just waited until I made eye contact with the person standing next to Erik. I nodded and he moved over about 2 feet closer so he could hear me. I asked if I could have a poster and he happily agreed. As he was turning toward Erik I asked, "Could you ask him to sign it to Mike? He probably can't hear me." However, Erik's hearing is apparently quite exceptional. Before I even had the words completely out, he turned slightly in my direction and stated rather firmly, "I can hear just fine thank you!" I knew instantly what he was thinking -- that I was assuming he couldn't hear because he couldn't see! He had no idea I was only referring to my shallow voice. He quickly went back to signing autographs and posters and I thought it best not to push the issue. I've learned that the first rule of holes is if you find yourself in one, stop digging. The rest of the week had some interesting things here and there, but it was Saturday that held the excitement. I had behaved all week and was ready to blow off some steam and do something fun before I went home on Sunday. Danny had the same type of week, so he and a friend of ours, Curtis, picked me up at the hotel around lunchtime.

Pam needed a break and just felt like relaxing at the hotel. I actually think she was content to just smoke a joint and enjoy being away from me for a day. It's a lot of work traveling with me and being my primary resource. She didn't just deserve some alone time; she deserved a damn medal. It was a very nice hotel equipped with pool, hot tub, bar, the works, so she had plenty to do. I, on the other hand, wanted to go out and see Los Angeles. Curtis, Danny and I left around lunchtime and went deeper into the city to meet their friend Todd. There was a Mexican restaurant that Danny said had the best margaritas around. When we pulled into the parking lot it looked like a complete dive. Fortunately, those are the places that usually have the best stuff. We all ordered margaritas - no salt, on the rocks and in Spanish (I had to learn, seeing as how I don't speak a word of Spanish). They were definitely good but came with a slight problem. I never really drank margaritas before. I had a good tolerance and could drink my fair share, but I also knew that different drinks affected me differently. I knew how many beers I could have or how many mixed drinks, how many shots, and even how many glasses of wine before I started feeling it. I had no idea how many margaritas. I learned very quickly -- it's not many! I had half a jag on by the end of lunch. Luckily our next stop was Griffith Park Observatory, where I could get some fresh air for a little while.

We made our way out of the restaurant and split into two vehicles. Danny and I in my rental van, Curtis and Todd in Todd's car. However, Curtis had the keys to the van. When that finally dawned on us, Danny blew up his phone getting him back to the restaurant. Eventually we got our act together and made our way to Griffith Park Observatory. We never actually went inside, just looked around at the view and took a few pictures. I think there was some type of light show inside, but I much preferred the view outside. The sweeping landscape of the city sprawled out before me along with the Hollywood sign, high on the neighboring hill, looked really cool, despite the hazy smog that lingered over everything. According to those guys, every year the Santa Ana winds come in and blow all of that shit out to the ocean, clearing the air and the view for at least a little while, but it hadn't gotten there yet.

Next, we hit a few more bars before deciding to recruit their buddy David to come out with us. Dave was one of their friends who wrote screenplays and was struggling to break into the movie business. At that point his biggest accomplishment was writing the script for a movie called U571. I think the story had already been written but he was hired to adapt it to a screenplay. It was a pretty successful movie, but he had just finished another script. He was really excited because this movie was about to be released within the next month or two. He kept telling me, "As long as you like fast cars and hot women, you'll love the movie!" I assured him that I indeed liked both, and that I would see it as soon as it came out. The Fast and the Furious ended up being a pretty good movie. The group of us made our way through a few bars and wound up at a Cheetahs strip club.

It was pretty late by the time we got there, considering we started around noon. Everyone was pretty rowdy, but definitely good-natured and harmless. I found out that Cheetahs is a pretty popular franchise, and for good reason. The women in that joint were ridiculously hot, but I don't think there was a real tit in the place. Every woman there looked like they had been surgically enhanced to Barbie Doll perfection. I was getting used to the prices of things being significantly higher in LA and fully expected the drinks to be even more so considering the atmosphere and scenery. Still, I was a little culture shocked when I sent Curtis up to the bar for two drinks and two shots. In 2001, things were quite a bit less expensive than they are now, drastically different when you compare small town to big city. Back then I would typically pay about $2 for a drink and $1.50 for a shot in my small-town bar. Obviously, the price would increase in the city, and significantly more so at a nicer place or a strip club. I gave Curtis a $20 bill and when he brought back the drinks and shots, he didn't miss a chance to point out I hadn't given him enough money. Thankfully, the shots were pretty damn big, so we didn't need to buy many of them.

As the drinks flowed and we enjoyed the show, Dave started peppering me with questions. People typically get much more comfortable, and inquisitive, after a couple of drinks and Dave was no exception. He was particularly interested in the violent nature by which I acquired my spinal cord injury. As a writer and filmmaker, I think it appealed to his creativity and desire to understand people and the stories that shaped them. He was also obsessed with gangs, violence and Los Angeles street life. I think he was amazed that gun violence reached so far into what he perceived to be quiet small-town life. On the lighter side of things, he got a real charge out of how I use my chair and maneuver around. I used my mouse stick to give him a high 5/fist bump that absolutely made his day. He wanted me to "fist bump" like that every time he saw me for years. Last, but definitely not least, he and Curtis were beyond amused at how the strippers dealt with my chair. They also started tipping the girls to see how many lipstick kiss marks they could leave on my face. I'm sure it was probably well-deserved payback. They kept declaring that since I couldn't wipe the lipstick off, the girls should see how many kiss marks they could leave. By the time we left it looked like someone beat the shit out of me! Not that I'm complaining, mind you. We finally got back to the hotel somewhere around 3 AM, I think. By the time Curtis and Danny helped lift me into bed and Pam got me positioned it was probably 4 AM, Sunday morning. Pam started my morning routine barely 2 hours later, 6 AM. She insisted on getting an early start, so we wouldn't miss our flight.

I was so hung over that I felt like that earthworm I ate, after I chewed it up. I grumbled and whined the entire time but was eventually in my chair by probably 10 AM. We made our way out of the hotel and headed toward the airport to meet the van rental guys. If I remember correctly, there was some confusion about when or where to meet. We ended up leaving the van in the parking lot with the keys locked inside. Next we made our way through the gates and to the terminal where we sat, for a good 2-3 hours because we were so early. Getting onto the plane and managing the wheelchair/disability aspect of the flight barely registers as a blip in my memory. The hangover and misery, however, are seared into my mind forever. I think the only way I survived the flight home was mimosas and no-doze. Sitting the way I do in an airplane seat, there is no relaxing. I sit upright with very little balance. I was too uncomfortable to fall asleep, but far too exhausted to stay awake. By the time the flight actually landed, with the time change, it was about 9 PM. We were the last ones off the plane and consequently the last ones to get our luggage. That made it about 10 PM when we finally got to my van. There was an ice storm that night and it took us an extra hour to get home. When I finally rolled into the driveway at about 1 AM, my parents met us and took over. Pam was exhausted, I was pretty much out of it and neither of us felt like dealing with the other. Luckily my parents were able to take over and get me out of my chair and into bed. It ended up being about two in the morning. I didn't think the trip would end up getting me home that late, so the attendant that was coming in on Monday morning was still scheduled for the regular time, 5:30 AM. Therefore, three and a half hours later, after one of the worst hangovers and roughest weekends of my life, the next attendant came in and begin getting me ready for work Monday morning. Still, I went to work and powered through, surviving the day, but learning a very valuable lesson. I've never, ever, since that trip went out and got drunk the night before I've flown anywhere. Ever. I don't learn lessons very well, or very quickly, but that one sunk in.

I ended up returning to Los Angeles several times, either for a week that included the technology conference or just a long weekend to visit with Dan and his friends. I think I was there a total of five times. On one occasion, it was a two-day stop on a really long weekend. I was receiving the Arthur A. Rubloff award in Arizona. The award was given to me for being a role model for people with disabilities, mostly due to my belief in making the most of life - with or without a disability. I didn't want to travel the entire way across the country for one night, so I arranged to stop by Burbank. Amy went with me that time, and our agenda was packed. It started when my attendant and I left Pennsylvania at about 9:30 AM on a Thursday, driving down to Virginia to pick her up. From there we drove to Dulles Airport and flew to LAX. We got a rental van, drove to Burbank and hung out with some cousins (at that time our cousin Rob was also living there). Next, we flew from Burbank to Phoenix and then drove from Phoenix to Scottsdale. We got to stay at the Biltmore, which was pretty impressive, but the following day had to drive from Scottsdale back to Phoenix and then fly from Phoenix to DC. By the time we were driving home, Sunday night, after dropping my sister off, we were pretty worn out. That trip was a blast, but it was definitely long.

One of the last times I was in LA was actually for a music video. Danny's friend Dave had found some success in writing but was looking to take the next step, producing and directing. In order to get some experience as well as get his portfolio started, he offered to make a music video for one of Danny's songs called Sunken Treasure. Apparently, Dave had always liked the song, but when he found out Danny wrote it when I was shot, he insisted on making the video. He wrote an eight-page script and bankrolled an initial $60,000, which would bloom into $80,000, to turn Danny's song into his directorial debut. His interpretation of the song, and consequently idea for the video, had nothing to do with my story of getting shot. Instead, it revolves around a soldier who gets killed in action and the effect it has on his loved ones. However, knowing where the song came from and knowing me, he insisted I come out for at least part of the video so that I could be in one of the scenes.

This time it was a quick trip, only for a long weekend, but was definitely full of excitement. A large group of us went out the night before, first, to dinner and then to a few clubs. We were a little rowdy, but nothing over-the-top. My attendant was a newer girl who was not much over 21, and after a few drinks was uncomfortable driving. Danny ended up driving the rental van and got pulled over for a DUI. Despite watching what he was drinking, he still blew .08, on the nose, and they wouldn't even consider letting him off. This posed a secondary problem though, how was I getting anywhere since the rest of the people in the van were absolutely hammered. My attendant, Dave, and one of their friends were all in the back seat, loaded. None of them could drive. As luck would have it, there were two police officers that had pulled us over. One of them drove the cop car, with Danny in the back seat, while the other drove my rental van. Once we were back at the hotel, the officer had me direct him how to operate the lift so I could get out. From there he proceeded to drop the keys in my shirt pocket, look me dead in the eye and say, "Now stay!" I figured my night was done. Unfortunately, I had no idea what to do about Danny.

I stayed up most of the night waiting for a phone call to my cell phone telling me what I should do. It wasn't until later that we all realized you can only make collect calls from a prison cell; and you couldn't call a cell phone collect. My phone ended up dying and I went to bed at about five in the morning. I got up about two hours later and turned on my phone. There was a voicemail. I figured Danny had found a way to call, but when I checked the message, I got quite a surprise. Since he couldn't call my cell phone collect, Danny had to call a landline. Apparently, the only landline numbers he remembered were his parents and mine. So, the voicemail I was listening to was from my father, he was saying, "Hey Mike, it's your dad. It's about 9 AM here on the East Coast and I got a message from Danny saying he's in jail? Can you call me back and let me know what's going on?" I don't know that I ever wanted to make a phone call less in my life. It all worked out though, they had actually let Danny out on his own recognizance.

When I talked to him that morning it was a pretty brief phone call. All he wanted to do was go to sleep. The video shoot was scheduled for later that day and he was up all night surrounded by gang bangers and drug addicts in a South Central prison cell. To make matters worse we had Mexican food at dinner the night before and Danny has always had a rather sensitive digestive system (years later he was diagnosed with ulcerative colitis that required multiple surgeries). He can laugh about it today, but that morning he was not happy at all. However, as rotten as that night was, he was about to end up with one of those perfect moments you just never see coming. We all met later that day at a bar where the video shoot was taking place. Dave had already been there for hours, making sure markers were set, camera angles ready, and everything was in order. The actors and extras were also all there, makeup done and ready to go. Part of the video included a group of single ladies sitting around a table, all of whom were absolutely gorgeous. Just as we had walked past them, we heard Dave behind us say to them, "Yeah, that's Soulsby, the lead singer. He just got out of County this morning." We glanced over and saw Dave nonchalantly walking away as though that was a regular occurrence, Danny in jail. They're reaction was priceless, and it was a 100% rockstar moment for Danny. The rest of the day was a blast. Danny, Curtis and Todd played Sunken Treasure over and over while Dave barked orders, turning his vision into reality.

Those first couple of trips to LA were awesome experiences, if for no other reason that it reinforced the idea that every problem has a solution. There were plenty of headaches and obstacles to navigate through those trips, but the rewards always outweighed the struggles by far. It also reinforced a common theme in my life, which is that things work out as long as I keep moving forward.

Chapter 28 - Automatic Triggers

I was riding in my van with a fraternity brother a few years later when he pulled into a convenience store. This was the same convenience store where I had stood for the very last time. It was where I was shot. I knew where we were going, and I was thinking about the fact that the last time I felt anything below my neck or had any control of my body was at that very spot. There wasn't a lot of emotion tied to it. Quite frankly I had only been thinking about it for a few seconds when Dave started apologizing and asking if I was okay. It took me a minute before I made the connection of why he was asking.

He said several times, really quickly, that he was sorry and didn't even think about where we were going. At first, I thought I had some bizarre look on my face like I zoned out or something. Then I realized he was worried I would be upset just being there. I have no doubt he was worried I would start revisiting that night. That I would become sad or angry or get flooded with any of the emotions that riddled my mind in the days and weeks that followed getting shot. But I was fine, I assured him, and it was true. It actually didn't bother me in the least, rather it was quite interesting.

Now that I'm in my forties, my friends and I have discussions occasionally that look back on "glory days." A time before aches and pains and sore muscles. Days we played football or rugby for hours, went snow skiing, or wrestled around with limitless energy. A time when our bodies bounced back easily from even the worst of 15-hour construction days in the hot sun. We talk about things being a little easier, physically, because of that resilience. That didn't mean we were miserable in our aging bodies, just accepting of the fact that the natural progression of aging makes our bodies work a little differently. Sitting in that parking lot, trying to picture where the payphone was several years earlier and thinking about pre-paralysis, it was a lot like those conversations. I was just doing it 15 years earlier, and by myself. It simply felt like I was reflecting back on a time when my body worked a little better (even though it worked a whole lot better!).

It took a little more reassuring than I was used to, but eventually I convinced him that I was fine. He gave me a little look, albeit a skeptical one, and went into the store. It was an unusual conversation. One thing the people close to me understood pretty quickly after I got home was that they did not need to tiptoe around anything; and I made it a point to emphasize "anything." I had already gone through the anger, denial, grief and all the other shit that rattled around inside my brain after I got shot. I did it once, I didn't want to revisit it. I figured the best way to avoid that was to make sure nothing was off limits. There were no sensitive spots that people couldn't discuss. There were no little topics or ideas that needed to stay hidden in the shadows, where they would undoubtedly fester and grow. I was going to make sure there were no delicate questions that would bruise my fragile psyche. Fuck that; my psyche was already broken once. It took a lot of work to repair it. I didn't - and don't - have anything even remotely like PTSD. I sure as hell wasn't going to self-induce it! I didn't realize it at the time, but what I was doing was eliminating automatic triggers.

As a teenager I had tons of automatic triggers, I think most of us do (especially during our teenage years). Songs were probably my biggest culprit; simply because of how often a random song pops up on the radio. For me, songs mostly triggered thoughts of old girlfriends. Which as a teenage guy brings an onslaught of emotion, and usually disproportionate to the reality of the girlfriend or breakup. Places can do it, like where I had my first kiss. Landmarks can do it, like where I encountered my first bully and got beat down. Smells, like perfume. People, like the parent of a friend who passed away. Lots of things... in fact, just about anything. The emotions triggered could be anything from brilliant to horrendous, from crushing to elating. Apparently, I had learned something from those experiences, because after I was shot, I began deliberately choosing what triggers I permitted... and more importantly, what they were triggering.

I never avoided talking about getting shot or about the guy who shot me, Dan Moyer. I never avoided the convenience store where I was shot or talking about what I could and could not physically do or the implications of paralysis. To me that was handing over control, and I wasn't going to do it. After all, let's say I needed to avoid the convenience store. Did that mean I had to take an alternate route to campus? It's a chain of stores, would I start needing to avoid all of them? I don't think so. No way. I was in control of my mind; I would choose where to place my focus. I can recognize things for what they are, but I'm the one who gets to choose where the most emphasis falls. The day I was shot, April 16, remains a pretty strong trigger, so I began to make a point of celebrating why I was thankful, what I had accomplished, each time that day rolled back around. I'd give the feeling of loss its moment, recognizing it, but then send it on its way. If something was going to trigger a visit back to when my life changed, I was going to choose what aspects of that change mattered most. I was the one that got to rank them in order of importance, and all the negative shit that I already dealt with was, for damn sure, going at the bottom of the list!

PART SIX - Stories, Lists, and Laughter

My Mother's Laugh

I've many treasures in this life of mine
With every breath with every sign
But my mother's laugh, so true and clear
is a jewel I hold so very dear

a laugh so brilliant and divine
an infectious flutter stopping time.
it can rise above for all to hear
and make my worries disappear

It's illuminated throughout my life
reaching from afar appearing near
And brought me more than once
From deafness again to hear

ask me why I have such courage
and seemingly have no fear
It's blessings such as this
My mother's laugh, so true and clear

M Kiel

With the advent of social media, particularly Facebook, I had a platform to share what I was thinking and how I was celebrating the things for which I was thankful every April 16. I didn't do it right away. Typically, for the first, well, many years, I celebrated April 16 very subtly. I went out for a drink or just sat outside and soaked in the air. After a time, though, it started to appeal to me to put something poignant on Facebook. Sometimes it was subtle, like "What a long, strange trip it's been..." with a couple of smiley faces or something of the like. Other times it was a little more philosophical. One of my favorites was on year 22, when I paralleled the 22-year anniversary with the 22-caliber pistol with which I had been shot. I posted a quick note that said, "The best advice I've ever been given was from my father when he said I didn't have enough room in my heart for both love and hate; one will consume the other. So I had to choose. Those words of wisdom allow me to look back and smile on the 22 years that matter instead of dwelling on the 22 caliber that doesn't."

Others were lists, like ranking the best of stupid things people have said to me. Instead of writing the entire story, such as I did earlier about the woman in Erie at the Playhouse or my cousin Danny's neighbor, I summarized them so people on Facebook could zip right through. They looked like this:

1. From a woman in Erie, when I was in graduate school, who kept sneaking up behind me, grabbing my head and kissing me when I wasn't paying attention:
Her: you're really cute, better than that jerk over there staring at me
Me: who would that be?
Her: my stupid husband...
Me: WTF?

2. From a random stranger who walked into the bar and directly up to me:
Moron: so, why are you in a wheelchair?
Me: I got shot in college
Moron: cool!

Me: WTF?

3. From cousin Danny Boy's redneck neighbor in college after I had convinced him I had a microchip in my brain, that whatever I thought the chair would perform and if he held my hand and concentrated hard enough the chair would react to his thoughts.
Me: you have to keep your eyes shut and concentrate really hard...
Him: I have a great idea! (Jumping up and opening his eyes)
Me: yes... that would be?
Him: My dog is really smart and knows his way around town. You can put him on your lap, tell him where to go and he could think so the chair drives you where you want to go!
Me: WTF?

4. From an elderly woman (again random) upon entering the bar:
Her: Excuse me, would you mind if I said a prayer for you?
Me: Thank you, I appreciate the gesture (attempting to be polite)
Her: (screaming by the way) "May the power of the Lord heal you, demons be gone... rise and walk!!" (All while grabbing my face and pinning my head against my headrest)
Me: WTF?

5. From a random guy at the bar (I may need a new hangout), out of absolutely nowhere I hear a voice above my head:
Him: I have a quad
Me: Huh?
Him: I saw you sitting here in this thing and figured I'd let you know I have a quad
Me: Good for you... I am a quad...

6. From an attendant in the shower:
Me: There is a spider above you.
Her: Aaarrrggg ... get it, GET IT!!
Me: Have we met...? WTF?

7. From an attendant who was wiping my nose when I had a cold:
Me: I can't stand it when my nose gets stuffed up, I don't have the lung power to blow my nose.

Her: I wish God could give you one good blow every now and then.

Me: All I did was agree... she got embarrassed anyway.

8. From a 50-year-old guy at The Olde Keg one night:

Him: Hey buddy you okay?

Me: Yup

Him: Good to see you still get out!

Me: Yep, every once in a while I sneak past the guards

Him: Good for you! But let me ask you this... can you still have sex?

Me: Sure... unless that's an offer.... WTF?!

9. From a fraternity brother who was trying to understand my spinal cord injury after helping lift me into bed around 6 AM after an all-night party in college:

Him: Can you feel this?

Me: What?

Him: Your legs?

Me: No... but for crying out loud stop ripping the hair out my legs, you nut job!!

And my all-time favorite...

10. From an attendant the first time she was shaving my face and trying to get below my lower lip:

Her: Hey, put your tongue back in there... I wasn't finished yet!

Me: I didn't say a single word... her face was red enough... :-)

Still others were lists that included places my chair has been, or random favorite memories and drinking toasts (and the toasts I usually made up on the fly). They are just fun ways to reflect back on the experiences I've had since getting shot. Some of them were lessons learned, but most were rooted in humor and laughter. They are the stories I love to tell and the things my friends and I laugh about over and over. In my opinion, they are the perfect way to celebrate life every April 16. I can think of no better way to embrace life than through humor.

The following includes a few more short stories and lists that I posted each year on the anniversary of April 16th. Some of them may sound familiar and some I have elaborated on in greater detail. A few of the stories appear in multiple lists because they are worth repetition. Thankfully these lists are difficult to narrow down because my life includes just that many moments of hilarity.

The Race

On a nice summer day, I'll occasionally drive my chair from my parent's house into town. It's only about a mile, but there aren't many sidewalks along the way, and I have to cross Route 53 which is fairly busy. The vehicles move pretty quickly on that road. On the upside, there is a stoplight where Main Street intersects with 53, which provides a crosswalk, making things a little safer and easier. Once I get past that point it's mostly clear sailing. I just stick to side streets, which is a more roundabout route but safer, especially when I'm driving along the side of the road due to the lack of sidewalk. All in all, it's like taking a nice relaxing walk, with the exception of the occasional person who feels the need to stop and make sure I'm okay. The intent is always genuine and kindhearted, so I usually let it slide. However, I often wonder what these people would say if I responded with, "No, I actually need a ride. Can you help get my 400 lb. wheelchair in the back of your car?"

On one such afternoon, I had made my way into town and found out that my cousin Janae and her husband Wayne were at Chuggy's, a local bar. At that point I had only been in there once since getting injured. I had been in there on occasion prior to that, but simple math would reveal that was before I was 21 and therefore an entirely different story. The reason I had only been there once after I was shot was the eight steps up to the front door and the six or seven leading up to the back door. I was carried up, and then back down, the front steps once. It was pretty hairy, and the risk/reward was definitely out of balance. I usually go to The Olde Keg, which has zero steps and an awesome atmosphere. However, after talking to Janae, she set out on a mission to figure out a way to get me into Chuggy's that didn't involve risking a brain injury.

When I arrived outside, they were debating whether or not it would be easier to carry me up the back steps. Considering most of the people willing to lift my chair were already half in the bag, I was leaning toward just meeting them up at The Olde Keg a little later. That's when Janae's light bulb went off. She directed us to wait right there and went jogging down the back alley behind the bar. She came back several minutes later carrying two boat ramps. She said she borrowed them from someone's backyard and just left a note. They worked perfectly, allowing me to drive right up in through the back door. Luckily, they were either not missed by their owner, or Janae's note did its job because they were still there, outside the back door, when I was ready to leave.

After I was safely inside, I parked next to Wayne at the end of the bar. I use the word "safely" very loosely here, because anyone that knows Wayne knows very well that sitting next to him at the bar was never very safe, considering the number of shots he loved to order. That day was no different, in fact it may have been a little worse if that's possible. At that point Wayne was in the midst of battling cancer. He would have alternating weeks where he would feel horrible one week and rejuvenated the next. Usually, after being given an experimental cocktail of chemotherapy he would feel terrible for a week or so. Then, being one of the most resilient SOB's on the planet, would feel much better for about a week. He took advantage of those weeks he felt strong. If there's one thing Wayne was good at, even before cancer, it was living in the moment and soaking up every minute.

The shots started almost as soon as I got settled in. When I was in my mid-20s Wayne had turned me onto Rumplemintz, which is a 100 proof peppermint schnapps that I still drink to this day. But after several years he had migrated over to Sambuca, which is an Italian liqueur that tastes like licorice. I wasn't always a very big fan of licorice, so when he ordered shots for everyone, my request was Rumplemintz. Now Rumplemintz and Sambuca look almost exactly alike, both are clear, and both are served chilled. The combination of Wayne's tendency to be a wise ass, and my naïveté to not check the shot before I drank it, resulted in me getting a Sambuca. I would really like to be able to say that I learned a lesson and paid closer attention next time, so I wasn't tricked again, but sadly I cannot. Wayne got me at least four more times. In my defense, I was at least questioning what he was ordering and not fully trusting him, but he was feeding me the shot and wouldn't let me get close enough to smell it. Finally, I decided the only way I was getting out of Sambuca was to order something that looked different, so I could see the difference. The next round of shots, I ordered a Jägermeister, which is dark in color and would be impossible to mistake for the clear Sambuca. When the shots were served up and Wayne fed me mine, it almost came out my nose. I had forgotten that Sambuca comes in two flavors, clear, otherwise known as White Buca, and dark, otherwise known as Black Buca. Black Buca looks exactly like Jägermeister. He got me again.

After that many shots, I figured it was wisest to take a break from my good friend and run away to the Keg. I had learned years earlier that I could only sit beside Wayne for a certain amount of time before risking a wicked hangover. Luckily, the boat ramps were still propped up at the back door and I was able to navigate my way out with a little assistance. I told Janae and Wayne I would see them at the Keg and headed on my way. Once I arrived at my next stop, the first person I saw upon entering the door was my friend Baxter, who is also notorious for shots. The first thing out of his mouth was that he had been there for a while and I needed to catch up. I told him I had just spent a few hours with Wayne. He laughed and immediately switched gears, suggesting that maybe he was the one that needed to catch up. We avoided shots for a little while but eventually ended up doing some more. Thankfully I was able to order what I wanted.

Eventually, someone suggested a shot of Tequila. I'm pretty sure it was my buddy Chris, who everyone else calls Dino. There were only two or three people that cared for tequila, the rest disliked it. Baxter and I hated it. This prompted one of those really good ideas that usually only surface between midnight and 1:00 AM after a long night of drinking. I suggested that since we both hated tequila so much, we should race around the block, with a shot of tequila as the stakes. The five or so people in our group also felt this was an excellent idea and we all began to walk outside. Apparently, we weren't being very subtle with our discussion. As we spoke, on our way to the door, we attracted a rather large audience. Once we were outside, we had a crowd of about 10 or 15 people watching while we discussed the rules. I would head south on Main Street and Baxter would head north. We would then round our respective corners at the end of the block, so we were running towards each other down the alley behind the bar. This way we would pass each other to ensure the other wasn't cheating before we rounded the opposite corners that would lead us back onto Main Street. The last person to arrive at the front door of the Keg was the loser and had to do a shot of tequila.

The crowd started laughing as Baxter stretched. He was adamant that it was going to be a difficult challenge. He told several of the people watching that he had followed me in his truck on several occasions and witnessed firsthand just how fast my chair could go in high gear. Meanwhile the two of us were going back and forth making sure the other wasn't going to back out of the shot if they lost. We both swore and promised up and down that if we lost, we would do the shot. We got ready and on our marks as someone in the crowd counted down from three. When they yelled go, we both took off at full speed. After about 20 yards down the sidewalk I turned around and looked behind me where I could see Baxter rounding his corner. It had just dawned on me that the air had become quite cold. I looked at the crowd, who were all staring at me curiously, and said, "It's really cold out here. I think I'll just do the shot."

I went back into the bar and waited near the entrance. Eventually, Baxter came walking through the front door, huffing and puffing, completely winded. I looked at him and said, "You win." Between gasps of breath, he was able to force out a few "son of a bitch" and "asshole" comments, but otherwise he had to go and sit down in a corner and use the wall to help keep him propped up. Apparently, all the running got his blood moving and flowing so much that it took him from a little drunk to, in his words, full out hammered.

I did the shot, and it was as disgusting as I expected. I even had a slightly more difficult time than anticipated, mainly because I was laughing. As Baxter got his breath back, the cries of "Asshole!" coming from the table where he was sitting got louder and louder. Doing a shot of tequila is nasty enough, but to try to have someone else feed it to you while you're laughing is actually rather difficult. Still, at the time it was worth it because it was cold outside. Reflecting back now, it was even more worth it because the story is so much fun to tell. It's even better in person when he can tell his side of the story and what he was thinking as he was racing down the alley. Especially when it dawns on him that he's the only one running.

On April 16, 2018 I was trying to figure out a good way to celebrate a quarter of a century with a spinal cord injury. I decided to list 25 different things, ranging from funny things I remembered to important moments that left an impact. I also mixed in a few toasts I created and an occasional tidbit about myself I felt like sharing. The list turned out great. You might recognize a few of the moments or memories because they're just so funny I've repeated them in multiple lists.

Memories, Moments, Tidbits and Toasts from 25 years

1. Moment: The moment it dawned on me that mulch was flying through the air, 5 feet high in an arc behind me because I was stuck in the decorative landscaping in the hotel lobby. Alcohol may have been involved.

2. Tidbit: My friends and I enjoy challenges, and laughter, so much that Dave, who's completely blind, successfully fed me a pastry at a Board meeting, just for the fun of it. Aside from a few crumbs that fell to the floor, not a bit ended up on my shirt. Also enjoyable was watching Ryan fight off tears of laughter as he stood beside us.

3. Memory: Just a few years ago I was showing some friends (both women) some pictures on my phone. As I flipped through picture by picture by using my mouth stick, one of the women remarked, "My God you can do that better with your mouth than I can my hand!" All I said was, "that's not the first time I've heard that." I don't know that I've ever seen anyone's face turn that red quite that quickly.

4. Moment: The moment the flight attendant told us, as the plane began to descend, that our direct flight home was not so direct. That we would actually be changing planes in Denver and would have about 20 minutes to catch our connecting flight…. It takes 20 minutes for the plane to unload…. I'm the last one off…. Our connecting flight is 40 gates away…. My chair is stored in luggage…

5. Memory: Stacking multiple Ziploc bags full of ice on my head and shoulders at the Jimmy Buffet concerts because it was 100° in the shade.

6. Toast:

Here's to the world we'll see
and to our lives and what may be
to the road ahead and the path behind
to friendship abound and the ties that bind

– M Kiel

7. Memory: The recline function on my wheelchair stopped working and the company from Pittsburgh couldn't send someone for several days. I couldn't go without it, so my dad got creative and bypassed a few wires. The result was a working recline, but only if someone else manually flipped switches and pressed certain buttons (in very specific orders). When the technician finally arrived and saw the contraption my father had rigged up, he said, "Um… Can you contact your dad? This looks like a bomb and I'm afraid to touch it!"

8. Memory: When my friends Tammy and John discovered that I had never followed up with a physiatrist after I left spinal cord rehab a decade earlier. They insisted I make an appointment in Pittsburgh. Tammy helped me find someone good and John insisted on driving me (even taking the day off work). When John arrived at my house that day, I asked him if he could pick up my records from my family doctor while I finished. The physiatrist wanted my history. No problem, he said. A few minutes later I heard the door open and him yell, "You're an asshole! Try going for a checkup every now and then!" I had forgotten that I very rarely went to my family doctor either, so my medical records only consisted of about two pieces of paper and easily fit in a business envelope.

9. Toast:

To those who are here
and those who are not
to the friends we have
and the family we've got
to the stories we've made
and those yet to be told
to this moment right now
and what the future may hold

M Kiel

10. Tidbit: One of my favorite quotes isn't something I discovered; it was something Amy did. She had a signature at the end of her emails that was a quote by Kurt Hahn. It read, "There is more in us than we know. If we can be made to see it, then perhaps, for the rest of our lives, we'll be unwilling to settle for less." I think the only thing I like more than that quote is the fact that my sister taught it to me. She's wise beyond her years. She must've had some kind of awesome influence like an older sibling...

11. Moment: That moment I realized swinging my mouth stick around, hitting myself in the stomach and poking myself in the arm trying to kill a jumping spider looks COMPLETELY different to someone else standing any further than 5 feet away... They can't see the spider...

12. Memory: Happy hours on the deck. They can include two of us, 50 of us or any number in between. Regardless of the number of participants, happy hours always include laughter, music, and the "5 o'clock somewhere" flag flowing in the air.

13. Memory: After hanging out with Wayne at Chuggy's all afternoon, I joined some friends at The Olde Keg. By the time midnight or 1 AM rolled around (which is when all great ideas emerge) I believe Dino began suggesting shots of tequila. My friend Chris Baxter and I both hated the idea of tequila, especially at that time of night. However, I saw a great opportunity for a bet. We decided to race around the block and the loser would have to do a shot of tequila with Dino. As we walked outside, we must not have been very quiet because a rather large crowd followed us out. We agreed on rules and promised no cheating. He would run in one direction; I would head in the opposite. That way we would pass each other going around the block to double check no one was cheating. The crowd counted down 3... 2... 1... GO! He went in one direction; I went in the other. I made it about 15 feet before turning around, looking at the crowd and saying, "It's really cold, I think I'll just do the shot." As Chris disappeared around the corner, I went inside where it was warm. 10 minutes later when he walked/staggered through the front door wheezing I said, "You win!"

14. Toast:
> Here's to a drink and here's to a shot
> and here's to the woman that Matthew got
> he said she's smokin and knows how to please
> but now he's itchy and scratchy and it burns when he pees
> so a word to the wise, because he's obviously not
> pick your pussy with caution but feel free with your shot
> – M Kiel

15. Memory: I have convinced many people over the years that I operate my chair through magnets that are sewn into my skull. These magnets are synchronized with magnets embedded in the headrest of my wheelchair. I usually end the story by describing that when I activate the magnets, they pull on the chair about as hard as I'm pulling on someone's leg. What can I say? I'm easily amused.

16. Moment: That moment I got busted while recapping one of those magnet-in-my-brain stories for a group of friends at The Olde Keg. At their request, I began telling one of these stories and all I heard was my friend Katie slamming her fist on the table and yelling, "You son of a bitch! You told me that story!" I apparently forgot to tell her the last part about pulling on her leg...

17. Toast:

Here's to the voices
that influence our choices
and affect decisions we make
when we roll the dice
may it be worth the price
of the penance we'll have to take

– M Kiel

18. Moment: Sitting, face in the wind on the top deck of a cruise ship at midnight as it sails full speed. The warm air moving so fast it feels as though it can blow all the shit and sadness, all the fear and frustrations buried deep within straight out of me and into the black night.

19. Tidbit: I was shot in April, right before finals. My professors all gave me the grades I had at that point, so the semester counted. It wasn't categorized as incomplete. Two months in ICU, two months in rehab and I returned home in August. Since that spring semester counted, I was technically still enrolled at Penn State. With the help of family, friends and fraternity brothers I was able to create a schedule of classes and continue that fall without ever missing a beat. I had no idea what I was doing and made everything up as I went. It was often 90% chaos, often frustrating and overwhelming but a hell of a great adventure!

20. Moment: That moment, on this day 25 years ago, when there were so many 18-20-year-olds in the lobby/waiting room of the ICU in Johnstown that the hospital staff had to ask them to move to a different floor.

21. Memory: Amy, brother-in-law Pete, Janae, Vanessa and I all went to Key West to celebrate Amy's 40th birthday. Little did we know we had scheduled our trip for the beginning of "Fantasy Fest." This meant we were treated to the perfect combination of Mardi Gras and Halloween which included body paint, costumes and a bicycle run comprised of about 5000 zombies. For the record some of the body paint was amazing; others were… well… not…

22. Moment: That moment I realized a nun was actually shuffling me into a strip club. Aunt Gigi had overheard my brother-in-law and I chuckling as we walked past a gentleman's club in New York. She took it upon herself to address the accessibility of the entranceway (which had a step), asking the bouncer if he could get my chair into the club. Next thing I knew Pete and I were on our way in, Gigi was laughing, and my sister was ready to strangle all three of us.

23. Tidbit: I was receiving an award in Arizona but didn't want to go through all the hassle of trip planning for only two days, so I ended up creating a whirlwind adventure. My attendant and I left Pennsylvania early Thursday morning, drove to Virginia and picked up my sister. The three of us drove to DC and flew to LAX. After landing, got my rental van and drove to Burbank Thursday evening. Hung out with cousins and friends until Saturday. That morning we flew from Burbank to Phoenix and then drove to Scottsdale. Saturday night we attended the event. Sunday, we drove back to Phoenix and caught our flight to DC, then drove from DC to Virginia, dropped Amy off and got home Sunday night. It was exhausting but we came away from those four days with a good 10 or 12 stories/memories.

24. Memory: I brought Pete a souvenir from Atlanta. It was a cigarette lighter in the shape of the same kind of pistol with which I had been shot. I felt it was important for me to find a way to leave no doubt in anyone's mind that there would be no limits when it came to humor. Nothing was off the table. Limits were for the limited. I felt, and still feel, that humor is our greatest ally in the darkest of times. It has the ability to poke holes through the blackest of night and the deepest of despair. In doing so it can allow in a little bit of light, and with it, hope. Bonus memory... I had forgotten the pistol shaped cigarette lighter in my carry-on bag as I tried to make it through airport security in Atlanta when I was coming home from Shepherd Spinal Center. It lit up every alarm in the joint and had security flying out of the woodwork!

25. Moment: That moment I understood my father's advice. That my heart wasn't big enough for love and hate; that I needed to make a choice because one would consume the other. It's made all the difference in these past 25 years. Thanks Pop.

Sexiest Man in the World

The first few trips I took made me anxious to see where else I could go, what was next, and what else was out there waiting to be experienced. Unfortunately, I had a long stretch of time where I didn't have a consistent attendant that could travel. No one to just pick up and go. That is until Sarah. Sarah lived, and grew up, less than a mile up the road. Since she is about 15 years younger than me, we didn't know each other growing up, but that changed after her second day on the job. She started a little bit like Bernadette, beginning with the shorter, less involved shifts and then quickly picking up more and more hours until she was one of my main people. Her second shift was throwing me in bed one Friday night, which is not very involved. I do just about everything in the morning, so at night I just have to get in bed. She had already done it once and was comfortable with the routine. When she got there Friday night I was sitting with my parents and some of their friends having a drink. Despite having just met her, I had a ton of faith in Sarah, so offered her a drink. Her response was hilarious. She just stared at the whole group and you could read on her face that she was wondering if it was a test. I assured her it wasn't, through a couple of chuckles, and I had my dad mix her a drink.

It didn't take long for me to realize that she was a free spirit and the perfect person to help me travel more, not to mention some of my meetings that were held across the state. At one point, during about a 5 ½ year time span, we went to San Diego, California and Orlando, Florida (this time flying) and went on six cruises, two to the Bahamas, two to Bermuda, one to the Caribbean and one "Cruise to Nowhere" that just went out to sea and back. We started with the cruises, the first one out of Baltimore sailing to Bermuda for five days. I had never been on a cruise ship and didn't know anyone in a wheelchair that had either. So, it was back to making things up as I went. Sarah helped a lot; she was game for just about anything. The cruise was a success. I didn't get an accessible cabin but found out I didn't need one. While planning things out, I discovered that the Junior suites were a little bit bigger and had a wider entry, which is all I really needed. Our state room attendant even fashioned a ramp so I could get out onto the deck. One of the more memorable moments of that trip was a "Sexiest Man in the World" competition. When Sarah saw it on the schedule, she made sure to have me up and ready in time. After I was in my chair, I headed up to the pool deck while she finished getting ready. We had made a bunch of friends, but for some reason I couldn't find any of them. I grabbed a drink and sat by the pool as the competition began. When Sarah got to the pool deck, a few minutes later, I had already joined the competition and was making my way across the deck in front of the six or seven bikini-clad women who were judging.

About eight of us took turns walking back and forth in front of the women. The first time was an introduction, our name and where we were from. The second time, we were supposed to dance. Some of the other guys were pretty good. I went last, and when I got in front of the women, reclined my chair and spun around in a circle. The third time, everyone was supposed to flex and show off our muscles. A few of the guys were sculpted, and a few others were, well, just *not* (to be polite). That didn't stop anyone from flexing though. It was meant to be funny. Again, I was last, but I obviously couldn't flex anything. So, when I got in front of all the judges I looked back at my competition, and then to the judges and just stuck my tongue out. My tongue is rather long and can reach below my chin. It usually gets a reaction. It did that time as well, from all of the judges. I won the competition and was given a medal declaring me "Sexiest Man in the World."

Cruise to Nowhere

Our second cruise was the "Cruise to Nowhere," out of Norfolk, VA. That one found five of us, my friend Pete and his wife Jill, Sarah, Bill, and me arriving over an hour after the ship was set to sail. We had left early to account for traffic, but not early enough, even though Sarah drove so fast she got a ticket. We had underestimated the amount of traffic and then ran into a couple of accidents. When we pulled up to the port, we were all shocked to see the ship still there. Turns out, there was a tiny sailboat having trouble with its anchor. It was in the way, and the cruise ship couldn't depart. We pulled up to the security guard and I explained that we were supposed to be on the ship. He was absolutely awesome. Not only did he radio the ship, convincing them to let us on, but he also said he would park my van and leave the keys for the security personnel that would be there when we returned on Sunday. So we ended up parking my van on the dock merely feet away from the ship and leaving it in a stranger's hands, still running, as we rushed on to a makeshift gangplank, all the while being applauded by the passengers on the top deck, who had been patiently waiting to leave. At some point during the radio conversation between the security officer and the ship they must have referred to us as "The Party of Five," because for the rest of the trip we were referred to as The Party of Five.

I'm pretty outgoing, so each time we went on a cruise it was typically only a matter of hours before Sarah and I had a group of new friends. On one of the Bahamas cruises there was a comedy club that had several showings per day. The earlier one was typically more family-friendly, while the later one wasn't. Sarah and I had already gone and thought the comedian was really funny. He was one of those guys that free rolled by picking people out of the crowd and poking fun, and he could get ruthless. We were sitting in the back because we got there late, but anyone within the first row or two he annihilated. When we told our new friends how good it was, they wanted to go and sit in the front row. I was all for it, but I had to warn them that if they were sitting in the front row with me, they wouldn't go unnoticed. I had no doubt he was going to rip us apart. Either they didn't believe me or didn't care because they really wanted to go. We got there early and got front row seats.

Sure enough, soon as he started, he glanced over in our direction several times while he was picking people out of the crowd. I could read it on his face, he was sizing me up to see if I had a sense of humor. Eventually he looked our way and spoke directly to me, asking how I was enjoying the cruise and was it accessible. Now, when we first entered, the crewmember seating people announced to everyone that it would help the flow of traffic if, after the show everyone left by the exit on the far right. It just so happens, that doorway had steps. When the comedian asked me how I liked the ship, I smiled and told him it was awesome except we were just told that when we leave, we had to use the steps. He got this instant grin from ear-to-ear, knowing I had just told him I have a sense of humor and to feel free. He threw a couple of shots my way, but I'm pretty quick-witted and did a good job of deflection by making fun of the other people in my group. Hey, I warned them ahead of time, maybe not that I would throw them under the bus, but better them than me. When he went after Sarah and the others in our crowd, they tried making fun of him right back, which didn't work. He had a microphone. They didn't. Nonetheless, we were all cracking up. He was really good, especially in making fun of our group.

The only downside came later, and unexpectedly, when Sarah and I were walking through the casino. We were still chuckling about some of the one-liners, when this guy who was absolutely hammered approached us. He started telling me how horrible it was that the comedian was making fun of me. I tried briefly to explain that people in wheelchairs can have a sense of humor as well as everyone else, but it was obvious I wasn't going to get anywhere. I took off, but Sarah didn't escape quickly enough. He grabbed her arm and started telling her how amazing she was for taking care of me. My attendants get that a lot (so do my friends and family). Quite frankly it is beyond irritating, not just for them but for me. To make matters worse he started saying to Sarah, "Do me a favor, jerk him off. Just once, just jerk him off. Do it for me, please." There are so many disturbing things about that I'm not quite sure where to start. I am not sure if I should have been more concerned that he was telling my attendant to jerk me off in the middle of the casino, or that he was asking her to do it "for him!" Either way, Sarah and I both told him he was an ass and took off. However, it did only take us about 3.4 seconds to start laughing about it.

About Me

1. I'm definitely a wise ass... but I'm really good at it
2. I tend to sing in the shower... and the car... and at work... well, you get the picture
3. I tend to make up my own lyrics
4. I tend to get yelled at for those lyrics... especially at work
5. I absolutely love the feel of the sun on my face, a warm gentle breeze and the sound of nature cascading around me. When you can allow your mind to let go and your senses take over, everything but the moment dissolves away. In capturing that moment, you capture something truly special, and it just might be the essence of being alive
6. The only thing better would probably be the sound of a little kid laughing or the power of a hug from a 2-year-old
7. Mid's Chocolates' chocolate covered caramels and meltaways are up there as well....
8. I fuss with my hair way too much, but it is the only part of my body I have control over shaping... so that probably won't change anytime soon :-)
9. I'm often much less confident and much more afraid than I ever appear
10. My family is ridiculously huge, crazy and can be completely overbearing... I love it and would not change any aspect of it for all the money in the world. They have been a tremendous support and have influenced who I am in nearly every way since the day I was born. They are resilient, they are close-knit and boy oh boy are they ubiquitous. To witness a family gathering you would truly be in the presence of Irish Catholic... when looking around all you would see is people, children and alcohol, but most importantly you would see love
11. Everything I am can be credited to my father... or should I say blamed on...
12. I love writing, but often find myself with writer's block. I can be far too critical of myself
13. If I had to choose between the ability or desire to sing, I would choose desire in a heartbeat
14. I've learned the hard way, you can ask Janae, that wheelchairs, alcohol, and mulch make for a very, very bad day... :-)

15. Big hair '80s music always makes me smile and laugh about my misguided youth

16. One of my favorite lessons in life was taught to me by a wise young woman years ago ... "There is more in us than we know, if we can be made to see it, then perhaps, for the rest of our lives, we will be unwilling to settle for less." That wise young woman... my baby sister...

17. Capt. Morgan & Coke should never have anything floating in it, not even fruit. The only thing that should be floating in alcohol is my liver

18. I have had unparalleled success in my friendships for the better part of my life. That was never more evident than immediately after I was shot, and continues to this day

19. My wheelchair is the ultimate idiot magnate. The most bizarre person in any establishment (especially those that serve alcohol) will make their way to me eventually and feel compelled to share their life story

20. I've come rather close to biting several of these people

21. I thoroughly enjoy giving guest lectures, especially at the collegiate level. I think public speaking is actually a lot of fun, especially when I have an audience that likes to interact. I've been told I'm fairly good at it

22. I have felt an overwhelming desire to die as well as live. Experiencing the former has made the latter infinitely more precious

23. There's a line from a movie called Perfect Warrior that's brief but poignant. There are no ordinary moments. It has stayed with me since I saw it and hopefully continues to do so for a long time. It's something far too often taken for granted, there are no ordinary moments, something special is always happening.

24. I live for April 1st

25. Women in my office become rather dangerous April 2nd

26. I absolutely believe in destiny. I think this world was created by someone or something with very specific intentions. That being said, I also believe that our destiny, or where we end up is probably the most insignificant aspect of our lives. What we do along the course of our journey is what defines us

27. Cogito ergo sum

Places My Chair Has Been

On April 16, 2013, I posted another list to commemorate the 20th anniversary of my injury. This one I framed as "Places My Chair Has Been." I used that format to summarize some of the really funny stories I had collected over those two decades. Some of them, again, are repetitive because they show up in other lists and a few of them I've elaborated on and told the full story earlier. Reminding myself, and the world around me, just how funny these things are every year on April 16 is, I think, the perfect way to manage my automatic triggers.

1. **Miniature elevator:** It was so small that my toes were pressed against the grate in front, my back wheels against the grate behind and both armrests rubbing the walls on either side. I'm not claustrophobic, but after the hotel employee closed the door, he neglected to tell me that he had to operate it from the next floor. The five-minute wait was not very pleasant.

2. **Locked inside a minivan:** This has actually happened at least three times, the last of which involved a very interesting conversation with an OnStar representative. My repeated explanation that I was paralyzed and locked INSIDE the vehicle kept getting met with awkward silence. It wasn't until afterwards that I realized she was wondering if I can't open the door how the hell am I driving…

3. **Locked inside a hotel room:** This has also happened on several occasions. The most recent of these included my sister deciding that the lock was not enough and finding a way to activate the panic latch. You know, that bar that goes across the door so it can't be opened more than half an inch. The one that's impossible to place on the door unless you're inside. That one. She latched it. Then, without thinking, proceeded to walk out through the adjoining doors and close them behind her. To me it's just overkill… Closing the door is enough, I can't open it anyway, regardless if it's locked or not.

4. **Locked inside a movie theater:** We were the last ones in the theater. My uncle Pat and cousin Rob walked out ahead of me

and allowed the door to close. Patiently waiting, I hear a small knock and then the following: "Mike, can you reach the door handle?" Of course I replied, "Yeah, actually I can. I've just been faking it because I like the parking spots."

5. **Stuck in mulch in the lobby of a hotel:** After my aunt and uncle's wedding in Pittsburgh, I took a wrong turn out of the elevator. I ended up in between a few plants, wheels spinning and mulch flying... a lot of mulch flying. Alcohol may have been involved.

6. **Upside down against a fence in the Blue Ridge Mountains of Virginia:** The night before my cousin Dave's wedding, a steep hill and wet road pretty much turned my chair into a toboggan. Once it caught the edge of the road it flipped upside down. After a few cousins kindly put me back on all four wheels, I was bombarded with family including two "doctors." Well, the two doctors were a dentist and a biology professor. Considering I didn't chip a tooth and I wasn't failing bio, I told them to scram and had a drink.

7. **Empty at my parent's house:** I, on the other hand, was in a lawn chair in the middle of the woods about 10 miles away drinking beer around a campfire just days after I got home from spinal cord rehab.

8. **In a rental van:** I've been in plenty of rental vans, but the time deserving of this list was in California and the rental van had been commandeered by the LAPD. When we arrived at the hotel the officer looked me right in the eye and said, "Now stay." I figured that was a good point to call it a night.

9. **On a van lift:** Again, another common occurrence. My old full-size vans had an elevator type lift that would raise up and down about 3 or 4 feet. I was on and off of this lift many times a day, so you wouldn't think this would make the list either. Except that on this occasion I was sitting out on the lift suspended about 3 feet in the air while the van was driving across the parking lot.

10. **Dragged up a flight of stairs by a four-wheeler:** There's not much more to elaborate on here, the video does a much better job of that. However, the fact that I was dressed as Superman might be noteworthy.

11. **Carried up and down stairways:** My fraternity began doing this immediately upon my return home. Usually it was only one flight of stairs, but those stairs were typically old, wooden and extremely narrow leading into basements of houses. However, they have covered everything from three flights of stairs in Buffalo 20 years ago through two flights at our 20th anniversary last fall.

12. **Venetian rolling sidewalk:** During my first visit to Las Vegas we were returning from Margaritaville and my friend John indicated we should take a shortcut. He, Seth, and Chad (who uses a manual wheelchair) all headed onto a moving sidewalk that went up like an escalator and had rails on either end. With my attendant and cousin behind me I figured there was no harm in following. The last thing I saw as it dragged me along was a little "No Wheelchairs" symbol, the little Ghostbusters circle with a line through over top of a wheelchair. The moving sidewalk went up about two or three stories when I noticed the three in front of me disappear. When I reached the crest, I realized why no wheelchairs were permitted. It went straight back down. I began sliding and bouncing off of the rails, while Chad had popped a wheelie so he didn't tumble ass-over-tin-cups. The people in front of them flat-out ran. Luckily Chad was quick enough to dart out of the way at the bottom as I slid behind him, dragging my attendant and cousin along.

13. **Outside with a bear:** Twice

14. **On a tow truck:** My van broke down on Route 219 in PA and, apparently, it's extremely illegal to stay inside a towed vehicle. Who knew? Luckily, the guy that eventually showed up didn't seem to care. It was quite a view from the top of the rollback.

15. *As a tow truck:* I would often have people rollerblading and holding onto the back of my chair. However, it was a friend in graduate school who was paralyzed from the chest down using me as a tow truck that makes this list. He didn't want to drive his chair to the bar, so he held onto the back of mine and I towed him there. Unfortunately for him as we entered the parking lot, I hit a bump and my chair stopped dead. This had the interesting effect of catapulting him around me like a slingshot directly into a parked car. He didn't hold on for the ride home.

16. **Middle of a cow field:** My pranks and wise ass comments went far enough to prompt retribution by several fraternity brothers in Edinboro. Don't remember exactly what I did, but it prompted a few of them to turn my chair off, take it out of gear and push it into the cow field next to my apartment. You would think I'd learn from that experience.

17. **Florida spring break:** At a club in Daytona Beach during spring break, all you could drink for $20 and several wet T-shirt contests that night. No other story here, just a really, really fun memory!

18. **Reclined at the opera:** Chair reclined back at the opera. I shall elaborate no further for fear of self-incrimination.

19. **Surrounded by great family and outstanding friends**... without which none of the previous experiences matter one damn bit!!!

20. I left this one open with a request that anyone else feel free to post or private message me a favorite memory of a place my chair has been.

Perfect Practical Joke

My buddy Baxter had a prank pulled on him that our friends have been laughing about for years. It was an epic prank that not only had multiple parts but lasted several years. It started one December when he began receiving letters in the mail -- not email, actual mail, postage and everything. The letters were from someone named Zelda with the first one thanking him for the lovely gift of a partridge in a pear tree. The second letter, which he received a day or two later, was another thank you, this time for two turtle doves. The third was about three French hens and the fourth about four calling birds. The letters were being written as if Baxter had sent this woman Zelda extravagant gifts based on each of the 12 days of Christmas. In the first few letters she was flattered and signed "With Love" or "Affectionately Yours" until about the fourth one, the one with four calling birds. That one was still signed "Affectionately," but the way it was written, she appeared to be getting a little overwhelmed. She was back to being enamored on the fifth day, with five gold rings, but everything went downhill from there.

Starting with the sixth day, six geese a-laying, her responses began taking a different tone. By the time the letters get through maids a-milking, lords a-leaping, and pipers piping her responses are not just frustrated but exasperated, and absolutely hilarious. She asks if he's a sadist and talks about the birds shitting all over her yard, the Lords leaping all over the maids, her neighbors taking a petition to have her evicted, and eventually she threatens retaliation. The very last letter is from her lawyers stating that they have filed a restraining order on her behalf, the house has been condemned, and she has been committed. If you Google Agnes and the 12 days of Christmas, you can find the actual letters. Apparently, it's been around for quite a while. I think it was an email chain that made its rounds years ago.

I believe Baxter discovered the letters online relatively quickly, or he had seen them somewhere before. He's got an engineer brain, so attention to detail is a fundamental part of who he is. That meant he was looking for clues everywhere. He took note of where the postage was stamped, which was a neighboring town. He compared the handwriting on the outside of each envelope, making sure it was always the same (which it was). Those 12 letters, sent back-to-back over a few weeks, were funny enough on their own. But the prank didn't stop there. He started getting other letters, cards, and even presents, from Zelda over the years. Everything from postcards from Florida and California, to a cheese platter from Wisconsin. There were even a few packages of M&Ms, with his face on them, that were sent to Chuggy's and to his parents' house. I think my favorite, though, was his birthday present from Zelda.

Apparently, he was on his way home from work and talking to his friend Kristin on the phone. As he was approaching his house, he told her that someone left a present on his mailbox.

When he opened the bag, he started describing to her what was inside. Women's underwear. Both he and Kristin tell the story the same way, that he opened the bag and said, "There's women's underwear in here... Big women's underwear. Really big... THEY'RE

DIRTY!!... DIRTY... THEY'RE DIRTY UNDERWEAR!" Kristin said in addition to his screams of "dirty" she could hear him throwing things, in an obvious attempt to get away from the underwear. She makes no bones about it, she was on the floor crying laughing, and says she may have peed her pants.

Watching and listening to Baxter tell that story is one of the funniest things I've ever seen. He has kept all of the different things Zelda sent him over the years in his ongoing investigation of "Who is Zelda?" Everything from the original letters and postcards to the little notes that came with the gifts. He's compared handwriting on every one of them, which has always been the same, despite some of these things coming from the other side of the country. He's had many theories over the years, most of which center around his friends as culprits. However, if things work out right, he's finally finding out, by reading this section in this book, that I was Zelda the entire time. I used my dad to sign all of the letters and cards. He wrote the notes and addressed the envelopes, all in a uniquely shaky handwriting. Sometimes I would have him do it ahead of time, then give the item to someone else to mail once they reached a destination like Florida. On one occasion, I had a friend of mine, Curtis, who is great at forging handwriting, send him a few postcards from California. I just gave Curtis a sampling of Zelda's handwriting and he did the rest.

Redneck Elevator

Pete Noel worked for my father roughly since the time we met in ninth grade. That was one of the many cool things about my dad owning his own contracting business, that my friends and I had easy access to a job where we could earn money. At other times, like when we got into trouble, it was a serious drawback. Getting grounded pales in comparison to some of the hard labor jobs we were assigned, and when they were handed down as punishment there was no juicy paycheck waiting at the end of the week as a reward for the blisters and fatigue. Pete and I both put in our fair share of hours that were free labor, but even those times were of value. Looking back now, the ability to do a lot of that work has saved Pete quite a bit of money with some of his home improvement projects.

A few years after Pete got married, he and his wife had my dad build their house. However, with everything that he learned from working all those years with my dad, he was able to save some money by leaving the basement unfinished and doing it himself when time and finances allowed. Pete learned from the best. My father is not only talented but meticulous and has built some really impressive homes, so Pete was able to do a pretty good job himself on that basement. He put in a really nice bar, big-screen TV, air hockey table and the works, all decorated in Pittsburgh sports themes. It turned out great, an excellent man cave perfect for Steeler parties and gathering friends. There is one catch though, it's not a walk-out basement, there are about 20 steps down into it.

The landscape and terrain where Pete built his house did not allow for a walk-out entry of the basement, so we were bound to have some problems with wheelchair access. Initially, he was always quick to point out that he deliberately made the stairway leading down from the garage into the basement extra wide so a few people could carry me down in my chair. My response was always that we weren't going to be young enough to do that forever, so we had to put our brains together and get creative. The chair and I together probably weigh close to 450-500 pounds. Somewhere in that creativity between a few of our brains came the idea for what is now referred to as the redneck elevator.

There are many parodies and jokes between Facebook, social media and comedic websites that poke good-natured fun at creative solutions to unusual problems. This would definitely fit among those. It is a fairly simple idea. Two pieces of plywood, each with a 2 x 4 running along either long end for support, are laid flat on top of the staircase leading down from the garage. This creates what is essentially a sliding board in place of the stairs. Next, I simply back my wheelchair up to the top of the ramp/sliding board. The chair and I together are too heavy, and with the stairs covered there is no footing for people to actually carry or even guide my chair down. Not to mention it's extremely steep. Pete will pull his four-wheeler up to meet the front of my chair and then fasten the cable winch from the front of the ATV to the frame of my chair. Then, with the four-wheeler and cable winch bearing all of the weight, one person eases out the cable while several others balance my chair as it gets lowered down into the basement. At the end of the party/night it gets hooked up again and I get drug back up the same way.

This is quite a sight to see and very ingenious if I do say so myself. The first weekend we tried it out was for a Steeler party. Pete was getting ready to have a Halloween party later that fall and we needed to test the system and see if it worked properly. My father was on a golf trip with several friends and my mother was planning on watching the game at home with several of her friends. She gave me a ride up to Pete's house and promptly left, proclaiming she was not sticking around to watch. She often tells the story of returning home and explain to her friends what we were attempting. Somewhere around halftime they asked her if she thought I made it into the basement okay. Her response was that I either made it safely and I was happily watching the game or lying in a pool of my own blood and everyone was too afraid to call her. When my father was asked if he knew what we were doing, he admitted to building the ramp before he left on the golf trip. To this day, though, one of the funniest reactions was from Krista. We had just gone on our first date the previous Friday and it had gone pretty well. She wanted to see me again, so I suggested something on Sunday because the Steelers were playing in the Super Bowl. After a few options were discussed, she was okay with going to Pete's house for his Super Bowl party. When we got there, she realized we were going to the basement and asked how I was getting there. I motioned to the back of the garage and told her to look over the 4-foot-tall brick divider that separated the stairwell from the vehicle area. As she peered over top of the wall, she could see the boards fastened neatly on top of the stairs. The look on her face was priceless when she spun around and declared, "I am NOT watching that!!"   I chuckled and told her I would meet her downstairs. I wonder if it impressed her on some level as we continued to date for over a year after that.

The Old Shoes

There is an old saying about refraining from judgment until you've walked a mile in another's shoes. Then you can say whatever you like because you're a mile away and you have their shoes. Both the original bit of wisdom toward patience and empathy as well as the joke, make me think back to the actual shoes I wore prior to my injury. I had only two options, Timberland boots or high-top sneakers. The Timberlands were your typical work boots, and they were never tied. Likewise, my sneakers were never tied either. I always kept the shoelaces barely sticking out the top loop, yet each string was knotted around itself to ensure it would not slide back inside the shoe. This made it easy to simply slip my feet in and out. I typically wore shoes until they were ready to fall apart, so by the time I was injured those high-top sneakers had quite a few miles on them. They were pretty beat up.

Although they were comfortable and worn in, they were ratty and no longer provided the support I would need while sitting in a wheelchair. I needed an upgrade to something that would protect my feet from pressure sores which meant brand-new sneakers. Therefore, like many of the other comforts and conveniences I had been accustomed to, I had to forgo my broken in shoes for something more logical and appropriate. It wasn't until several weeks after I had returned home from rehab that I noticed those shoes still sitting by the door. I never thought much about it until I realized after a month or two that my father was wearing them occasionally. He wore them to run out and get the mail, take the garbage out, cut the grass, mainly simple errands around the house or quick trips uptown.

The symbolism struck me immediately. Whether it was deliberate and conscious or not, he was literally walking in my shoes. It had been apparent from the moment I was shot that he would have given anything to trade places with me. He would have willingly taken my journey as his own, and I have no doubt he would have done it fearlessly. I, on the other hand, would have never traded places even if I could. I've said before that I would not even wish to see the guy who shot me in such a position.

We spoke a lot that first year about regaining movement, about a cure, and about walking again someday. During that time, he was not only walking in my shoes, but more importantly walking beside me every step of my journey. It made me push forward and brought out a resilience that I was unaware I possessed. As my old shoes began to fall apart on his feet, my life began to stabilize and strengthen. As the ability to walk became less important, the opportunity to continue life's journey took its place. By the time my beat-up old sneakers were held together by nothing more than duct tape, falling off his feet, I had begun owning my life and living it fully. I'm not sure at what point those old shoes were tossed out, but they seemed to have served their purpose. As they became weaker, I became stronger. As I became stronger, I think walking in my shoes became less important. To this day, though, he continues to walk beside me every step of the way, and for that I am truly blessed and thankful.

EPILOGUE - *A Parting Thought*

My Uncle Joe always emphasized the importance of taking advantage of opportunities. His philosophy makes sense. He thinks it's important to plan ahead and set goals, but when an opportunity presents itself, run with it... at full speed! I may not have chosen my journey, but I'd like to think I've taken advantage of it. I've learned and grown in ways I would have never imagined possible. I've experienced things, both good and bad, that have allowed me to become the man I am today. I've been blessed with friends and family who have placed me on their shoulders, sometimes literally, to lift me up and propel me forward. They have empowered me beyond limits. It's because of them that I continue running, full speed, adrenaline pumping and air beneath me, without hesitation and despite fear, toward every new obstacle for which I will never be prepared yet will undoubtedly overcome.

ABOUT THE AUTHOR

Michael A. Kiel was born on August 9, 1973. He attended Penn State University for three years, then transferred to Edinboro University where he graduated with a Bachelor's Degree in Psychology in 1997, and a Master's Degree in Rehab Counseling in 1999.

He and a partner, Pete Noel, opened The Underground Health and Fitness Center and operated it for nine years, selling it in 2006.

He is employed at the Hiram G. Andrews Center in Johnstown, PA through the University of Pittsburgh. Mike was named to the Pennsylvania State Board of Vocational Rehabilitation by Governor Ed Rendell and continues to serve under Governor Tom Wolf.

He is also a Board Member of the Portage Area Regional Endowment Fund.

His interests include dabbling in the stock market, playing chess, watching movies and enjoying the company of his two nephews.

Mike resides in Portage, PA.

Acknowledgments

First and foremost, I would like to thank Michele Kupchella Adams (without who, there would, I'm guessing, be lots more sentences like this...!). In addition to her editing and organizational contributions, I want to thank her for all the love and support. Without her, this book would have never been completed.

I'd also like to thank my parents and their crowd, the baby boomer group that are too numerous, and too notorious to name. Thank you for the modeling of friendship and support and the crazy Christmas parties from which I was banned as a kid, avoided as a teenager, and came to embrace as an adult.

Thank you to all my friends and family for pushing me to write. The only thing more brilliant than my friends and family is the fact that it's nearly impossible to tell them apart.

There are more stories than I can count and more people to thank. If you're not in this book, trust me, you're in my heart. To try to include them all, I'd still be writing, probably around page 832, which I'm guessing would be in the neighborhood of halfway done.

In Memory of Aunt Gigi
Gigi's Eulogy
SR. REGINA KIEL, RSM
Sept. 10, 1944-Dec. 13, 2016

Love. There's no other way to begin this; none. Of all the words I'm going to try to put together here, *that* one had to be first. Love. It was the only thing that mattered to her and the measuring stick to which she held all things, especially herself. Gigi had this giant well of love inside her, and from it she drew brilliance. She drew strength, kindness and beauty, she drew genuineness and creativity. From that well she drew an astonishing perspective on life that flowed through everything she did, every belief she held, every piece of art she created and every hug she embraced. The only thing more amazing is the way she allowed that love to not only flow through her but continue into everyone else around her. It's why she connected with so many, so often and so deeply. You could just feel it when you were in her presence. Her love had a gravitational pull like no other. She would be so proud right now to know that's the legacy she's leaving behind. To know the first thing we think of when remembering her is how much she embodied love. Her eyes would light up, her chin would lift as the grin spread across her cheeks and she'd say, "Yeah, that's right!"

30 years ago, almost to the day, my grandmother's funeral was held in this very church. I was in eighth grade and 13 years old. My grandfather had passed away just a few months earlier, so Gigi, my dad and the rest of my aunts and uncles had a pretty tough time. I was serving as an altar boy for the Mass and sitting right over there. Gigi got up to give a reading, standing here at this podium. I remember her voice beginning to shake and I could see her hands trembling. I walked up behind her and gently placed my hand on her shoulder. Over the years she would tell this story from her perspective. She would talk about how she felt a sudden sense of calmness and was able to continue on, finishing her reading. From my perspective, the moment I touched her shoulder I felt her energy and strength. Her shoulders straightened up and her voice steadied.

Gigi always got so much strength from connecting with others. I think that's how her giant well of love got replenished. She could connect with someone in a heartbeat, effortlessly. Whether it was about creativity and art, which of course was her specialty, or if it was about current events or history or a movie or an old beat up car. She was just easy to talk to. A friend of mine told me the other day that Gigi always made her feel like an old friend. That from the first time they met their conversations felt warm and comfortable. One of the things she said that really hit home was that Gigi made her feel like the most important person in the world when they spoke. I think she probably had that impact often, on a lot of people.

She never had much time for rules or authority (great qualities for a nun in (non-in) the Catholic Church). Her position was always that there is only one true authority, Jesus, and he has only one rule, love each other. It became her mantra, "All the love I can give." She embodied that belief and led by example. In doing so she promoted her faith without actually promoting it, she encouraged belief and spirituality without persuasion. It gave her a type of freedom to engage people in such unique ways that even the most delicate discussions, the kind that are so important yet people often avoid, were not only freely debated but joyfully and laughingly challenged. She empowered people to find their own beliefs and there was never, ever a wrong way. The only criteria were that those beliefs allow someone to live a good life, and of course, love.

She was godmother to a few of us but played the spiritual guidance role for just about everyone. For me, she is hands-down the greatest spiritual influence I could have possibly been blessed with growing up. I remember the first time I questioned what I was learning in grade school. I was talking to her about the difference between spirituality and religion, which can be a pretty complicated topic. She destroyed it in about two seconds. She boiled it down to that one simple thing. Love. The only thing that matters when our time here ends is how much we've loved. She told me plainly, the rest of it is man-made and can be subjective. Jesus said to love. That's it. She made it simple. She had a knack for doing that, and I think that's why so many of us valued her opinion so highly. I know I'm not the only cousin that went to her for advice. I'm probably not even the only one to call her at 2:30 in the morning! But she would always answer that call, no matter what. For someone who took a vow of poverty and was supposed to have so little what she had to give was so absolutely immeasurable.

She didn't just share herself and her beliefs with the world, she shared her talent and her amazing artwork. She worked in jewelry and sculptures, in paintings and photography. She worked in any medium in which she could find beauty, and she could always find it… anywhere. Each object she crafted, especially her jewelry, was such a labor of love. She would often describe the healing process of creating a specific sculpture. She used to point out how many of her pieces started with a tightly closed knot, empty circle or hole at the base. Then, from that base, the piece would expand and flourish outward. The symbolism of healing and growth was unmistakable. I think the only thing she may have loved more than creating art was explaining the process to others and teaching them how to create it themselves.

When we were kids, many of us spent time during the summers visiting her and working with her in Studio One. We would help her with inventory and cleaning or anything else that she needed. More importantly though, she taught us how to make jewelry and helped instill in us a love of all kinds of art. Everything from making rings and necklaces in her studio to taking pictures while hiking at Ricketts Glen. She always had a keen eye for photography, obvious by the thousands and thousands of pictures she had stockpiled in multiple crates in her apartments. Thank God for the digital age! Although, now we have these tiny memory cards hidden everywhere…

Those three aspects of Gigi, embodying love, connecting with others and the creative artist, weren't just random qualities that Gigi possessed. They were something more. Her own personal Trinity. It was something she cultivated over a lifetime. Deliberately and for one simple purpose, to share all the love she could give. So it's with a heavy heart and a trembling voice I'll struggle to whisper farewell. But the memories of her love and laughter and warmth will remain with me forever. They'll lighten my heart and steady my voice and allow me to put forth all the love I can give. Until we meet again Gigi, I love you so very much.

M. Kiel